CONTENTS

THE ETRUSCAN CITIES AND ROME

H. H. Scullard

CORNELL UNIVERSITY PRESS
ITHACA, NEW YORK

CORNELL UNIVERSITY PRESS

First published 1967
Second printing 1976

International Standard Book Number 0-8014-0373-1
Library of Congress Catalog Card Number 67-20631
Printed in the United States of America

ASPECTS OF GREEK AND ROMAN LIFE

General Editor: H. H. Scullard

★ ★ ★

THE ETRUSCAN CITIES AND ROME

H. H. Scullard

LIST OF ILLUSTRATIONS

PLATES

FIGURES

PREFACE

IT IS NOT POSSIBLE to write a history of the Etruscan cities: their own records have largely perished, while Greek and Roman writers were mainly concerned with later episodes in their history at a time when they came into contact with Rome. However, if the contribution of ancient writers, which forms the basis of our knowledge, is somewhat patchy and meagre, our other source of information is varied: the results of archaeological work reveal something of the physical appearance of the Etruscan cities and of their cultural, artistic, economic and social life, while epigraphy throws a fitful light on some aspects. Thus despite the enormous gaps in our knowledge, we know enough to see that each Etruscan city enjoyed an individual life and development of its own, and an attempt may be made to bring together in outline some of this scattered knowledge, and to look at the separate cities in their historical and topographical setting. But first we will look briefly at the more primitive cultures of the land in which Etruscan civilization developed, and later at Etruscan Rome and the stages by which the cities were absorbed into Rome's ambit and gradually became Romanized.

The field is vast, the attempt hazardous, but it seems worth while to collect some of the material which is both widely dispersed and rapidly increasing, and to draw attention to some of the highly controversial questions, not least those concerning the early history of Rome, that are being keenly debated by scholars at this time. If over-all agreement cannot be reached on many points, at any rate the fervour of current discussions indicates the widespread interest in this field. Though a sketch of this kind necessarily involves over-simplification of complex issues, that risk must be run if a brief survey of the present state of these problems is to be attempted.

Some readers may feel that I have mentioned too many place-names, but this has been done in the hope that this book may be of some use to visitors to Tuscany: few things are more irritating than having to waste time in seeking to localize some name; for instance if one looks for the Etruscan and Villanovan sites at Bolsena, much time may be spent in enquiry if precise details are not known. Even with so spectacular a find as the archaic altars at Lavinium, local enquiry at Pratica may not always lead one directly to the site, and though the surrounding fields are very pleasant, one may lack the time to wander. As a guide in this connection, as in many others, George Dennis' *Cities and Cemeteries of Etruria*, though over a hundred years old, is still useful.

In a book of this scope an author's debt must clearly be widespread. Here I would acknowledge primarily my great indebtedness to the works of Professors L. Banti, J. Heurgon, and M. Pallottino, as well as a host of others. I am extremely grateful to my friend Professor A. Momigliano for having found time to read my typescript and for his comments: the conventional disclaimer that such a kindness implies the reader's approval of any views expressed in the book, is surely scarcely needed in a work on so controversial a subject: Etruscology is not a topic which easily breeds unanimity of opinion.

Finally, I should like to express my thanks to Dr Anne Ward, Mr Jean-Claude Peissel and the staff of Thames and Hudson for their help, particularly with the illustrations.

King's College, London
July 1966   H. H. Scullard

CHAPTER I

EARLY ITALY

ETRUSCAN ORIGINS

'THE ETRUSCANS', as we call them, are the Tyrsenoi or Tyrrhenoi of the Greeks, and the Etrusci (Tusci) of the Romans; they called themselves Rasenna.[1] Classical writers reveal them as living in a definite place (essentially modern Tuscany) and at a given time. They were gradually conquered by the Romans and incorporated in the Roman state, with the result that the distinctive features of their culture had been largely absorbed by the beginning of the Christian era. The other end of their history is more dim because it extends back into prehistoric or proto-historic times, but Herodotus and all other classical authors, except one, record that the Etruscans came by sea from Asia Minor and settled in Italy. The exception is Dionysius of Hali-carnassus, who lived at the time of Augustus: after enquiring into the matter he decided that they were indigenous in Italy, and not settlers from overseas.

Until comparatively recently the problem of their origins has bulked large in learned discussion: was Herodotus or Dionysius right?[2] Latterly, however, the emphasis has shifted from an apparently insoluble problem to the agreed fact that Etruscan civilization, as we know it, developed on Italian soil. Thus the question is now often regarded as one of formation rather than of origin: what elements, in Italy and from overseas, combined to create the culture? Furthermore, there is the problem of time. During the seventh century BC there was a culture in Etruria with strong individualistic features, which everyone agrees can legitimately be called 'Etruscan'. But how far back does this go, or in other words at what point in time does the use of the word 'Etruscan' in an Italian context begin to have any valid meaning? In recent years salutary warnings have been given against regarding the Etruscans as a clear-cut and closely-knit racial, cultural and linguistic unit, at any rate in the early days of their development. Thus the question arises: what is meant by a people or nation, and by what criteria is this Protean entity to be judged to exist? No one would accept ethnic characteristics as the sole factor; Nazi folly might cling to the idea of the existence of a 'pure' race, but mongrel Englishmen and Americans knew that nations could not be defined by the concept of a single ethnic unit. On the other hand a nation may have a predominant physical type, shown by the shape of the skull or by a blood-group. A common language may seem the most binding link, and despite the existence of some bilingual communities it may often prove to be so (especially in a literate society with a common literature). But language alone is no decisive factor: many Africans speak English or French as their first language without having become English or Frenchmen. Again, a culture shared is a bond of unity, but not necessarily of nationhood, as can be seen, for example, from the distribution of the products of western European or Japanese industry. When the archaeologist finds objects of one culture intruding into another context, he must be cautious before presupposing a movement of people. Again a nation, no less than a primitive tribe, may be united by a predominant religion, and the religious beliefs and practices of prehistoric peoples may be reflected, though often somewhat darkly, in their archaeological remains, not least in their burial rites; but beliefs may change or interact, so that the use of inhumation and cremation in the same society need not necessarily indicate the presence of two separate 'peoples', though of course this may prove to be the explanation.

All this is very obvious, but neglect of such simple considerations has often helped to add further confusion to a problem which already depends for its solution on extremely diversified and specialized evidence. Dr Ward-Perkins with eminent common sense has gone to the heart of the matter: 'In asking the question "Who were the Etruscans?" we may really be asking several related but quite distinct questions.' Who were they racially or linguistically or culturally? A question may produce an answer which is relevant to historical make-up, language, culture or political framework, but which should not be widened to include other aspects. And again, the element of time is of paramount importance. Can we rightly apply the word Etruscan to any culture in Italy before the seventh century, or is it wiser to label the previous century as proto-Etruscan; if so, how far back can any 'proto-Etruscan' period be traced?

This brings us back to the question of origin, unfashionable though it may be. Professor Pallottino has drawn a helpful analogy in pointing out that the modern historian is more concerned with ethnic formation than with provenance and does not, for instance, ask where Frenchmen came from originally, but rather how the French nation took shape on the soil of France. Celtic Gauls, Romans, Burgundians, Visigoths and Franks, all made their contribution in race, culture and language in varying degree. He therefore applies this principle to the Etruscans. From one point of view this is unexceptionable; no one supposes that vast hordes of hundreds of thousands of Etruscans disembarked from their ships on the shores of an almost empty Etruria. If they did come from abroad, their numbers were limited and they mingled with the Iron Age population (the Villanovans) whom they found in occupation of the land; from this mingling, which in the course of time was subjected to strong Oriental and Greek influences, Etruscan civilization of the seventh century emerged. Seen thus, the problem *is* one of formation, whether the ethnic elements were both foreign and Italian, or essentially only Italian as Pallottino believes. But if there was any foreign ethnic element, then an attempt to assess the extent of its influence must be made. As Dr Ward-Perkins has pointed out, the analogy of the Norman occupation of Sicily and southern Italy in the eleventh century AD, which lasted two centuries, warns us that archaeology may not reveal the full story. Since the genius of the Normans lay primarily in administration and war, their direct impression on the material remains is comparatively small: they produced a Siculo-Norman civilization, but its cultural roots were Arabic and Byzantine.[3] If the Etruscans were a similar small dominant minority, there is still the problem of trying to define the elements which contributed to the fully developed civilization, since few would believe that the invaders brought with them a completely developed culture.

But however obscure the facts may be, not everyone will be happy to let sleeping dogs lie, though the great scholar Mommsen was content to dismiss the question of Etruscan origins as on a par with that of Hecuba's mother, 'neither capable of being known, nor worth the knowing'. Man is by nature curious: he even wants to know whether the universe originated from 'continuous creation' or a 'big bang', and similarly whether the Etruscans originated by 'continuous creation' in Etruria, or as the result of an 'explosion' in Asia Minor which hurled some of them across the seas. Cosmic theories may not worry the man in the street. He may not be very excited to be told that at the beginning of 1966 the evolutionary Big Bang hypothesis seems to be defeating the Steady State theory; he might even reflect that either theory would explain only the development and not the origin of the universe and that the origin of the material of the galaxies would still remain unexplained. So too he may feel that the historian's primary task is to show him Etruscan civilization as it was and the way it developed in Italy. To appreciate its cultural richness he need not worry about the origins beyond a given point. Yet beyond that point lurks the haunting question of 'whence?' The problem should not be completely elbowed out of the picture, and that for at least two good reasons: 'it is there' as a perpetual challenge, and, for historians, the authority of Herodotus is involved. It we could dismiss his evidence out of hand, many might be content to believe that the archaeological evidence pointed as much in one direction as the other. But he cannot be so dismissed: he may be wrong but at least his view must continue to be discussed until it is proved to be wrong— or right.

Thus an understanding of the Etruscans must be approached by way of their geographical and historical setting. This means that before considering modern theories about their origins in more detail (see pp. 43ff), we must look briefly at the early ethnology of Italy, since Dionysius and some modern archaeologists believe the Etruscans emerged directly from the matrix of Neolithic, Bronze Age and Iron Age Italy, while everyone would agree that their early days were inextricably bound up with the Iron Age Villanovans and that the basic population of Etruria in the 'Etruscan' period was Italian Villanovan.

PREHISTORIC ITALY[4]

After long centuries when life in Italy had not progressed beyond the level of Neolithic culture, man gradually gained knowledge of metals and skill in their use. In the Alpine regions and the plain of the Po men slowly acquired knowledge of copper from Hungary and Bohemia. By 2000 BC 'warrior' immigrants, whose stone battle-axes are associated with the Indo-Europeans, were reaching north Italy from the Balkans, while the Bell-beaker culture from Spain reached the Po valley. This Chalcolithic or Eneolithic culture, a typical site of which is Remedello near Brescia, flourished in the northern plain of Italy and spread southwards to Tuscany; here between the Arno and Tiber, especially in the heart of Etruria around Lake Bolsena, the so-called Rinaldone culture is found.

As supplies of metal and skill in working it increased, from c. 1800 a Bronze Age culture emerged in two main areas, the north and the Apennines. The 'Apennine' Bronze Age culture spread along the mountain back of Italy from Bologna in the north to Apulia in the south. These people were pastoralists, moving between semi-permanent winter settlements on lower ground (often only caves by water-courses) and summer pastures high in the mountains, but by the twelfth century they had become somewhat more stable and practised some agriculture. They comprised the descendants of the Neolithic population, intermixed with some 'warriors' who may have come in small groups from overseas (from the Aegean world) and landed either on the west coast or in Apulia, and who probably spoke an Indo-European language. The semi-nomadic life of the population would help to spread the use of the rudimentary Indo-European speech, from which the later Umbro-Sabellian dialects will have developed in the central Apennines. Further, unlike the northern Bronze Age folk, they buried their dead.

The most famous of the northern Bronze Age people are those whom archaeologists have called Terramaricoli (from the remains of their settlements of terramara, 'dark earth'). Until fairly recently they were considered to have had widespread influence, ultimately spreading southwards through Etruria to Rome. Now, however, they are regarded as a more local group who settled in the middle Po valley, having come to Italy from the area of the middle Danube in the north-east. They brought a distinctive pottery with them, great skill in bronze-working, the custom of cremation and in all probability an Indo-European language or dialect. They practised agriculture and stock-farming, and used the horse for draft purposes. In the course of time this group seem to have made peaceful contacts with the Apennine folk. Some of the latter appear to have moved northwards and settled in open villages in the area near the Adriatic and the mouth of the Po, e.g. around Imola; they perhaps supplied some of the bronze of Etruria to the Terramara people who worked it up and exported the finished products not only to Etruria but also down the Adriatic coast to the south of Italy. Increasing trade led to interchange of people and of their ideas as well as of material objects throughout parts of continental Italy where the final stage of the Bronze Age is now sometimes named the Pianello horizon (Pianello lies inland from Ancona). This stage is marked by the introduction of cremation and urn-fields into districts where previously inhumation had prevailed. However the effects upon the rest of Italy of any partial fusion between Terramara and Apennine cultures that occurred in the north must not be exaggerated; the old Apennine culture with its practice of inhumation persisted well into the Iron Age in much of central and southern Italy. Thus for instance although Timmari in south Italy adopted cremation for some time, Torre Castelluccia near Tarentum apparently did not take to the idea : ten cremation urns found there may represent settlers from the north whose native practice failed to impress the inhabitants with the desirability of abandoning their customary burial-rite.[5]

The transition from the Bronze to the early Iron Age is obscure. When the Iron Age was fully established much of northern and central Italy, west of a line from Rimini to Rome, was occupied by a people whom archaeologists have called Villanovans, after a typical site discovered at Villanova, some five miles east of Bologna. The dating of the stages of this transitional process is highly controversial. In fact only two firm points of reference exist: these are provided by contemporary datable developments in the Greek world, one at each end. The full flowering of the Bronze Age Apennine culture coincides with Mycenaean III A and B (c. 1400–1200 BC), that of the Villanovan Iron Age culture in Etruria with the beginning of Greek colonization in Italy at Ischia and Cumae (from c. 750 BC). The intervening gap has been variously reconstructed, one problem being the chronological relationship between the urn-fields (cemeteries of ashes buried in urns) found north of the Alps and those to the south. The supporters of a 'high' chronology reduce the length of the transitional period and assign the beginning of the Iron Age to c. 1000, while the champions of a 'low' chronology prolong a Sub-Apennine and Proto-Villanovan period to c. 800 and shorten the first phase of the Iron Age; others put the transition about 900. But whatever the date of its emergence, Villanovan culture is in fact only a label invented by modern scholars, and Professor Pallottino rightly warns that it is misleading to think of the Villanovans as a large ethnic unit rather than as a collection of cultural entities. But since it is agreed that in the eighth century, if not earlier, there existed in and beyond Etruria a fairly homogeneous Iron Age culture and that this provided the framework in which Etruscan civilization emerged and developed, we must now look at Villanovan culture and then consider its genesis.

Its most distinctive mark was the use of cremation and of biconical urns in which the ashes of the dead were preserved. The urn was covered with an inverted bowl, and was put in a round hole in the ground, sometimes enclosed by small stones or a rectangular cist. Within and around it were placed various small ornaments and implements, such as brooches, bracelets and razors; the number of weapons found does not suggest widespread warfare. One branch of this culture developed north of the Apennines, another in Etruria. Whereas the northerners covered their urns with pottery bowls, many of the southerners used helmets for this purpose, while others (more particularly in Latium) used urns, modelled like huts, in place of the northern type of ossuary (*Pls.* 2, 7). The south also displayed other local forms both in the pottery, which was incised with geometric patterns, and in tomb-furniture. We must now look at the two groups, since both are relevant to our subject: the southerners because their culture developed into Etruscan civilization, the northerners because at a much later stage their land became part of the Etruscan 'Empire'.[6]

THE NORTHERN VILLANOVANS[7]

These were settled in an area roughly corresponding to the modern provinces of Bologna, Faenza, Forlì and Ravenna stretching from the Panaro eastwards to the Adriatic and lying between the Apennines and the course of the Reno. The key position was centred on Bologna where in the eponymous village of Villanova a typical cemetery was excavated in 1853. Four periods have been distinguished, Villanovan I–IV (according to the older nomenclature San Vitale, Benacci I and II and Arnoaldi), which tentatively may be dated: I until *c.* 750 BC; II a very short period; III *c.* 750 to *c.* 625/600; IV to 550/500. Then about 500 the Etruscans arrived and established a town called Felsina, cheek by jowl with the Villanovan settlement. The development of metallurgy, even in the preceding Bronze Age, stimulated an increase of population in the area of Bologna, which was favourably placed astride the early trade-routes. The settlement drew its supply of copper (and later of iron) from Tuscany; in return it exported agricultural products, salt, and manufactured metal work, together with amber which it had imported from the north. The two main areas of early Iron Age occupation were the zone of Bologna and Imola, and eastern Romagna (Verucchio, San Marino, Rimini); they command the entrances to the Reno and the Marecchia valleys, two of the main passes over the Apennines southwards to Etruria. In the more open Bolognese, agricultural settlements were scattered on the plain and the lower slopes of the outlying Apennines, while in Romagna from Imola eastwards settlements occupied strong and more centralized positions. Villages might gradually cluster together, as at Bologna, and some form of union develop, but it is too early to think in terms of towns in this pre-urban age. The basis of economic life was still agriculture and stock-breeding, but the production of goods became more professional. Metal-working naturally demanded an increasing degree of specialization, while a change from home production to embryonic factory work is indicated by the greater uniformity of the pottery in Period III. Further, metal ossuaries began to replace the earlier pottery ones. Commerce also increased, and other goods beside raw metal began to cross the Apennines from Etruria, for instance some gold work, which was soon imitated locally in silver and bronze. The growth of the population is shown by the number and size of the cemeteries: many now lie beneath modern Bologna and some huts have been preserved in the pedestrian subway under the Piazza Maggiore. This flourishing settlement has been called 'the Birmingham of early Italy', and its mineral wealth is brought home in striking fashion to the visitor to a room in the Bologna Museum, which contains nothing but an overwhelming mass of bronze implements, no less than 14,838 objects which were all found in a massive jar in a hut and weigh altogether nearly a ton and a half.

Increasing wealth naturally provoked social changes. Whereas the uniformity of the early ossuaries suggests a fairly even distribution of wealth with relatively little social differentiation, Periods II and III saw some individuals and groups beginning to emerge above their fellows. Although a change from round to ovoid and then to rectangular dwelling huts may not have had much significance, the grouping together of collections of huts was important. These larger groups of people would be economically stronger, and the *gens* was perhaps replacing the family as the unit of importance—but since burials had always been individual, man apparently was not regarded as a mere cog in a tribal system. The discovery of many horse-bits indicates an increasing use of the animal, but whether a new social class of aristocratic 'knights' emerged cannot be said. A flask (*askos*) shows a horseman armed with shield and helmet (*Pl. 6*). Although few arms survive, military activity may have increased in the late period under Etruscan influence, but at most we should deduce a citizen-militia, not a 'warrior-class'. In this later period also Villanovan art underwent some modifications; the patterns on pottery were now produced mechanically by wooden stamps instead of by hand; geometric patterns gave place to schematic figures of animals or men. The inspiration of this new influence, which was 'orientalizing', probably came from Etruria, just as the gold jewellery was imported from Etruscan Vetulonia. It is now becoming increasingly clear that during Period IV Villanovan culture was subjected to strong Etruscan influences. This is illustrated by two recent discoveries of great significance. An 'orientalizing' gravestone (*stele*) has been found at Bologna in connection with a tomb of Villanovan III, while the great archaic *tholos* tomb found at Quinto Fiorentino near Florence (see p. 168 and *Pls. 84-6*) shows one of the routes by which these influences could penetrate through the Apennines. This development culminated when the Etruscans advanced over the Apennines, established Felsina, and spread into the Po valley (see pp. 198ff).

THE SOUTHERN VILLANOVANS

With the Southern Villanovans, we come to the area in which Etruscan civilization first emerged in Italy: whatever the Etruscans owed to foreign influences, racial or cultural, their debt to the Villanovans is beyond all doubt, since many Etruscan settlements are found on the same sites as earlier Villanovan villages. Further, whether the relationship of Etruscans to Villanovans was that of a tree to its roots or of a grafted shoot to its alien stock, it is equally certain that Villanovan culture was the Italian soil in which Etruscan civilization grew up and flourished. Even so strong a believer in the eastern origin of the Etruscans as Randall-MacIver could write, 'we may detect in the Villanovans the real backbone of the Etruscan nation'.

Villanovan culture in Etruria closely resembled that found north of the Apennines, and the minor differences need not be stressed.

The people lived in huts which can be reconstructed from the clay replicas that some groups used as cinerary urns in place of the more normal biconical type; these hut-urns are found in Etruria, for instance at Vulci and Caere, but they are more common in Villanovan settlements south of the Tiber. The foundations of three such huts were found in 1948 on the Palatine hill at Rome, cut into the tufa rock (*Pls. 1, 3*); they are roughly rectangular (some $13\frac{1}{2} \times 11\frac{3}{4}$ feet). The disposition of the post-holes enables the wooden superstructure to be reconstructed. A central wooden pillar held a ridge-piece, from which a gabled roof descended to, and extended beyond, the upright sides of the hut. In front of the door was a small porch or an extension of the roof; possibly there was sometimes a side window. The roof and walls consisted of wattle and daub (branches and thatch laid on a coating of dry clay). Remains of charcoal and ash attest a hearth inside the hut, while fragments of cooking-stands, smoke-blackened household utensils and charred animal bones reflect the family meal. Clusters of these huts formed village-settlements, and recent work at Veii (see p. 106) shows that groups of such 'villages' might be built around a central strong-point, and thus ultimately fuse into a 'town' or at any rate, into what became a town during the Etruscan phase. The fact that the pattern of Etruscan settlement was in many cases already established by the Villanovans in the eighth century suggests that the latter should be given more credit for social organization than they have sometimes received.

The Villanovans' material goods and chattels were often excellent, thanks to their skill in metallurgy and pottery. Outstanding among the bronze work were crested helmets, ornamented with rows of engraved bosses in repoussé; the technique of these helmets is purely Villanovan and the strictly geometric decoration lacks any trace of the more luxurious floral or animal designs which appeared later. Other types of helmet are cap-shaped and 'mushroom-topped' (*elmo pilato*). Such helmets or pottery models of them were often used as covers for the cinerary urns. Typical were bronze antennae- and T-shaped swords, semi-lunate razors, buckets, girdles and fibulae (*Pls. 4, 5*). Of the pottery, the biconical or two-storied urn was the most characteristic; it was decorated with incised geometric patterns, often meanders. This urn was used exclusively in the earliest cemeteries, where it was placed at the bottom of a pit (*pozzo*) several feet below the surface of the rock. A second phase developed (*c.* 750–700) when inhumation appeared alongside cremation, the bodies being laid in trenches (*a fossa*). The objects placed in the graves became finer, especially the bronze work which included the lively little figures in the Wiry Geometric style (see pp. 290f), and imported objects became more common; Greek painted pottery began to appear, since now the Greeks were establishing the earliest of their colonies in Italy. In the seventh century, during the next phase, inhumation became the normal form, with the dead laid in chamber-tombs cut into the rock. This corresponds with the beginning of the 'orientalizing' phase, when the funeral equipment becomes richer with the importation of more Greek and oriental objects, including work in gold and silver, and the use of iron becomes general. These changes naturally took place earlier in the settlements near the coast, which were more open to foreign influences; in distant inland areas the time-lag was considerable. Thus at Clusium cremation persisted much longer and inhumation is not found much before the sixth century. There is in fact greater local variation among the Villanovans in Etruria than among those at Bologna whose culture was more homogeneous; north of the Apennines, Villanovan culture was not much affected by external influences before the middle of the sixth century, and its society was little changed until Etruscan settlers arrived at the end of that century. The Villanovans in Etruria, however, were much more exposed to the varied influences from the Aegean, and when we see the orientalizing movement sweeping over Etruria, we feel that we are moving, or have moved, from a Villanovan to an Etruscan world. This transition may appear gradual, but between its beginning and end profound changes had been effected: not only had small villages become wealthy cities, but men were beginning to use the Etruscan language. By that time either 'the Etruscans' or Etruscanization had arrived, and we have reached the heart of the 'mystery' of the Etruscans. Why did a relatively homogeneous Iron Age culture, which covered so much of central and northern Italy, develop into what we call 'Etruscan civilization' in one area and in one area alone? That, as we shall see, is the crucial question.

Southern Villanovan culture was not confined to Etruria, but is found in Latium and farther south. This Iron Age civilization, which flourished in the Alban Hills and at Rome, used to be known as 'Southern Villanovan', but it is now more often called *cultura laziale*.[8] It differs in some details from Villanovan in Etruria, but in all essentials the two may be regarded as one. One characteristic of Latium, already noted, is the standard use of the hut-urn in place of the biconical ossuary; Latin pottery, too, has a strong local flavour. The culture lasted (from the tenth?) to the seventh century, and is exemplified by the eighth-century hut-foundations on the Palatine at Rome, whose inhabitants were buried *a pozzo* in what later became the Roman Forum. At these sites, unlike those in Etruria, Villanovan culture did not merge gradually into Etruscan: again, the crucial question is 'why not'? Their Etruscanization came at a later stage of their history when some, including Rome, were seized by Etruscan rulers.

Recent evidence has revealed 'Villanovan' settlements in two isolated areas of Italy. One is north of Fermo in the Marche near the Adriatic coast, some forty miles from Ascoli Piceno, where an eighth-century cemetery was found in 1956 with 120 cremation tombs of the Villanovan type and burials. The other is in the south, around Salerno and in Campania. At Pontecagnano, some six miles south of Salerno some 330 tombs, dating from the eighth century to *c*. 550 BC, have been found in excavations which started in 1958. The earlier ones comprise a Villanovan cemetery, with biconical urns, often covered with pottery helmets, parallel to material from southern Etruria. There were also *a fossa* inhumations; these predominate in Phase II. Later, from the early seventh century, an orientalizing phase (III) occurs, with Protocorinthian pottery and light *bucchero*, to be followed later by heavy *bucchero* and Corinthian pottery (Phase IV). At Capodifiume, four miles north-east of Paestum, similar Villa-novan pottery occurs. Sala Consilina in the Valle di Diana also reveals cremation urns and inhumations, and the inhabitants apparently exchanged goods with those of Capodifiume. In Campania too evidence of Villanovan settlements is now coming to light. At Capua itself some Villanovan cremations have been found, together with some inhumations; the Villanovan material is more closely related to that of central Etruria (Vulci and Bisenzio) than to that of southern Etruria. Near the famous temple of Diana Tifatina also there are some even earlier Villanovan cremations. Indeed the extent of this Iron Age penetration in Campania is only beginning to appear; it may well be that the convenient label 'Villanovan' will have to be abandoned. How some of these settlements developed an orientalizing phase, is a matter which is linked with the problem of the 'coming of the Etruscans' (see pp. 191f).[9]

WHO WERE THE VILLANOVANS?

'Villanovan' is a useful label to cover a common culture, but it can be misleading if it creates the impression of a unified racial and linguistic block. There may have been such a homogeneous unit, but we cannot be sure: for instance, much of the culture of the Southern Villanovans could have come to them by borrowings from and contacts with the northerners, who could have been of a different racial stock and have spoken a different language. Such doubts were felt less keenly a generation or so ago, but they lie behind the present unpopularity of enquiring into Etruscan origins: race, culture and language may be united to form a 'people' or a 'civilization', but it is equally true that different peoples may have one or two of these elements in common. We should therefore be chary of supposing that the Villanovans of Etruria were necessarily identical with those who lived around Bologna in all essential respects.

Did the Villanovans come from anywhere? If not, they must have been autochthonous, and they presumably spoke an early 'Mediterranean' language and not an Indo-European tongue. In that case the Etruscans who followed them could have inherited their speech, and there would be little objection to regarding the two as a single people at different stages of its development. If, however, the Villanovans did come to Etruria from outside Italy, they could have brought with them an Indo-European dialect, and since virtually everyone agrees that the Etruscan language was not Indo-European, then the Etruscans are less likely to be of Villanovan origin. While it is generally accepted that Etruscan civilization owed much to the Villanovans, the crucial issue is whether men of alien stock, speaking another tongue, came into Villanovan Etruria and so interacted with the Villanovans as to produce what we call Etruscan civilization; in that case if the original speech of the Villanovans was Indo-European and since Etruscan was not, then the probability of an eastern origin for the Etruscans is greatly increased. Thus the question of Villanovan origins becomes important, if not *per se*, at least in so far as it has any bearing upon what language they spoke.

The problem of the introduction of Indo-European into Italy is highly complex, and we must limit ourselves to a few aspects of it, despite the hazards of oversimplification. At the beginning of the Iron Age there were, in addition to the Villanovans, various other groups of cultures: the Golaseccan culture in Piedmont and Lombardy, and the Atestine in Venetia in the north; the Fossa Grave culture in Campania and Bruttium (modern Calabria) and Apulian in the south; and the Picene on the east coast. No epigraphical evidence survives to show what languages these peoples spoke at the beginning of the Iron Age, but later the majority were Indo-European speaking. More significant are the tribes of the central Apennines, where the Bronze Age 'Apennine' culture had flourished. Whatever their cultural pre-history, the Iron Age peoples here shared a linguistic group of Indo-European dialects, the Osco-Umbrian or Umbrian-Sabellic; as these spread out, we find Umbrian in the north, Sabellic ('Italic') dialects in the centre, and Oscan (the language of the Samnites) in the south of this area. These dialects are closely related to Latin, but they are even more closely related to each other. As to the racial stock of their speakers, these were probably descendants of the 'Apennine' culture, reinforced by some Indo-European-speaking peoples from overseas (the Aegean world in general: *cf.* p. 19). Like their predecessors, they buried their dead. Their occupation of the central highlands blocked the eastward expansion of the Villanovans and later of the Etruscans. Thus central Italy was sharply divided by a line which ran from near Rimini to just south of Rome: to the west were the Villanovans who practised cremation, to the east the Indo-European-speaking highlanders who inhumed their dead, including the people of southern Picenum; the linguistic affinities of northern Picenum are less clear. This Rimini–Rome line has figured large in many arguments, which assumed that it formed a cultural, ethnic, or linguistic boundary—or all three.

The basic problem is to determine from what direction the Indo-European dialects reached Italy and to what extent their arrival involved the migration of peoples who spoke them. Were there large-scale immigrations, or did the dialects spread by infiltration? If the spread of the dialects presupposes mass movements, were the individual dialects peculiar to the individual groups of speakers from the beginning or did the differences arise when they were already acclimatized *within* Italy? Amid such a welter of problems, we can only glance at some aspects. Since the concept of a group of correlated Indo-European languages involves the probability of a common 'ancestor', all the Indo-European dialects in Italy probably originated from a common source, perhaps more immediately the Danubian area. But did the Indo-European dialects reach Italy from the north or from the east? For some dialects a reasonable answer can be advanced. Messapic, spoken in the heel of Italy, was probably introduced by the migration of Illyrian tribes from the other side of the Adriatic; a similar source is probably responsible for Venetic in the north (and perhaps for 'East Italic' in Picenum), while the dialect of the Raeti (north and west of Venetic) is partly Illyrian and partly Celtic (at a later date it was influenced by Etruscan). But where do Osco-Umbrian and Latin stand? Did they come from the north (*e.g.* via Austria) or from the south-east (*e.g.* via Albania)? The classic modern theory has been that two waves of peoples who spoke Indo-European dialects came down from the north of the Alps: the first group, who cremated their dead, settled west of the Rimini–Rome line and the second, the Sabellian-Italici, who buried their dead, settled east of the line.

The second part of this view is open to serious objection: it would seem that if large numbers of inhuming Italici came from the north, some traces of their line of advance through north Italy would have survived. These Italic dialects therefore may well have spread from eastern or western parts of Italy among the Bronze Age peoples of the central Apennines without the mass immigration of invaders. And the older inhabitants naturally retained their practice of inhumation. But as regards those settled west of the line, namely the Terramaricoli, Villanovans and Latins, the theory of their northern origin is still widely held. On this view therefore the Villanovans must have been an Iron Age people who came from over the Alps, cremated their dead and spoke an Indo-European dialect; some pushed southwards to Etruria where the Bronze Age settlements appear to have been sparse. Here they developed until Etruscans arrived from overseas with their non-Indo-European language, which gained the upper hand. This view rests on the many links that Villanovan culture had with the urn-fields of central Europe; these are found in Hungary in the early Bronze Age and spread thence in the late Bronze Age to other parts of Europe, including Bohemia. The method of burying the cremated ashes is the same; and there are similarities between the artefacts of the various urn-field cultures, such as biconical urns, hut-urns (on the Elbe), bell-helmets, crested helmets (Germany and France), antennae swords (Middle Elbe, etc.), bronze girdles, and birds' heads ornaments. Further, there are sufficient early examples in the European urn-fields to suggest that these settlements are earlier in date than those in Etruria.[10]

Other archaeologists argue that the urn-field culture reached Etruria not by land from the north but by sea from the East. A highly confident summary of this view is given by Mrs Richardson: 'Prehistorians have recently determined that the first settlers of the Iron Age, the so-called Villanovans, a cremating people with many connections with northern Europe, actually came to Italy by sea from the eastern Mediterranean some time between 1000 and 900 BC.' Incidentally, she goes on to identify the Villanovans with Pelasgians and believes that a second migration brought the Etruscans to Italy from the east much later (early seventh century). But this view involves the acceptance of some very dubious recent theories such as that of H. Müller-Karpe, who suggests that close cultural connections existed between the Latin urn-field cultures and the early Iron Age civilization of Crete.[11]

This view would certainly not be accepted by Professor Pallottino, who believes that the Villanovans were autochthonous and that the urn-field culture reached them from outside. For him the creation of Villanovan culture was the result of a long process. Some factors such as cremation and biconical urns were imported 'perhaps even by means of more or less numerous immigrants. One can think of arrivals from the continent by land, as reflected by the spread of the urn-fields of central Europe and connected with the cremations which appear in northern Italy at the end of the late Bronze Age. But one can also think of arrivals from the south by coastal or sea routes, if account is taken of the fact that the proto-Villanovan cemeteries in Etruria and some of the earliest cremations of the same Villanovan cemeteries of the great southern Etruscan cities come into the proto-Villanovan framework of South Italy (Apulia and Sicily) and of the Adriatic'. Thus for Pallotino Villanovan civilization is a native growth, based on the Apennine Bronze Age culture, which absorbed external elements but without profound ethnic changes.[12]

Pallottino also believes that linguistic waves of Indo-European dialects reached Italy from the east across the Adriatic, and pushed the earlier non-Indo-European languages (Ligurian and Tyrrhenian) to the north and west. The first wave was proto-Latin and reached Italy even before the Bronze Age, *i.e.* before *c.* 2000. It was later pushed westwards by the subsequent wave of Umbro-Sabellian dialects which established themselves in southern central Italy where the Apennine Bronze Age culture was relatively uniform. Thirdly, an Illyrian wave got no farther than the east coast. On this linguistic map of Italy Pallottino imposes the archaeological map, and finds that the Indo-European languages fall to the east of the Rimini–Rome line in the inhumation area, and the non-Indo-European to the west: thus the

Villanovans, whose area lies to the west of the line, did not speak
Indo-European. This argument, however, has not won over all
the philologists. E. Pulgram, for instance, has pointed out that
the two maps do not correspond: the archaeological picture
belongs to the tenth-ninth century, the linguistic to the sixth-
fifth (the time of the earliest inscriptions). Thus like is not compared with like, and it does not necessarily follow that, because
non-Indo-European (*i.e.* Etruscan) was spoken in Etruria west
of the line *c.* 500, the inhabitants of this area cannot have spoken
Indo-European in *c.* 900. In regard to the presumed movements
of peoples behind these waves (*e.g.* 'the Umbro-Sabellian wave
drove back these proto-Latin people': Pallottino), Pulgram wrote,
'I wish to reject the migrations . . . since there is simply no
evidence for them at this point.' Some would not go as far as
this. Thus G. Patroni went only half-way: he accepted that there
was no migration to explain the origin of Osco-Umbrian
dialects (their seeds, he believed, were introduced by infiltration
by speakers of Indo-European), but he believed that Latin was
brought in by the Villanovans, who spoke it. Pulgram, who
rejects the Villanovan immigration, does however believe that
the originators of the Villanovan culture probably spoke Indo-
European. But as yet no firm correlation between linguistics and
archaeology can be established.

Thus in regard to the Etruscan problem, to which we must now
turn, we are left with four possibilities: that the Villanovans
brought an Indo-European tongue with them into Etruria,
coming either from the north or by sea, or that they were in some
sense autochthonous and either acquired an Indo-European
tongue, or developed into Etruscans whose tongue was akin to
their own. While large-scale immigrations may find few supporters nowadays, at least it is very far from certain that Etruscan
civilization and language were basically a native growth in
Etruria.[13]

CHAPTER II

WHO WERE THE ETRUSCANS?

THE LITERARY SOURCES

THE ETRUSCANS first appear in Greek literature in the epic poet Hesiod (*Theogony* 1010) who wrote that Agrius and Latinus, the sons whom Circe bore to Odysseus, 'ruled over the famous Tyrsenians, very far off in a recess of the holy islands'. This suggests that there were Etruscans in Italy (and even in Latium?) in Hesiod's day, but it throws no light on their origin.[14] Of this Herodotus gives the first account (1, 90). After eighteen years of famine Atys, King of Lydia, decided to send half his people to seek new homes; when lots were drawn, one half stayed with him, while his son Tyrsenos led the others to Smyrna, built ships and sailed off. After passing many peoples they 'at last came to the Ombrikoi [Umbrians in Latin], where they founded cities and have lived ever since. They no longer called themselves Lydians but changed their name to Tyrsenoi after the king's son who had led them.' Herodotus is merely repeating a Lydian account, but while he does not vouch for it himself, there is no suggestion that he doubted its truth.

Various versions of this story circulated later and some were mentioned by Dionysius of Halicarnassus who wrote during the reign of Augustus. The Lydian origin of the Etruscans was in fact accepted by most classical writers (*e.g.* Timaeus, Lycophron, Strabo, Appian, Plutarch, Cicero, Virgil, Catullus, Horace, Tacitus and Pliny). Mere repetition cannot turn fiction into fact, but the list is impressive. Strabo (5, 2, 2) adds a piece of native Etruscan tradition when he says that Tyrsenos, after arriving in the land which he called Tyrrhenia, put Tarchon in charge as colonizer and founded twelve cities. Tacitus (*Ann.* 4, 55) records a meeting of the Roman Senate in AD 26 at which envoys from Lydian Sardis referred to their 'kindred country' of Etruria and explained the link by repeating the story of Tyrrhenus' voyage from Asia. Thus the Lydian origin was generally accepted at this time, and appears to have been the version officially adopted in Etruria itself.

Dionysius alone rejected the Lydian origin, and believed that 'the Etruscan nation migrated from nowhere else but was native to the country' (I, 30). He had two reasons. First, he could find no similarity between the Etruscans and Lydians of his own day in language, religion or institutions. But this is not surprising, since many centuries had passed, Etruria had been virtually romanized, and the Etruscan language had probably largely died out. His second reason is more serious, namely that Xanthus of Lydia, who lived about the same time as Herodotus and wrote a history of his country, showed no knowledge of a Lydian ruler named Tyrrhenus nor of any settlement of Lydians in Italy. But the historical reliability of Xanthus on the whole does not appear to have been very great: L. Pearson has written that 'It would be surprising if Xanthus earned the reputation as a trustworthy historian'. Thus the silence of Xanthus on this point may have no more, and perhaps less, weight than the statement of Herodotus.[15]

Dionysius also rejected the widely held view that the Etruscans should be equated with the Pelasgians. This view, which is reflected in a reference by Sophocles to 'Tyrsenian Pelasgians' in a fragment of his lost play *Inachus*, was given currency by Hellanicus, a contemporary of Herodotus, and probably slightly his junior. Hellanicus said that after the Pelasgians had settled in Italy they changed their name to Tyrrhenians.

Mystery surrounds the identity of the Pelasgians, partly because classical writers seem to have used the word in two senses, general and specific. First, the word was applied to a definite historic people or peoples. Thus Herodotus spoke of Pelasgians on the south coast of the Hellespont at Placie and Scylace, in the Troad, in Lemnos, Imbros and Samothrace, and in Creston between the Strymon and Axius rivers. Thucydides also refers to them in Lemnos, and both historians regard them as 'barbarians', that is, non-Greeks. Both writers also link them with the Etruscans.

Herodotus (1, 57) mentions the Tyrseni as neighbours of the Pelasgians in Creston (unless the reference should be to Cortona in Italy), while Thucydides (4, 109), speaking of the district of Acte in the area of Creston, says that it was 'inhabited by mixed barbarian tribes who speak two languages; there is in it a small Chalcidic element, but the greatest part is Pelasgic, belonging to those Tyrsenians who once inhabited Lemnos and Athens'.[16] Secondly, the Greeks used the word Pelasgians in a general sense for any prehistoric people, what we might call the pre-Indo-European Mediterranean peoples. This usage seems to go back to Homer, but it was perhaps Hecataeus of Miletus (c. 500 BC) who popularized the idea of the Pelasgians as the 'original race' or 'early men'.

In view of the vagueness in the use of the word Pelasgian, it might be tempting to suggest that any comparison or identification of Pelasgians with Etruscans arose from this wider application; Greek writers might have applied the same term to the primitive population of Italy as they used for this stratum in Greece. If this were so, the Pelasgians would have little relevance to the Etruscan question, but in fact many circumstantial stories were told, which may or may not contain some element of truth. Thus Hellanicus in a mythographic work, *Phoronis*, which dealt extensively with the Pelasgians, stated that in the reign of Nanas, who was fourth in descent from Pelasgus, 'the Pelasgians were driven from their land by the Greeks, and after leaving their ships at the river Spines (*i.e.* the Spinetic mouth of the Po) in the Ionian Gulf, they took Croton (*i.e.* Cortona) an inland city; and proceeding from here they colonized the country now called Tyrrhenia'.[17] This account of the origin of the Etruscans in Italy is full of error: there is no archaeological evidence to suggest that they arrived first from the Adriatic, their settlements in the Po valley were much later than those in Etruria, and inland cities like Cortona developed later than the cities on the coast like Tarquinii. Nevertheless it does add another testimony to the widespread belief that the Etruscans had arrived in Italy from overseas and that they had some connection with people or peoples in the Aegean world. This belief in an eastern origin combined with a Pelasgian connection is expressed by a writer of the late fourth century, Anticleides of Athens: the Pelasgians 'were the first to settle the regions round about Lemnos and Imbros, and indeed some of them sailed off to Italy with Tyrrhenos the son of Atys' (see Strabo 5, 3, 6).

This tradition posed a problem for Dionysius, who accepted a Pelasgian invasion of central Italy. Since he believed that the Etruscans were autochthonous and that the Pelasgians were Greeks, he had to deny the identity of the two people. Further, he was not willing to minimize the role of the Pelasgians, the reason being that he was writing an account of the origins of Rome in order to show that Rome was not a barbarian but a Greek city: he claimed that 'one will find no people that is more ancient or more Greek' than the early population of Rome, which for him comprised Aborigines, Pelasgians, Arcadians, the followers of Heracles and the Trojans of Aeneas.[18] Since he knew that the Etruscans did not speak Greek, the Pelasgians, even apart from their overseas origin, could not be the same people, and so the latter had to be removed from Italy. This he did by telling of a famine which led to disorderly emigrations from Italy and 'the Pelasgic nation was scattered over most of the earth'. The famine, incidentally, looks suspiciously like some reflection of Herodotus' story of the famine in Lydia, though in Dionysius' Italian context the subsequent migration appears rather as the result of the Italic practice of a Sacred Spring. After the Pelasgians had left Italy, Dionysius continues, their cities were seized chiefly by the Tyrrhenians 'whom some declare to be natives of Italy but others call foreigners' (1, 26): he then discusses the origins of the Etruscans for whom there was now more room after the departure of the Pelasgians.

It is difficult to make archaeological sense of Dionysius' picture of indigenous Etruscans overlaid by invading Pelasgians. The invaders cannot have been Greeks—archaeology makes this certain—but could they have been Villanovans? This view would be possible for those who hold the Villanovans to have been Iron Age invaders; Dionysius' Etruscans would then be equated with pre-Iron Age peoples who later ultimately superseded the

Villanovans and became the Etruscans of history. But those who believe the Villanovans themselves to be indigenous have no incoming people to equate with the Pelasgians: the Umbrians are excluded because Dionysius regarded them as a native people (2, 49), whom he distinguishes from the Pelasgians. But if we could accept Herodotus' eastern origin and Hellanicus' equation of Etruscans and Pelasgians, the position would be much clearer. Thus if Dionysius' autochthonous theory can be questioned on other grounds, its veracity is not strengthened by his Pelasgian story.

Beside literary texts, two important groups of documents provide possible evidence for Tyrrhenoi in the East; they come from Lemnos and Egypt.[19] In Lemnos, where the pre-Greek population was Pelasgian according to Herodotus (6, 137) and Tyrrhenian according to Thucydides (4, 109), the tomb-stone (*stele*) of a warrior was discovered in 1885, not dissimilar from that of Avele Feluske of Vetulonia in Etruria (*cf.* Figs. 1, 2 and p. 223). It not only shows his head in profile, but also bears two inscriptions in an alphabet which closely resembles that of old-Phrygian inscriptions of the seventh century. The language has some analogies with the tongues of Asia Minor, but philologists are in general agreement that both in its morphology and vocabulary it has many similarities with Etruscan.[20] When this document stood alone, it might have been dismissed as the epitaph of a foreigner who was buried in Lemnos, but more recently other short inscriptions have been found on vases, and these show that this was in fact the language spoken on the island before its conquest by the Athenian Miltiades (*c.* 500 BC). Thus we have a very important document, pointing both to Asia Minor and to Etruria, and it comes from the very island where Thucydides placed the Tyrrhenoi. Though it does not afford conclusive proof that 'Lemnian' and Etruscan were the same, or even dialects of the same, language, it provides a valuable link for those who accept an eastern origin and suggests that some Etruscans from Asia Minor may have settled in this Aegean island instead of continuing farther west. Those who reject an eastern origin have to explain away the similarities of language

Fig. 1 Funeral stele of Avele Feluske from the Tomb of the Warrior in Vetulonia, the city from which the Romans are said to have borrowed the fasces. Note, in this connection, that he carries a double-axe

Fig. 2 Funeral stele of a warrior buried in Lemnos, with an inscription in a pre-hellenic dialect which resembles both Etruscan and old-Phrygian, and thus may provide a link between Etruria and Asia Minor

as due to survival from a hypothetical widespread pre-Indo-European linguistic unit which once occupied a vast area in Italy and the Aegean until it was broken up by the advance of Indo-European: in Italy it was confined to Etruria, while in the Aegean relics of it were left in Lemnos.[21]

Egyptian documents may offer evidence for the presence of Etruscans in the eastern Mediterranean at a much earlier period. Two raids upon Egypt by the so-called Peoples of the Sea are recorded, one against Pharaoh Merneptah about 1219 BC and the other against Rameses III between 1165 and 1159. The forms of the names given in the hieroglyphics are not easy to interpret, but they show that the raiders included Achaeans, Philistines, Danaans, and perhaps Lycians, Sardinians and Sicels. One name, the *Trs.w* or Teresh, has often been equated with the Tyrrhenoi: the transliteration of the hieroglyphs is difficult, but the identification is attractive. Once again conclusive proof eludes us but it is possible that the ancestors of the Etruscans were among the unsettled peoples who were seeking new homes during the period of *Völkerwanderung* and general confusion which the Near East suffered towards the end of the thirteenth century. Egypt managed to repel the invaders, but the Hittite fortresses of Mersin and Tarsus which protected the plain of Cilicia were destroyed; here some Greeks may have settled, while the Philistines seized the coastal area of Palestine. Did some Etruscans from Asia Minor share in these troubled times and then find new homes in Italy? Is such a hypothesis, apart from any other difficulties involved in it, possible on purely chronological grounds?[22]

CHRONOLOGICAL ASPECTS

Herodotus, who does not date the voyage of Tyrrhenos, Atys' son, to Italy, records three Lydian dynasties. The Mermnadae, whose rule started with Gyges (716 BC according to Herodotus), were preceded by the Heraclidae to whom he assigns 505 years; these in turn were preceded by the descendants of Lydus, Atys' son. Thus a chronology based on Herodotus would put the Etruscan migration well back in the thirteenth century. This corresponds roughly to the Egyptian evidence, and a closer link has been sought on the assumption that Herodotus' story can be connected with a famine known to history. Merneptah (*c.* 1219) caused certain people 'to take grain in ships to keep alive that land of Kheta' (*i.e.* the Hittites), while there is Hittite evidence for a famine in western Asian Minor in or near Lydia in the time of king Tudkhaliyas IV (*c.* 1250–1220).[23] A slightly later date, near the beginning of the first millennium, might be deduced from the Etruscans' own system of reckoning by *saecula*. They believed that their nation had ten *saecula* to live, and although the precise length of some of them is doubtful, a rough calculation would put the beginning of the Etruscan era in 969 BC.[24] But any attempt to find Etruscans in the eastern Mediterranean in the thirteenth, twelfth or even tenth century leaves a gap of several centuries before the usually accepted date of their arrival in Italy in the eighth or seventh century.

How far back then are we justified in seeking 'Etruscan' evidence in Italy? While it is better to reserve the word Etruscan for the developed civilization of the seventh century, this may well have been preceded by a proto-Etruscan period in which the cultures of early Italy were subjected to some alien influences from the East. What then is the earliest object found in Etruria that is not Italic but oriental? The answer now appears to be the Mycenaean pottery found at Luni (see p. 96), but present indications are that this was the result of trading activity and is scarcely relevant to Etruscan origins. In general Mycenaean pottery found in Sicily and southern Italy reflects considerable commercial penetration, with trading-depots, if not full-scale colonies, at Taranto and Lipari.[25] These close contacts were apparently broken in the disturbed days of the thirteenth and twelfth centuries when Mycenaean power collapsed in Greece, but traces of Aegean influence in some pottery and architectural styles (apart from any alleged Aegean influences in the Alban Hills and at Rome)[26] continued while Italy was going through a transitional period between the twelfth and ninth centuries.

The evidence from Populonia implies some limited settlement as well as trade with the Aegean area. The crucial object is the grip-tongue sword, a type which appeared in the Aegean and eastern Mediterranean about 1250 BC by derivation from central Europe. Since it was much used in the eastern Mediterranean, some of the specimens found in Italy may well have derived from this area rather than directly from the north: in particular a type with a T-shaped projection of its top is of eastern derivation. Their distribution suggests that in the later twelfth and eleventh centuries after the period of the Sea Peoples, traders from the eastern Mediterranean brought these objects to the south-east coasts of Italy (*e.g.* to the Gargano peninsula) and to Sicily, and may have settled here and there. Some of them may have moved on and settled on the Etruscan coast about 1000 BC at Populonia. Here *tombe a fossa* have produced a bronze dagger which is regarded as an immediate derivative of the grip-tongue sword, together with some *a gomito* fibulae of the *occhio* type which occur in Sicily, while a chamber-tomb has yielded a sword with the T-type projection.[27] Further, the *tombe a fossa* may not represent merely the persistence of the 'Apennine' tradition of inhumation, because not only is there no other evidence for Apennine culture at Populonia, but fibulae *a gomito* have been found in a cemetery of *tombe a fossa* at Molino della Baddia in Sicily, which, like that at Populonia, is in an anomalous context, and even unique. Thus, the presence of imported objects and the choice of burial methods combine to suggest that Populonia received not only trade but also settlement from the east from *c.* 1000. The attraction must have been the mineral wealth of Etruria. At Populonia the *tombe a fossa* continued in use for a considerable period, and beside these are found cremations and chamber-tombs; the early small chamber-tombs date back to at least *c.* 750, and may be older; after 700 they become larger and more exotic. All this would suggest the possibility of a long period of gradual infiltration when settlers were winning control of the land from the Villanovans. Could this have been the long struggle with the Ombroi which Herodotus mentions?

We are now at the other end of the time-chart. By *c.* 750 Greek colonists were settling at Ischia and Cumae. The metal of Etruria must surely have attracted them farther north but they did not get beyond Cumae. The most obvious reason is that the

'Etruscans' were now strong enough to keep them out: in other words, during the period from the early tenth to the middle of the eighth century, native and foreign elements had fused. The reputation of the land had attracted sufficient Oriental settlers to develop its resources, and build and organize its settlements into cities; individual Greek settlers, like Demaratus of Corinth (*cf.* p. 85), might be welcomed, but any attempt to found an organized Greek colony would be repelled. Above all, it will have been in this long transitional period that the Etruscan language established itself in the land. This suggested development admittedly rests on slender evidence: it is a hypothesis (and one among many!), but at least it seems to fit well with the demands of chronology.[28]

ETRUSCAN ORIGINS—SOME MODERN VIEWS

The view that the Etruscans arrived in Italy from across the Alps now has little support, but when it was first put forward by N. Fréret in 1741 it was a bold challenge to Herodotus, based both on the fact that according to Dionysius the Etruscans called themselves Rasenna and on the assumption that this name could be linked to the Raetians of the Alps. The theory gained the authoritative support of Niebuhr who laid emphasis on a notorious passage of Livy (5, 33) which attributes the same origin to the Raetians as to the Etruscans. But since Livy in fact did not say that the Raeti spoke Etruscan, but only that their tongue had an Etruscan sound or accent (and a corrupted one at that), we do not need to accept his belief that the Raeti were actually an Etruscan people. True, Etruscoid inscriptions have been found in the Raetian Alps (in the area of Trento and the Upper Adige valley), but they are late (third and second century); Raetic is now recognized to be Indo-European (which most agree Etruscan was not), and the toponomy of the Raeti is Celto-Illyrian; and there is no archaeological evidence for Etruscan settlement north of the Apennines before about 500 BC. Thus the theory of a mass migration of Etruscans from the Alps to Italy has long been discarded, although the possibility of a northern origin did receive further support from archaeologists who believed in two waves of settlers in Italy from the north, namely the Bronze Age Terramaricoli and Iron Age Villanovans. Although most scholars regarded these newcomers as speakers of Indo-European dialects, a few, such as G. De Sanctis and L. Pareti, identified the Etruscans with them, and the Indo-European speakers with the older inhuming peoples. But this theory has been generally rejected.[29]

Thus if a northern origin is unacceptable, the two 'classic' modern theories of an oriental or an autochthonous origin remain, together with the more recent concept of 'formation' instead of 'origin'. Now let us see briefly how their champions handle the literary, linguistic and archaeological evidence. If for convenience we call them Orientalists and Autochthonists, it must be remembered that these labels are loose terms, each of which includes a great varieties of interpretation; the essential difference is that the Orientalists accept, and the Autochthonists deny, that Etruria received a considerable number of settlers who brought with them the Etruscan language.

Literary sources

The Orientalists accept Herodotus and reject the objections of Dionysius as inconclusive (the silence of Xanthus) or invalid (the alleged difference between Etruscans and Lydians in Dionysius' own day). The gap between Herodotus' date for the Etruscan arrival in Italy (the Trojan War period) and the date provided by the archaeological evidence (the eighth century) is explained either by supposing that Herodotus has misplaced his story in time or that in fact some Etruscans reached Italy in the confused period of the Peoples of the Sea after the fall of Troy and Mycenae. Thus F. Schachermeyr postulated two waves of immigrants (*c.* 1000 and *c.* 800), while J. Bérard regarded the eighth-century development in Etruria as a renaissance of an original Tyrrhenian–Pelasgian settlement of the Late Bronze Age;[30] others suppose that the settlement took the form of very gradual infiltration over a long period (see above p. 42).

To this the autochthonists reply by rejecting out of hand Herodotus 'legend' which may have arisen from similarity between the name of the Tyrrhenians in Italy and some town (Tyrra) in Lydia: Dionysius is to be followed. They would reject too the idea that the ancients knew of any 'Tyrrhenians' in the east before the fifth century: thus not only are the *Trs.w* of the Egyptian documents irrelevant, but even the Tyrrhenians in Lesbos are the creation of late learned speculation. Naturally, the traditions about the Pelasgians, together with Hellanicus' identification with the Tyrrhenians of Italy, are likewise to be thrown overboard. As to chronology, any settlement in the eighth century at the beginning of the historical period, must have been well known; it would surely have been recorded by other historians and could not have been detached by Herodotus from its historical context and retrojected some 500 years. In other words, it is argued, Herodotus' story and its chronology must hang together, and thus they do not make archaeological sense. Indeed, some would ask whether the archaeological evidence would ever have given rise to the hypothesis of Etruscan immigration into Italy, if Herodotus has never told his story: thus, for instance, it is argued that the cultural sequence in the cemeteries of Tarquinii suggests no ethnic change (*cf.* p. 86).

Linguistic evidence

The obscurity that surrounds the precise nature of the Etruscan language enables both schools to find support in it. Few believe it to be an Indo-European tongue—when this view was argued by W. Corssen in 1874, it was decisively refuted by W. Deecke in the following year—even if some still find some Indo-European influences in the speech as we now know it in the inscriptions. But if it is essentially a pre-Indo-European language, its affinities still remain uncertain. It was the verdict of a very distinguished linguist, R. S. Conway, that 'all roads lead to Asia Minor', and an important stage on that route is Lemnos, where the language has affinities with both Etruscan and Phrygian (see p. 38). Although such similarities may be admitted by the autochthonists, they can still argue that there is no convincing affinity between Etruscan and any known tongue of Asia Minor, such as Lydian, Lycian or Carian. For them Etruscan is the remnant of a pre-Indo-European language spoken in Italy and over a wide area, including Lemnos, before the coming of the Indo-Europeans.

The script in which the Etruscans wrote their language, throws an equally fitful light on the problem. It is commonly regarded as derived from a Western-Greek alphabet transmitted to the Etruscans from the Chalcidian Greek colony at Cumae, which was founded *c.* 750, shortly after the Greeks themselves had taken over a Phoenician (Semitic) alphabet and adapted it for their own use. A Greek inscription in the Chalcidian alphabet on a Greek Geometric vase of the eighth century has recently been found in the island of Pithecusae (Ischia), where Greek colonists from Chalcis and Eretria in Euboea had established themselves just before the settlement was made at Cumae on the mainland nearby.[31] For the autochthonists this development presents no difficulties: the more primitive native Etruscans simply adopted a script from the more civilized peoples who were establishing posts from which they might gain commercial access to the mineral wealth of Etruria. Nor need this view embarrass the Orientalists: since the Etruscans adopted a Greek script in Italy, either they did not possess one of their own when they were in Asia Minor or else they preferred the Greek alphabet to their own form of writing. The Greeks themselves had used Linear B in Mycenaean times and then after a period of interrupted literacy during the Dark Age (which admittedly lasted much longer than any reasonable period of Etruscan migration) they adopted the Phoenician alphabet. But there is another possibility which, if soundly based, would greatly reinforce the Orientalists' position. This is the theory that the Etruscans derived the alphabet, not from the Greeks of Cumae, but from an earlier form of Greek which they encountered when they themselves were in the east; this would have been a primitive form, earlier than the division into the 'Eastern' and 'Western' alphabets. The evidence is provided by the Etruscan alphabet of twenty-six letters which is inscribed as a model around the margin of an ivory writing tablet found at Marsiliana d'Albegna (see Fig. 3 and p. 126). It is written from right to left (unlike other Etruscan abcedaria) and dates from the first half of the seventh century. It gives

Fig. 3 Model Etruscan alphabet written on the edge of an ivory writing-tablet from Marsiliana d'Albegna and dating from the first half of the seventh century BC.

twenty-two North–west Semitic letters, in the Semitic order, followed by what the Greeks called upsilon, phi, chi and psi; it thus included the Phoenician samech, a letter which, though retained by the 'Eastern' Greek alphabet, was dropped by the 'Western'. It cannot, however, be said with absolute certainty that the western Greeks never used the letter samech, but only that since it does not occur in any surviving inscriptions, it is probable that they did not use it. Another fact, namely that the sign 8 occurs in both Lydian and Etruscan, may not be relevant, because it does not appear in Etruscan until near the end of the fifth century onwards when it was put last in the series of letters of the alphabet. Nor can much be derived from the hypothesis that the Etruscans used a syllabic script before they adopted the alphabet: syllabaries (*e.g.* CI, CA, CU, CE, etc.: see *TLE*, 55) do appear with Etruscan model alphabets, but they may not indicate more than methods by which writing or reading was taught by means of syllables. Thus, as so often, the evidence proves to be two-edged.[32]

Cremation and burial

On Villanovan-Etruscan sites the general sequence is cremation *tombe a pozzo*, followed and overlapped by *a fossa* inhumations which begin to predominate from *c.* 750; then came the increasingly elaborate corridor- and chamber-tombs. Does this variation in rite indicate a new racial element or merely a change in social custom? The Orientalists argue that, although inhumation was practised as far back as Neolithic times (when, however, the bodies were buried with knees drawn up, and not stretched out), the sudden increase during the eighth century of inhumation in what had previously been a cremation area, together with the novel aspect of some of the objects found with the burials, indicates the arrival of a new people. These people must have come by sea, because the earliest settlements in Etruria are those nearest to the coast, while the new burial rite superseded the old in south-west Etruria, but not inland and in the north. To these arguments the Autochthonists reply that the tombs from *a pozzo* to the elaborate chambers form an unbroken sequence, that *a fossa* are mixed with *a pozzo* at a very early stage, that burial is progressive (as in Latium in the eighth century, where there were no Etruscans), that cremation was not entirely abandoned at inland sites such as Clusium throughout the Etruscan period, and that it even reappeared to some extent in the sixth century in southern Etruria. It is also clear that eastern influences, no less than immigrants, would come by sea and therefore affect the coastal areas first.

The view that a change in funerary rites indicates the appearance of a new people was once widely held, but the fact that it is now regarded with considerable scepticism does not prove that it is necessarily wrong in specific cases.[33] And even if it is conceded that a break in the sequence is not sufficiently clear to convince everybody, one may still ask whether this was not to be expected. No one supposes that immense bands of Etruscans arrived from overseas together, and met with such fierce resistance that the warriors who fell were buried in large military cemeteries. If the infiltration was relatively gradual, men would be buried as and when they died over the years, and a changeover from cremation would be a progressive process. Further, the analogy sometimes suggested by the Autochthonists that cremation and inhumation flourished side by side during the Roman Empire as a result of social or economic, but not racial, causes, is not very convincing. We are not dealing with a highly developed civilization, but with relatively primitive peoples, among whom the initial impetus to make a change in so fundamental a matter as the disposal of the dead would surely arise from a more deep-seated cause than mere social fashion. True, that need not involve the arrival of a new people; it could equally mean the adoption of new religious ideas from contact with neighbours. The difficulty here is that the inhuming neighbours of the Villanovans were in the interior, while the new rite apparently arose first in the settlements near the coast.

A more fundamental question arises for the Autochthonists who believe that Villanovan merged into Etruscan. Villanovan culture, as we have seen, spread over much of northern and central Italy but north of the Apennines it retained its own characteristics and did not develop into an Etruscan civilization, which was not imposed on parts of north Italy until a much later stage. In other words, why did only one part (namely Etruria) of a large cultural area evolve in this manner? The Autochthonists could reply that it was more open to influences from the east; but were imported objects and the traders who brought them really a sufficient stimulus to create this striking development? These foreign influences had been at work for a long time. Even in the earliest period before 750, when cremation was almost the universal rite, a few Egyptian scarabs, amulets and thin gold plaques have been found at Tarquinia, while the much poorer burials in Latium have yielded traces of gold wire, together with crude human statuettes which are to be linked with the eastern Mediterranean rather than with the urn-fields of the north. During the next fifty years (c. 750–700) at a time when cremation increasingly gave place to inhumation, the contents of the *fossa* graves show increasing eastern influences, but these are Greek rather than oriental: while the small beads and amulets from Egypt and Phoenicia had no marked effect on the native artists who worked in bronze and pottery, imported Greek wares (and even pottery made by Greek artists who may have worked in Etruria itself) did affect the native pottery, which began to imitate Greek shapes and Greek Geometric decoration. A crucial question is the extent to which these changes should be regarded as the result merely of intensified contact with the east, or, as those who stress the change in the disposal of the dead believe, of 'Etruscan' influence. In other words, should 750–700 be regarded as advanced Villanovan or early Etruscan? What is beyond doubt is that this period was soon to be followed by a spectacular change, the full flood of the orientalizing period with its immense wealth and massive tombs containing ivory, alabaster, silver-gilt Phoenician bowls (*Pl. 27*), a new type of bronze sculpture and bronzeware with Assyrian style decoration. It is at this point that others would see the appearance of Etruscans.[34] And a cardinal question is why this orientalizing culture should have appeared only in Etruria and to some extent in Latium.

This brings us back to our original enquiry. Were eastern objects, traders and perhaps a few immigrant artists sufficient to stimulate these amazing changes? Granted that they might conceivably account largely for the artistic development, surely human agencies, and these on a much larger scale, are needed to explain the skills that led to the sudden flowering of city life and administration. It is true that the Autochthonist might answer that at this time the Villanovans were beginning to develop greater powers of this kind than we had previously suspected (*e.g.* the fusing of the villages at Veii into a larger community). In all these matters judgements tend to be subjective, but the speed with which city-life suddenly emerged in Etruria would seem to many to be explained more satisfactorily by the direct influx of a relatively small number of men endowed with administrative skill and experience, than by the hypothesis of gradual evolution from within. If, then, the main contribution of the newcomers was in the realm of ideas and 'invisible imports', there would be nothing strange in the supposition that they might also effect a change in burial habits in the course of time.

Parallels between Etruria and the East

The debt that civilization in Etruria owed to eastern influences is indicated by the modern term 'orientalizing period', the phase from c. 700 BC when the contents of the tombs became increasingly enriched with gold and silver works of art from Egypt, Cyprus, Phoenicia, Syria and Mesopotamia. But did a native people of Italy begin to exploit its mineral wealth and exchange this for the artistic treasures of the East, or was there already in Etruria the nucleus of a governing class that itself had come from the East? It cannot be denied that many parallels can be found in Asia Minor for many aspects of Etruscan civilization; even a scholar who is so strongly sceptical of oriental origins as Professor Pallottino, admits that the tumuli, chamber-tombs and rock-face tombs of Etruria and Asia Minor resemble each other. Yet despite this he believes that the tombs in Etruria were structurally part of a native development, although the spirit of the decorative elements was acquired from overseas. Further, as he points out, these imported oriental elements began to appear in Greece too, where no Etruscans settled, while in Etruria the orientalizing phase was succeeded by one of increasing Greek influences (Ionian and then Attic), and no one supposes that the Greeks colonized Etruria in the sixth century! But this formulation somewhat overstresses the point: few can doubt that foreign influences could become acclimatized in Etruria without immigration, but the fusion would obviously be explained more easily (though not necessarily more truly!) if such a movement occurred. Apart from the grave architecture, Pallottino can find no parallels between Etruscan civilization and the east during the Phrygian period (ninth to seventh centuries): there is no connection between Phrygian, Lydian or Lemnian pottery and that of Italy, nor did Asiatic Greek pottery influence the development of Etruscan bucchero ware; a widely diffused type of Asiatic fibula is rare in the west (the single example found in Italy was in Latium, not

Etruria); and although the bronze cauldrons recently found in the royal tomb at Phrygian Gordium resemble those from orientalizing tombs in Etruria (*Pl. 28*), they provide no link between Phrygia and Etruria, but merely testify to the wide distribution of the bronzes from Urartu (Armenia). Pallottino also stresses that the foreign elements in Etruria come chiefly from the cultural area of Egypt and Syria rather than from the Aegean-Asiatic zone of influence. This is a strong case, but except for the tombs, which may be significant, it is negative.[35]

Apart from any specific parallels, there are many similarities between Etruscan and Asiatic culture: the luxury of the Etruscans seems more oriental than Italic, together with their love of feasting, dancing and music, of games, jewellery and bright colours. According to classical writers the double-pipes were introduced from Phrygia, and the trumpet from Lydia (one tradition assigned its invention to Tyrrhenos), while even Dionysius, who denied any resemblance between Etruscan and Lydian customs, said that the purple robes of Etruscan magistrates resembled those of Lydian and Persian rulers. Some Etruscan usages, such as the long chiton and shoes with turned-up toes (*calcei repandi*) which are also found among the Ionian Greeks, could be Asiatic in origin without necessarily proving an Asiatic origin for their wearers. The Etruscan employment of matronymics, although not an exclusive use, nor one that affords evidence for a matriarchal society, was also customary among the Lydians. The Etruscan science of divination by means of the entrails and liver of sacrificed animals is widely recognized as derived from Chaldaea. Further, the general religious outlook of the Etruscans appears to reflect a non-classical mentality, but it is difficult to deny that this could have arisen from a primitive past in Italy rather than from the East. In assessing such factors as the religious mentality or attitude to life of a people whose literature does not survive to speak for them, judgement is likely to be subjective. It has been widely felt that Etruscan civilization had an essentially oriental element in it, but a general impression is not the same as proof. Since this is lacking, the cumulative effect of various items of evidence persuade some that Herodotus was right, but others can still maintain that all the oriental elements in Etruscan civilization were mere borrowings rather than inherited, even if they cannot point to any other local culture in the Mediterranean world that was as vitally changed as that of the Etruscans through purely 'commercial' channels.[36]

Biological Aids

The skills of physical anthropologists and medical biologists have been laid under contribution in attempts to determine the racial make-up of the Etruscans. The study of skeletal remains has been slow, partly because of the shortage of material that could be defined as Etruscan, since not every body found in Etruria could be so classified! G. Sergi, who examined 44 skulls from tombs in seven Etruscan cities, found 34 to be dolicho- or meso-cephalic, and 10 brachycephalic, but it would be extremely hazardous to identify the former with Etruscan invaders and the latter with a native population. From the variation in skulls A. Neppi Modona has concluded that 'they can tell us very little about the ethnic complex of the Etruscan people . . . on the other hand, an accurate and complete examination of numerous skeletons proved that the Etruscans were of medium height'.[37] Future work may be more productive in this field.

Another line of approach is the study of blood-groups, both those indicated by the evidence of bones and also those in the present population of Tuscany. The red corpuscles of the blood are agglutinated by two substances, one or other of which is present or absent in four human blood-groups, known as O, A, B and AB. The variations in proportion of these groups among different races is very striking: thus in western Europe the proportion is roughly 46%O, 42%A, 9%B, and 3%AB, while among the Basques group A forms only 20% and group B less than 3%. Further, these percentages appear to remain fairly constant for long periods in certain circumstances. Sir Gavin de Beer has attempted to apply this knowledge to the Etruscan problem.[38] He noted from the maps in Dr A. E. Mourant's work on *The Distribution of the Human Blood-Groups* (1954) that there was a large zone in central Italy where group A is some 20%

more numerous than in the surrounding regions, that within this zone is a smaller area which shows a percentage of group B nearly twice as high as that found in the rest of Italy, and that a similar distribution is found among the Armenians in Asia Minor; further, group B appears to be of eastern origin. But we must hesitate to conclude, with Sir Gavin, that this is evidence that the Etruscans came from Asia Minor. Apart from the immensely complex problem of possible changes in the ethnic population of Tuscany since Etruscan times, Dr Mourant has now revised his map and shows that 'there is a fairly progressive change from north to south (of Italy), but not an Etruscan enclave as appeared before'.[39] In 1958 under the auspices of the Ciba Medical Foundation a conference was held in London to consider how these advances in human genetics could be applied to Etruscan problems. The symposium of their proceedings is a fascinating volume, but despite all the detailed and valuable work that was put into it, the results are disappointingly small and emphasize the difficulty and delicacy of the problems and methods.[40] It may be that more satisfactory methods for determining the blood-group of old bones may be found, while the study of living populations will obviously be intensified. In the future the biological tools for ethnological research will no doubt be refined, but they have unfortunately not yet provided an Open Sesame to the problem of Etruscan origins.

IS RECONCILIATION POSSIBLE?

Since such a variety of theories is held in both the Orientalist and Autochthonist camps, it might be thought that, if the extreme views on both sides were abandoned, some reconciliation might be reached.[41] Thus, few of those who accept Herodotus now believe that large numbers of Etruscans arrived from the east with all the cultural characteristics that are later found in Etruria. The movement may have resembled those of earlier prehistoric times rather than later Greek colonization. Thus H. Hencken writes, 'if eastern Mediterranean newcomers brought an orientalizing civilization there (*i.e.* to Etruria), they were the last colonists of the old pattern. One can trace the individual items of their culture to various places in the eastern Mediterranean. But the eastern Mediterranean has not yet produced an Etruscan homeland complete with culture and language. Greek colonization was on quite another pattern. A partial analogy to all this can be seen in America, a country that is European in its origin and with very large continental elements but, despite its use of the English language, is widely different from both England and continental Europe'.[42] Some Orientalists would spread the process over a long period, others would limit it in time as well as in numbers, and many would be prepared to admit the increasing efficiency of Villanovan culture. On the other hand, few Autochthonists believe the Etruscans to have been completely immune from foreign admixture: thus Pallottino, who believes that Villanovan civilization developed locally upon Apennine Bronze Age foundations, yet admits the possibility of a limited infiltration of cremating peoples, whether from the north and the urn-fields of central Europe or even from the south by coastal or sea routes; he also allows the probability that later some orientals and Greeks contributed to the economic and cultural development of the 'proto-historic' centres of Etruria.[43]

But however much each theory is attenuated, an unbridgeable gulf remains, caused by the divergent aspects of language, race and culture. Thus those who would be prepared to attribute the oriental cultural elements to trade and thus eliminate from the problem an external eastern racial element, are faced with the question of the origin of the language. Some may be willing to follow Pallottino in believing that the language was, so to speak, always there, and to accept his views of the spread of the Indo-European tongues in Italy, together with his equation of Villanovans with a non-Indo-European stratum. But any who find his general linguistic pattern unacceptable, and believe the Villanovans to have been Indo-European, can hardly find a home for Etruscan in Italy: if it was a primitive survival, it can scarcely have 'gone underground' during the early Villanovan Iron Age to re-emerge with the Orientalizing period. Then again, why did it survive in Iron Age Etruria and not in Iron Age Latium with its kindred civilization?

Since interpretations of these interacting elements have often led to a monolithic conception of the Etruscan people and not to any agreed solution, Pallottino abandoned this line of approach and concentrated on the historical reality of the Etruscan nation in Italy: the origin of the ethnic, linguistic, political and cultural elements that contributed to its formation may be discussed, but the essential problem here is not provenance but ethnic formation, and this process took place on the soil of Etruria itself (*cf.* p. 32 above). A not dissimilar point of view was expressed, with much less soundness of judgement, by F. Altheim, whose book on *Der Ursprung der Etrusker* (1950) was more concerned with the formation of the League of Twelve Cities, with which he identified the rise of the Etruscan nation. Although he accepted an early eastern element in Etruria, he minimized its importance, and by this approach he concentrated attention away from remoter origins to developments in Etruria.[44] No doubt this attitude is fruitful and directs attention to Etruscan civilization as a more rewarding field of study, but if it is pursued too rigidly without sufficient reference to the wider context (and no one could accuse Pallottino of neglecting this) it cannot attempt to say whether there was an eastern racial element in historic Etruria or whence came the Etruscan language. If it attempts an answer, it can only lead back to the vicious circle of Orientalists and Autochthonists.

At this point the reader may feel somewhat baffled either by the complexity of the problems or the lack of clarity in the exposition, but to attempt to offer any 'solution' would be dishonest. There *is* no solution, and perhaps never will be. The discovery of an Etruscan inscription in Lydia would certainly help, but even that might not solve all problems! The evidence is such that the most a scholar should say is that the balance of probability seems to him to be so and so. With this reservation, a subjective sketch of what the writer thinks *might* have happened may be given, provided that the hypothetical nature of nearly all its stages is recognized, and it is realized that a fresh piece of evidence might any day change the picture. It may be assumed that in the turmoil and *Völkerwanderung* in the eastern Mediterranean following the collapse of the Mycenaean empire, some peoples from Asia Minor drifted westwards, ultimately settling where they could, in Lemnos and the coast of Etruria. A folk-memory of this and subsequent movements may have survived in Lydia where Herodotus heard the story of Tyrrhenos. What these wanderers took with them would be their language, and their skill and experience in war, administration and the arts of city-life. They were perhaps warrior bands, unaccompanied by many womenfolk. If individual landings in Italy were accomplished easily, the process may have continued over very many years, without great numbers being involved. In Etruria they may have found at first a sparse Bronze Age population, and then an expanding Iron Age Villanovan population which spoke an Indo-European tongue and cremated its dead. Superior powers of organization enabled the intruders to impose themselves as a conquering aristocracy; they intermarried with the Villanovans, their language and burial habits gained the ascendancy, they developed city-life and, by exploiting the mineral wealth of the country, they were enabled to build up an overseas trade which brought them many of the luxurious artistic products of the East. Thus with the dawn of the orientalizing period from the beginning of the seventh century, we find an Etruscan nation: the bulk of its population were Iron Age Villanovans whose latent abilities and tastes had been sharpened by gradually increasing pressure by immigrants from the east. If this picture has any relation to historical truth, then Seneca would be justified in his claim: 'Tuscos Asia sibi vindicat'.

CHAPTER III

THE LAND AND THE CITIES

THE LAND

THE DISTRICT known to the Romans as Etruria by no means co-incides with the area penetrated by Etruscan civilization; before 500 BC Etruscan influence and, to some extent, Etruscan domination had reached northwards to the plain of the Po and southwards to Campania. In 27 BC Augustus defined Etruria, the seventh of the administrative divisions into which he divided Italy, as bounded in the north by the river Magra (near modern Spezia) and the Apennines, and on the east and south by the river Tiber. But Etruria in the sense of the central area of Etruscan civilization may be defined as the country lying between the Arno, the Tiber and the Mediterranean; the whole of this area is bounded on the east by the Apennines whose lower slopes thrust into it, producing a land of hills and valleys. This definition, however, does not quite correspond with the modern *regione* of Tuscany (Toscana), which includes land north of the Arno (as the Augustan *regio*) but excludes both an eastern strip (thus Perugia is now in Umbria), and, more important, the southern area stretching from Lake Bolsena to Rome (now in the *regione* of Lazio), which may be regarded as the very heart of Etruscan power (Fig. 4).

This modern division reflects a very significant geological and geographical distinction: the area of Etruscan settlement falls into a northern and a southern sector, divided roughly by the course of the rivers Fiora and Paglia, the former reaching the coast near Vulci, the latter flowing into the Tiber just north of Orvieto. South of these rivers is a volcanic zone which continues south of the Tiber and includes the Alban Hills. It contains the craters of three extinct volcanoes, now Lakes Bolsena (amid the Volsini mountains), Vico (Cimini mountains) and Bracciano (Sabatini

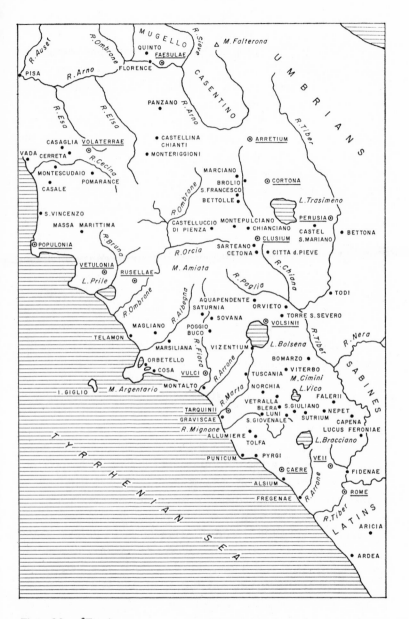

Fig. 4 Map of Etruria

mountains), and it consists mainly of tufa which has worn into peaks or plateaux, separated by deep valleys and gullies. The landscape is often wild, covered with oak or chestnut, but descending through brushwood and thicket into more gentle grassland slopes to the Tiber or the coast. The trachytic hills of La Tolfa, seamed and criss-crossed by gorges, form part of the wild region, which still retains much of its primitive appearance since it has not been widely settled in medieval or modern times. It was in this southern section that the earliest Etruscan settlements emerged, generally near the sea and not very far apart: Tarquinii, Vulci, Caere, Veii. Here beat the real heart of ancient Etruria (*Pl. 10*).

The northern section, north of the Fiora, falls into two parts: coastal and inland. Near the coast, which is marked by a few promontories and the marshland of the Maremma, isolated hills attracted early settlers at Rusellae, Vetulonia and Populonia. Inland settlement came somewhat later, but the countryside was much more attractive than farther south: here were the 'opulenta arva Etruriae' and the 'Etrusci campi', fertile alluvial valleys and plains and rolling hills of sandstone and limestone, stretching northwards from the mountain peaks of the old volcanic cones of Cetona and Amiata to the Chiana valley, Lake Trasimene and on to Arezzo. In this more spacious setting arose Clusium, Cortona, Perusia, Arretium and Faesulae. In this more smiling land, now decked with olives, vines, cereals and fruit trees, the later inhabitants proved less willing to abandon the earlier settlements which have been occupied continuously from Etruscan times throughout the Middle Ages until today; while the cities of southern Etruria decayed, these northern ones lived on to form a link with the city-states of Renaissance Tuscany.

Thus Etruria was a tangle of hills, predominantly sandstones, limestones and clays in the north, volcanic tufas and lavas in the south, cut up into sections by valleys and ravines. Except the surrounding Arno and Tiber, the rivers were relatively small. Apart from two tributaries of the Tiber, the Chiana and the Paglia, most of the other rivers ran from the hills down to the Mediterranean coast: the Cecina from near Volaterrae, the Bruna by Vetulonia, the Ombrone near Rusellae, the Albegna north of Orbetello, the Fiora by Vulci, the Marta by Tarquinii, and the Mignone farther south. Spring flooding could cause serious trouble in the Arno valley, as Hannibal found to his cost, and in the enclosed Clanis valley: in AD 15 the Roman senate debated a proposal that the Clanis should be diverted into the Arno. Even worse were the swamps caused by some of the streams draining down into the Tyrrhenian Sea: the water-logged Maremma was notorious in the Middle Ages as a malarial district, and it has been adequately reclaimed only in recent years. However, the plain between modern Grosseto and the sea was perhaps covered by shallow seawater in Etruscan times, with Vetulonia and Rusellae rising above this, while in Roman times it became a salt lagoon called Prilius; by the fourteenth century it had become a fresh-water lake, all too acceptable to the anopheles mosquito.

At what point in time malaria invaded Italy in general and this coastal area in particular, and whether this may have accelerated the early decline of some of the Etruscan cities, are controversial questions. By the second century BC places on the coast were regarded as unhealthy: Graviscae, near Tarquinii, even in 181 had an unhealthy climate ('gravis aer', according to Cato), which it retained in the fifth century AD when the poet Rutilius Nama-tianus wrote of the marshy smell which pervaded its ruins ('quas premit aestivae saepe paludis odor'). The younger Pliny also admitted that the coastal part of Etruria was 'gravis et pestilens'. With less justification this belief in an unhealthy climate was apparently applied to all Etruria because Pliny went on to tell his friend Domitius not to worry about his spending the summer at his villa in Tuscany, which Domitius thought to be *insalubris*: on the contrary the villa lay far from the sea in a very healthy position at the foot of the Apennines: he then described the climate, the countryside and the villa in most glowing terms. Further, the admitted swampiness of part of the coast does not necessarily involve ill-health (thus Strabo could note the healthi-ness of Ravenna amid its marshes) and still less the prevalence of malaria.[45]

Some historians believe that malaria was brought to Etruria by the invaders from Lydia or even it was there already to infect them. Against this is the improbability that the Etruscans would have chosen to land on an unhealthy shore, while it has been argued that if they came with the germs in their blood (and thus provided the mosquitoes of the swamps with the poison to pass on to others), they would scarcely have created and maintained for so long such a virile civilization. Against this objection is the fact that the Etruscans were skilled engineers who carried through great irrigation schemes (see pp. 68f). Thus proper drainage and the avoidance of stagnant water might well have enabled them to keep malaria at bay, even if they were not conscious of the link between the disease and the breeding-grounds of the insects; then as their power declined, the drainage systems were neglected and malaria became more rampant. This perfectly reasonable explanation of one possible factor in their decline must remain a hypothesis simply because of our ignorance. No solid evidence on the topic was advanced at the conference on 'medical biology and Etruscan origins', held in London in 1958, though this is the side from which fresh information might accrue. Meantime those who believe that malaria first came into Italy with Hannibal's troops from North Africa can scarcely be proved wrong: the question remains open.[46]

Another feature of the landscape that profoundly affected the pattern of human settlement was the forest, which in early times spread over large stretches of central and southern Etruria. This primeval growth, although not literally impenetrable for man, formed a daunting and decisive barrier, and helped to determine the ways by which men could advance inland. The greatest of these forests was the dread Ciminian, which stretched from the Monti Cimini, south of Lake Bolsena, to Monti Sabatini, north of Bracciano. This was regarded with awe as late as 310 BC, when it was first approached and penetrated by a Roman army under Fabius Maximus, who received too late a despatch from the Senate which in alarm had ordered him not to undertake this risk. The story may be exaggerated 'ad maiorem gloriae Fabii', but it reflects a realization of the barrier which in earlier times had separated the Etruscan peoples settled west of the forest (from Viterbo towards the coast) from the Indo-European speaking Faliscans to the east. Thus the forests, combined with the rivers and valleys, and the very complex formation of the mountains forced the early settlers to probe in different directions and to choose for their homes various pockets of land, often separated from one another by physical features that made communications difficult. Similar, but more marked, conditions in Greece led to the particularism of Greek city-state life; geography also ensured that settlements in Etruria followed a pattern which produced cities with individual characteristics and made any over-all political union difficult.

AGRICULTURE

We may now glance at agricultural life in Etruria, which is more relevant to city life than might at first appear: not only did it provide the economic basis of that life, but the fields were largely tended by men who lived in the cities if the evidence from around Veii may be taken as typical of at least southern Etruria. Here there are few traces of villages or scattered farms, but as in many of the more remote parts of modern Italy and Spain, the farmers lived within the protection of the town and rode out each morning to their fields.[47]

Apart from naturally fertile areas, agriculture depends upon man's ability to win suitable land from the grip of wilder vegetation, and much of Etruria in early times must have been very wild indeed. We should dismiss from our imagination pleasant memories of the smiling countryside around Florence today, and recall the daunting barriers of the Ciminian forest. As in modern Tuscany, vegetation was of two main forms: forests of beech and fir on the mountains, and wild macchia on the lower slopes which led down to the hillocks and plains where cereals and fruits might more easily be cultivated.[48] The more twisted and tortured contours of southern Etruria, though offering a possible foothold near the coast, faced man with a greater challenge than did the gentler country in the north. The pioneers who penetrated this formidable barrier and wrung from the wild sufficient land for cultivation, were of course the Villa-novans whose villages are found on most sites of later Etruscan cities. Wider occupation came during the 'Etruscan' period and was made possible by a great surge forward in engineering skill, displayed in land-reclamation, drainage, forestry, and road building (see pp. 68, 117). What lay behind this great advance must remain speculative: did the Villanovans suddenly develop latent talents in the technical field, or did these new techniques, arriving from overseas, find an apt labour force ready to learn how to apply them? Whatever their origin, they made possible the expansion of a virile population which spread farther into the country, producing sufficient food to nourish the increasing number of inhabitants.

It is not difficult to picture the fertile north, with its history of relatively continuous development until modern times, although even here the Val di Chiana was depopulated in the Middle Ages. More effort is required to realize the extent of the Etruscan population in the south beyond the immediate neighbourhood of the great cities: if even Vulci and Rusellae seem slightly remote today, how much more imagination is required to repopulate in the mind's eye the wild and rugged land around Bieda and Norchia with their rock-cut tombs (see pp. 93ff); yet these great cemeteries presuppose a large population, and indeed there are few parts of the country where the tangle of undergrowth does not still hide many indications of its lost population.

The pattern of economic life in Etruria at a much later stage is revealed in Livy's well-known passage (28, 45) describing the gifts sent by the cities to help Scipio Africanus equip his expeditionary force against Carthage in 205 BC. Caere promised grain and supplies of every kind for the crews, Populonia iron, Tarquinii linen for sails, Volaterrae grain and interior fittings for the ships. Arretium promised three thousand shields, the same number of helmets, fifty thousand javelins, spears and lances, together with axes, shovels, sickles, baskets and hand-mills for forty warships; in addition 120,000 pecks of wheat were also offered. Perusia, Clusium and Rusellae promised fir for shipbuilding and a great quantity of grain. This indicates that the chief grain-producing areas were Volaterrae, Arretium, Perusia, and, further south, Clusium and Rusellae, and it was no doubt

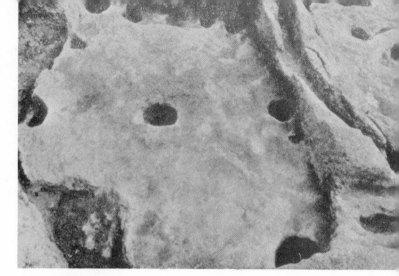

1   Foundations of Iron Age
'Villanovan' hut on the
Palatine hill at Rome.   Note
arrangement of post-holes and
the drainage channel between
two huts.   The porch is at the
top of the picture.   See p.25.
2   Cinerary urn in the form of
such a hut.   See p.22.   3   Model
reconstruction.

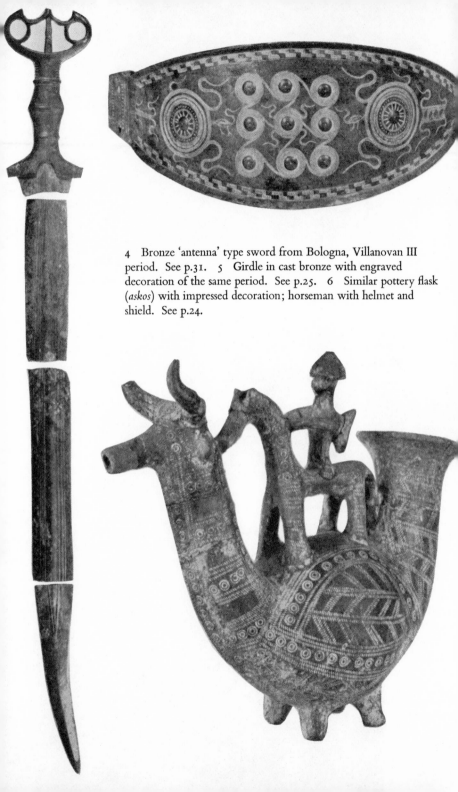

4 Bronze 'antenna' type sword from Bologna, Villanovan III
period. See p.31. 5 Girdle in cast bronze with engraved
decoration of the same period. See p.25. 6 Similar pottery flask
(askos) with impressed decoration; horseman with helmet and
shield. See p.24.

7 Biconical pottery ossuary
of standard Villanovan form,
covered by a crested bronze
helmet. From Tarquinii.
See p.22.

8   The Certosa bronze *situla*, from Bologna, of *c.* 500 BC. The third band depicts scenes of country life See pp.8, 203.   9   Part of painting in the Tomba della Caccia e Pesca at Tarquinii. Note the fisherman in the boat and the slinger on the rocks aiming at wild duck. See p.67.

these areas that Varro had in mind when he wrote at the end of the Republic that 'in rich soil, like that in Etruria, you can see fertile crops, land that is never fallow, sturdy trees, and no moss anywhere' (*R.R.* 1, 9, 6), or when he spoke of seed giving a return of fifteen-fold 'as at some places in Etruria' (1, 44, 1).

One of the chief crops was *far*, emmer (*triticum dicoccum*), the staple diet of early Italy. Since it was unhusked and not suitable for bread-making, it was pounded and eaten as *puls* or porridge. But later so-called 'naked' species of wheat were developed which made possible the production of bread and pastries.[49] During the Roman Empire the emmer of Clusium (*far Clusinum*) was famous for its whiteness (Columella 2, 6) and weight (Pliny *NH*, 18, 66). Clusium and Arretium were also well-known for the flour yield of their wheat (*siligo*). How far any of these refinements had been developed in Etruscan times we do not know, but the main diet of the early Etruscan, as of the early Roman, must have been *far*.

Not much is known about wine and oil in Etruria. Fenestella,[50] an Augustan writer, said that the cultivated olive was not known in Italy, Spain or Africa in 581 BC. Olive oil, however, must have been used from early times and was imported from Greece in the vases that are found on most Etruscan sites. Indeed an early Etruscan inscription (*TLE*, 762) on a pot refers to its function: *aska eleivana* means a vase (*askos*) for oil (*elaion*). How soon the Etruscans started cultivating their own olive trees is not known: they are not mentioned in later literature. Etruscan wines, known in Greece from the days of Alexander, are mentioned by Dionysius (1, 37) alongside Falernian and the wines of the Alban hills. Those of Graviscae and Statonia and especially of Luna are praised (Pliny *NH*, 14, 67). Other wines mentioned are those of Tuder, Florentia and Arretium (Pliny *NH*, 14, 36); that from Veii was little esteemed. The wine that was most widely cultivated in Etruria was Apianae, a name which Pliny (*NH* 14, 24) derived from bees (*apes*) but which more probably came from a grower named Appius. This was a sweet wine, a muscatel. But our evidence is for a period many centuries after the great days of Etruria, and even then it does not single out any Etruscan cities as especially famous for any particular fruits or vegetables, although these must in fact have been widely cultivated: when Varro said that Italy was everywhere planted with trees so that it looked like one great orchard, he did not except the Etruria of his day.

There is, however, one comparatively early source—the floral decorations on Etruscan paintings and other works of art. But care is needed; Etruscan art borrowed much from oriental sources, so that native and borrowed have to be distinguished, while the borrowings may have been either artistic or actual. Five native plants have been noted: artichoke, convolvulus, ivy, dwarf palm and oak. Non-indigenous plants are crocus, acanthus, laurel, cypress, lily, pomegranate, apple, date, olive, poppy, pine, rose and vine.[51] A less pleasing list of ill-omened flora has been preserved by Macrobius (3, 20, 2), from a work on 'Prodigies relating to Trees' by Tarquitius Priscus: they are buckthorn, dogwood, fern, black fig, holly, wild pear, butchers' broom, eglantine and bramble. If these recall the world of the macchia, the earlier lists reflect the cultivated gardens of the nobles, whose luxury is depicted in the frescoes of the tombs of Tarquinii.

We are well informed about the implements with which the Etruscans worked their land. Many are depicted on works of art, while actual tools have been found, especially at Telamon and Luna, which can be seen in the Florence Museum. Iron tools include hoes, pruning-hooks, bill-hooks, sickles, a scythe for corn, a ploughshare, two ox-yokes and a plough not unlike those used in Tuscany today. Further, a hoard of votive tools of bronze was found, probably dedicated to celebrate Rome's victory over the Gallic invaders at Telamon in 225 BC.[52] A simple plough comprises a long handle turning back at one end to form a hook. A more advanced one consists of a long beam to which the yoke was fixed, with a pointed ploughshare and a handle with cross piece; it is depicted on the *situla* from Certosa (p. 203) where a ploughman is carrying it over his shoulder on his way to or from his work (*Pl. 8*); it is also seen in the bronze group of ploughman, plough and two oxen from Arezzo.

Our evidence for stock-farming is late. Columella records that the oxen were thick-set and powerful workers; those bred in the

Apennines were very tough but not handsome. The white oxen of Falerii were popular for religious sacrifices in Rome, where the cheeses of Luna were also esteemed. The antiquity of the sheep-rearing industry in Etruria is reflected in the fact that in Varro's day the wool on the distaff and spindle of the Etruscan queen Tanaquil was still preserved in the temple of Sancus at Rome, while in the shrine of Fortune was kept a royal robe which she had made for Servius Tullius. The spinning of wool no doubt was one of the main occupations of women in early Etruria, as it was at Rome. Horses were bred for war and for racing, and pig-breeding was widespread; Polybius noted that, unlike Greece, where the swineherds drove their animals before them, in Etruria the herds followed the swineherd to the sound of a trumpet (*buccina*).[53]

Agriculture was supplemented by two of the oldest human activities, hunting and fishing. Forests abounded with game, which included boars, deer and hares. Varro records a game preserve of 40 *iugera* near Tarquinii and larger ones at Statonia and elsewhere. Whether Etruscan nobles had staked out their claims in this way we do not know, but hunting scenes enliven tombs at Tarquinii, while the Certosa *situla* (p. 203) shows a hunter driving a hare into a net and two men carrying on a pole the stag they have caught while a dog runs underneath. Further, the famous painting in the Tomba della Caccia e Pesca at Tarquinii illustrates both activities (*Pl. 9*). On a cliff a man is aiming his sling-stones at a flock of the wild ducks which abounded in the lakes and marshes. At the foot of the cliffs in the sea is a boat from which a fisherman is casting his line while dolphins are leaping ahead. Pyrgi had a reputation for its fish, and we hear of watch-towers for spotting tunny-shoals on the coast at Populonia and near Cosa. Beside fresh-water fish, sea-fish were raised in the inland lakes of Bracciano, Bolsena and Vico a long time before the days of Columella, who records the fact (8, 16): whether as far back as Etruscan times we do not know, but the tables of the Etruscan nobles could groan under a variety of fish, game and meat.[54]

The forest, beside supplying game, offered timber. Fir was provided by Perusia, Clusium and Rusellae for Scipio's fleet (*cf.*

p. 64). Virgil tells of the fir of Caere and regards the pine as a typically Etruscan tree (*Etrusca pinus*), while Rutilius speaks of the pines of Graviscae and Pisa. In Pliny's day the Romans liked the firs of the Etruscan coast better than those of the Adriatic: they were closer grained and more durable. Two species of oak have been found in an analysis of charcoal used in the Fucinaia Valley, while a wooden sarcophagus from Falerii is also made from *quercus cerris*. Other specimens analysed revealed beech, elm, willow, box and other woods.[55] Thus the Etruscans had at hand good supplies of timber for building their farms, houses and temples as well as for shipbuilding.

Successful farming involves proper control of water-supplies, and in this activity the Etruscans had great technical skill. In parts of southern Etruria and Latium the countryside is almost riddled with artificial tunnels (*cuniculi*), whereas in other parts of Etruria they are much scarcer. The reason for this is largely geological: the volcanic tufas of these districts are much more easily worked than the harder limestone and travertine areas. These extensive underground drainage-ways, which were cut in order to reclaim waterlogged valleys for cultivation, have recently been carefully studied. No less than 28 miles of *cuniculi* have been identified on the south-west flanks of the Alban Hills, and some 16 miles have been mapped around Veii: here they generally follow the line of the valleys which run south-east. Some seven examples are known near Caere. They consist of horizontal tunnels, roughly $5\frac{3}{4}$ feet high and half a yard wide, just large enough for a small man to pass along. At every 30 or 40 yards a vertical shaft runs from the ground level to the tunnel. These shafts would be cut first, and pick marks on the walls of the tunnel show that it was cut out in both directions from the base of each shaft: the debris would be taken to the surface in baskets by rope or hand. The tunnelling between the shafts was done with considerable accuracy; usually the error at the point of junction can be measured in inches or less. One fascinating result of these *cuniculi* is that they enable us to get a glimpse of the Etruscan countryside as it was in Etruscan times. Elsewhere surface drainage has roughened and cut up the terrain, but where the *cuniculi* carried off the surface water underground the land has remained more smooth, gentle and undulating, as revealed especially by air photography in the territory of Veii (*Pl. 11*).[56]

The political implications are no less remarkable. Schemes on this scale require a large organized labour force and a central authority powerful enough to impose a uniform plan over a considerable area in which, no doubt, various land-holding interests were involved. In other words Veii must have had a firm grip on the Ager Veientanus. Other engineering achievements were not only the drainage of the Forum at Rome through the Cloaca Maxima (*cf.* p. 248) but also the draining of the Alban Lake. It is said that when the lake overflowed in 398 BC an Etruscan soothsayer (*haruspex*) revealed to the Romans that according to the Books of Fate (*libri fatales*) of the Etruscan *disciplina* they would not capture Veii until they had drained off the overflowing lake: this they are said to have done. It is a fact that a tunnel (*emissarium*) was built to serve as an overflow for the lake: it is over 8000 feet long, some 5ft × 4ft, and runs from below Castel Gandolfo to La Mola. Although an arch at the outflow dates only from the first century BC, the tunnel is much older: it could be early fourth century or before, *e.g.* sixth century. If, as Roman tradition asserts, it was built at the time of the Roman siege of Veii and if the Romans in fact captured Veii by means of tunnelling (*cf.* p. 269), the two operations may have somehow become linked. But the point here relevant is that the Romans regarded the Etruscans as hydraulic experts, and Livy says that it was the *haruspex* who explained to them the proper method of doing the job. Once again, we can only wonder whether or not native Villanovans developed these skills internally. What is clear, however, is that by their technical prowess the Etruscans were able to reclaim land from forest and flood and also to exploit the mineral wealth of their land.

MINERALS AND MINING [57]

Italy is not very rich in minerals, but most of what she has is concentrated in Etruria. This fact goes far to explain the basis of the flowering of Etruscan civilization, whether the metals are regarded as the magnet that first drew the Etruscans to Italy or as the material that the Villanovans began to exploit. The skill of Etruscan goldsmiths was outstanding, but it is uncertain whether they got the ore from local sources, later forgotten, or imported it from northern Italy or beyond. Some silver was mined in the district between Volaterrae and Populonia, but copper and iron provided the main wealth. From Volaterrae down to the Campigliese and Massa Marittima, at Populonia and Fullonica, in Elba and on Mount Amiata are numerous traces of workings, galleries, caves (still recalled by such names as Cento Camerelle and Cavina), trenches, piles of slag and even remains of furnaces which show how the Etruscans developed this basic industry.

Beside copper, iron and argentiferous lead, tin ore was worked (although its presence was not known in modern times until 1875). The first ore to be exploited was copper, with which tin, in the proportion of 8–15%, was alloyed to produce bronze. This is illustrated by some bronze plates inlaid with the then rarer metal of iron, found at Populonia (see p. 143), while the whole history of this city shows that its early prosperity was due to bronze, and only later did it become the great iron-working and producing centre of Etruria. The gradual supersession of copper and tin-working by iron mining may have been due in part to the increasing availability of other sources of supply (*e.g.* Spain, Brittany and Cornwall), partly perhaps to the supply running out: at any rate pseudo-Aristotle, *De Mirabilibus Auscultationibus* 29 (possibly third century BC), records that in Elba copper had not been found for some time before his own day, though iron workings were plentiful. This abundance is attested by Virgil (*Aen.* 10, 174): 'insula inexhaustis Chalybum generosa metallis', and by Diodorus (5, 13) who records that Elba was called Aethalia 'from the smoke (*aithaolos*) which lies so thick about it. For the island possesses a great amount of iron-rock, which they quarry in order to melt and cast and thus secure the iron, and they possess a great abundance of this ore.' Later much of this was shipped across to Populonia for more skilled working than could be achieved on the island. Anyone who has walked across the fields of Populonia knows that they are still full of pieces of iron slag, and many a traveller to Elba will have seen the smoke rising from the furnaces of Fullonica and Piombino which are still supplied with ore from the local mines.

The ore was extracted either by open-cast mining near the surface, like much of the iron in Elba, or by underground workings often with galleries at different levels where the metal could be raised from one level to the next by means of vertical shafts. One such mine in the Campigliese in the Val di Fucinaia (Forge) appears, from pottery found there, to have been worked as early as the eighth century, while some actual furnaces are preserved. They are built in the shape of a truncated cone (6 feet at the base), lined with tiles and divided into two chambers by a perforated partition which rested on a column of quartziferous porphyry. The upper chamber was filled with pieces of copper ore and some charcoal (*quercus cerris* and *pinus aucuparia*), together with some quartz and silicon to separate out the iron. A fire was lit in the lower chamber, which had a square door at its base to regulate the combustion; the iron oxide then collected in the upper chamber, while the molten copper ran through the perforations into the lower one. Traces of furnaces for iron smelting which have been found at Populonia are of a simpler type, of clay-lined sandstone; in consequence their working life was short. Examination of the residue from this process, preserved in the mountains of iron slag at Populonia, reveal a rather low degree of efficiency, and much of this material has in fact been worked again with profit by modern industrial methods; this was started in 1915 when iron was scarce during wartime. Whether the better type of furnace owed anything to external influences is uncertain: parallels have been sought as far apart as among the Philistines and the La Tène Celts.

The quantity of iron smelted at Populonia, whether from mainland mines or brought over from Elba, was immense. The weight of the surviving slag-heaps has been reckoned to be 2,000,000 tons, and an annual extraction of ore has been put at 10,000–12,000 tons for some four centuries. Such rough estimates depend on the length of time during which the process was continued, but they give a striking idea of the scale of the industry.

Of the more human side of the workings our only testimony consists in the survival of some miners' clay lamps. Finally, it may be well to recall how fortunate the Etruscans were not only in their mineral wealth and their skill in exploiting it, but also in that their land was so well wooded and thus could supply plentiful timber for the furnaces.

Beside the minerals, the Etruscans made good use of the stone of their land. Stone for building material was mainly volcanic, including a compact hard grey tufa known as *nenfro*. In general, communities would use the local stone that was most accessible. In the south the Sabatini volcanoes were active for three periods, starting in the Pleiocene era, each of which provided building material when the ash had solidified into rock. First came the dark grey ash which hardened into tufa (*capellaccio*); this is ugly and friable but easy to cut. Then came a layer which was deposited from Civita Castellana to Fidenae in the south (Fidenae tufa), a rough tufa containing black scoria or charred obsidian. Lastly comes a friable greyish-yellow stone which stretches from Prima Porta, just north of Rome, to Nepi in the north. It was quarried in an area known as Grotta Oscura and was later used extensively by the Romans after they had captured Veii; they probably used the old Etruscan quarry and may well have put to work Etruscan prisoners who knew how to handle the stone.[58] This Grotta Oscura stone greets the eye of the modern visitor to Rome who steps out of the main railway station and sees in front of him the 'Servian' Wall (*Pl. 113*). Other building stone was used locally elsewhere, and in the north the alabaster around Volaterrae provided good material for a local industry in funerary urns. This area also produced sulphur. The marble deposits farther north were not worked until Roman times.

Thus nature had well provided the inhabitants of Etruria with mineral wealth which would yield building stone for cities and raw materials which their inhabitants could trade for luxuries from overseas. Nature too had provided land fertile enough to support a large population. But it was man's effort and still more man's technical skills that made possible the flowering of a rich civilization in this land.

BOUNDARIES

The Etruscans set great store on the rights of property and the careful marking-off of land-holdings of various kinds, both public and private. We know something about this from an Etruscan prophecy, delivered by a prophetess Vegoia to a certain Arruns Veltumnus who was apparently a priest or prince from Clusium. It is preserved in Latin in a collection of documents, the *Corpus agrimensorum Romanorum*, which dealt with land-surveying and boundary-marking. Some *libri Vegoici* were preserved in Rome, together with the Sibylline books, in the temple of Apollo on the Palatine, while a fragmentary *elogium* from Tarquinii suggests that the *haruspex* Tarquitius Priscus, who lived at Rome at the end of the Republic and was a friend of the scholar Varro, had produced a poetic version of the religious mysteries which had been revealed to Arruns, probably through Vegoia. Thus the text in the *Agrimensores* may well derive from Tarquitius, and is almost certainly a piece of genuine Etruscan tradition.[59]

Vegoia starts with cosmology: 'know that the sea was separated from the sky', a remark which has been thought to echo a Chaldaean tradition.[60] She continues: 'when Jupiter (*i.e.* Etruscan Tinia) had claimed for himself the land of Etruria, he determined and ordered that the plains should be measured and the fields marked out. Knowing the greed of men and their desire for land, he wished everything to be established with boundaries.' Vegoia goes on to say that anyone who moves boundaries fraudulently will be punished by the gods; further, the crime may be committed by slaves against their masters, but equally by masters against their *servi*, who are thus shown to have been in occupation of land. The prophecy of Vegoia may have been used in 91 BC as propaganda against the land schemes of the tribune Drusus, but it reflects the older sociological and religious thought of the Etruscan discipline: the sacredness of boundaries, *tular* in Etruscan, was divinely ordained and guaranteed.[61]

This word *tular*, which occurs in nine inscriptions, applies according to Professor S. Mazzarino to five categories of land.[62] First, the land of a city demarcated by a sacred boundary which the Romans called *pomerium*. An inscription from Perugia (*TLE*,

571) reads: *tezan teta tular*. Whether this means precisely *auspicii urbani finis* or not, *tular* here almost certainly refers to the *pomerium* (*finis*) of the city. A second type of *tular* embraces the wider territory of a city beyond the sacred *pomerium*, its *ager publicus* or *territorium*: this is the *tular spural*, referred to in an inscription (*TLE*, 675, 676) from the territory of Faesulae, which is followed by the names of the magistrates who had been responsible for the delimitation; Roman parallels to such formulas are found. A third use is applied to the boundaries of a cemetery in the district of Clusium; here *tular hilar nesl* (*TLE*, 515) probably means *finis territorii mortuorum*. This is also followed by the name *au latini* (Aulus Latinius), in whom Professor Heurgon would see one of the followers of Sulla whom the dictator settled on the land here, because the name is followed by the word *claruchies* which must be a late borrowing of the Greek κληροῦχος, a colonist.[63] A fourth usage applies to private property such as a farm: *tular alfil* (*TLE*, 530) gives the owner's name in the genitive. Lastly an inscription from Cortona (*TLE*, 632) refers to *tular rasnal*, the frontiers of the Etruscans, conceivably referring to the Etruscan League.

The *terra Etruriae* is probably mentioned in one of the longest surviving inscriptions, that on the *cippus* of Perugia (*TLE*, 570). Despite great obscurity the inscription clearly refers to the laws on the delimitation of land (*tular* appears in the form *tularu*); it contains several references to measurements (*e.g. naper* xii), and is concerned with a case about proprietary rights of members of two families, Velthina and Afuna. It contains the phrase *helu tesne rasne* which Mazzarino has translated *terrae iuris Etruriae*. This may well be right, but his attempt to see the spread of the use of *tular* farther afield in Italy is more hazardous. Thus the so-called Table of Veleia, which deals with Trajan's alimentary arrangements for Veleia near Placentia, mentions an estate named Tullare (modern Tollara); here Mazzarino would see an Etruscan delimitation (*tular*) 'fossilized' in the name Tullare.[64] It is also quite uncertain whether the Umbrians adopted the word *tular* in their *tuder*, which occurs in the Iguvine Tablets from Gubbio, or in the place name Tuder (modern Todi) between Umbria and

Etruria.[65] What is clear from all this somewhat ambiguous evidence is the importance which the Etruscans attached to the proper demarcation of private and public property.

CITY FOUNDATIONS AND TOWN-PLANNING

The Etruscans were the first builders of cities in central Italy: before them only Villanovan villages existed. The foundation of a city was a combination of religious lore and architectural skill. The Ritual Books of the Etruscans laid down directions for founding cities and consecrating altars and temples which would secure the inviolability of the walls and the religious security of the gates (Festus 358 L); each city had three gates, according to Servius (*Aen.* I, 422).

Lacking much direct Etruscan evidence, we must see what the Romans thought about Etruscan procedure. This was a matter which greatly interested them, since they believed that they themselves had inherited this *Etruscus ritus* in the founding of their own cities: thus even early Rome itself, the *urbs quadrata* on the Palatine (see p. 246), was reputed to have been laid out on these lines. According to Plutarch the method which Romulus, advised by Etruscans, followed was this: first a centre was chosen, where a pit (*mundus*) was dug, into which first-fruits were thrown. From this centre a circle was marked out around it. The founder, having fitted a bronze share to a plough and having yoked to it a bull and a cow, cut a deep furrow round the boundary lines, while those behind turned the clods inwards toward the city and allowed none to lie turned outwards. With this line they marked out the course of the wall; it was called *pomerium*. Where they planned a gate, they lifted the plough-share over the ground, leaving a vacant space; all the wall was regarded as sacred but not the gates, since otherwise necessities, which might be unclean, could not have been brought into the city. Thus through this sacred boundary the population within was secured from all unseen dangers without.

The Romans, however, believed that their earliest settlement, Roma Quadrata, had been laid out in the same way as their later colonies and camps by a process which went back to Etruscan augural methods. The augur after taking the auspices orientated the site by use of a surveying instrument, the *groma*, a word which derives from Greek γνῶμα or γνώμων but the modification of the Greek ν to r reveals that the word reached the Romans through the Etruscans. Placed at the centre (the *mundus*), the *groma* provided the cardinal points; from it two main axes were marked out, the *cardo* running from north to south and the *decumanus* from east to west. These two lines, intersecting at right-angles, formed a frame on which a regular grid-system of lesser streets could be constructed.

Although there is no good reason to doubt that the concept of the sacred *pomerium* and a religious inauguration of cities was genuinely Etruscan, quite recently doubts have arisen about this quadripartite axial arrangement as applied to Etruscan cities: it is of course abundantly attested for Roman colonies and camps. The difficulty arises from the fact that it is not found at the Etruscan city at Marzabotto (see pp. 205f) which is one of the very few to have revealed its internal structure. Though laid out on a rect-angular grid, the central feature of the two main roads crossing in the centre is apparently absent; rather it has one broad *decumanus* and three broad *cardines*, and thus it conforms more to the so-called Hippodamian pattern of the Greeks. Much has recently been learnt about the latter, not least from air-photography. It is now clear that the principle of planning which Hippodamus used for the Peiraeus at Athens in the second part of the fifth century is in fact somewhat older. The grid pattern is based not on an axial crossing of *cardo* and *decumanus* but on a pattern of alternating wider and narrower divisions. This is seen in a number of Greek colonies in the West, such as Selinunte, Paestum, Naples, Locri, Metapontum. At Selinunte the present evidence puts it as early as *c.* 500 (some say *c.* 550). It is therefore claimed that Etruscan Marzabotto, which was founded *c.* 500, followed a Greek pattern. One of our leading authorities even goes so far as to reject the urban interpretation of Roma Quadrata and the Etruscan origin of the technique of the *groma* as a false attribution by Roman scholars of the late Republic, together with all sacral inspiration behind urbanization.[66] But this surely is to go much too far. Marzobotto is evidence for what the Etruscans did *c.* 500, not for their practice of 200 years earlier. How, for instance, can we tell that any earlier axial pattern was not adapted to a 'Hippodamian' one when the Etruscans, knowing about the new Greek fashion, decided to found one of their latest cities?

Any help that archaeology might give is unfortunately limited and, as yet, indecisive. Excavation in the past has concentrated largely on the cemeteries rather than the cities, none of which has been fully or systematically investigated. A beginning has now been made at Vulci and Rusellae, so perhaps more will be known about the earlier phases before too long, but the sites chosen for the cities reveal much. In unsettled conditions a naturally strong position would be sought. High ground, especially if partly surrounded by water, would be ideal. Thus in southern Etruria towns are often found on hills which rise where rivers or streams meet. Natural defences could be improved by trimming rock-faces, and city walls do not appear to have been early. The oldest known wall is at Rusellae where a sun-dried brick wall of the seventh century underlies a stone circuit-wall of the first half of the sixth, but in general many cities, like Veii, do not appear to have needed walls until Roman power began to challenge them about 400 BC. But such strong natural sites are not so common in the less contorted northern part of Etruria, where isolated hills without river defences were chosen; some, like Volaterrae or Orvieto, might be naturally strong, but others, like Clusium, were more open to attack. Few cities (except Populonia, as noted by Strabo) were actually on the coast, because of lack of harbours, while a site slightly inland would give better protection against piratical raids. When the cities grew and their commerce expanded they could use smaller settlements on the coast; even such great trading centres as Corinth and Athens were not on the water's edge.

In regard to town-planning this evidence means that the Etruscans were not usually faced (as they were at Marzabotto) with a comparatively level stretch of open ground where they could trace neat rectangular patterns, although some of the plateaux themselves were broad and fairly level. Here some system may have been used early. How the later Roman *decumanus-cardo* system found at Vulci is related to the earlier Etruscan plan is not certain; at Veii the internal streets seem to radiate from a centre; but in the sixth-century cemetery of Crocifisso at Orvieto the rectangular tombs, like houses, are arranged in parallel lines. At some of the larger sites such as Veii, Vulci and Caere, not all the area may have been 'urbanized' at once, but some of the ground may still have been farmed for some time. At steep hill-towns like Vetulonia, where the streets do not seem to cross at right-angles, chessboard planning would have been thwarted by the twisting contours. The various factors that each city had to contend with will be seen later, but in general, even if we grant to the Etruscans the ritual lore involved in city-founding to which the Romans testified, little can be said with assurance about the street-planning of their early cities. But the rules for the plan and orientation of their temples and sacred buildings may have introduced some symmetry in the public buildings even from early times. Let a great authority, A. Boëthius, sum up: 'nothing in our literary and archaeological material indicates that the old Etruscan towns had any regular plan or shape. But it seems likely that the Etruscans . . . had certain architectural ideas which were alien to Greek architecture and which had no background in what we know about primitive architectural attempts in Italy. The predilection for symmetrical and axial planning of public squares and temple courts seems to have been as characteristic of the Etruscans (and of the monumental architecture of the Orient) as it was alien to the Greeks in classical and early Hellenistic times.'[67]

It is not very easy to visualize the appearance of Etruscan cities in any detail. In general the earlier ones were hill-top settlements, many of them without walls until *c.* 400 BC (*e.g.* Veii, see pp. 107f: though Rusellae had strengthened its hillside some two hundred years before this: *cf.* p. 133). If the inhabited part did not cover the whole hill-top, it could be guarded by a ditch across the hill (as at San Giovenale and Luni: *cf.* pp. 96, 97). Elaborate gates, such as those at Volaterrae and Perusia (*Pls. 68, 77, 78*), with arches and sculptured figures set in them, were late developments. The arrangement of the private buildings within the older towns will probably have been fairly haphazard, until more regular planning was aimed at where the ground allowed this. Greater order will have prevailed in the siting and planning of the temples, though there is no archaeological evidence to attest the statement of Servius (*ad Aen.* 1, 422) that Etruscan *disciplina* required three temples in a city.

Since no Etruscan temples earlier than 600 BC are known, it is likely that open-air sanctuaries with altars were used at first; there is a later example at Marzabotto, while a small stone base from Clusium may be the model of one. The foundations of an early temple (first half of the sixth century) on the Piazza d'Armi at Veii forms a rectangle nearly twice as long as it is broad, but the typical early Etruscan temple was much more square (*e.g.* the Portonaccio temple at Veii: *cf. Pl. 38*) and conforms to the type which Vitruvius (*de arch.* 4, 7) attributed to the Etruscans: a wide frontage which measured slightly less than the depth of the building from front to back. The front half had a colonnaded portico, while the back half comprised three *cellae* for three deities or else one *cella* with two *alae* at its sides (*cf.* those at Rome, Veii and Marzabotto: pp. 252, 107, 206). Later temples approximated closer to the plan of Greek temples, being longer and narrower: thus the Ara della Regina at Tarquinii (*Pl. 14*) was peripteral, having colonnades on all four sides. The reason why only the stone foundations of Etruscan temples survive, in contrast with the still standing columns of so many Greek temples in southern Italy, is that their superstructure was made of less durable material: the main framework was of wood which was covered with bright and gay multicoloured terracotta ornamentation. The columns were not very high and were set well apart. The roof was low-pitched and broad, with eaves projecting beyond the side-walls, and decorated with terracotta antefixes and acroteria. Before the fifth century the pediment was open and revealed the roof-timbers, but was later decorated with terracotta figures of deities (as at Pyrgi: *cf. Pl. 36*).

Temples were set in a sacred precinct, usually against the rear wall, with a space in front which contained an altar. Of other

public buildings we have little evidence: a Roman deposit at
Vulci (*cf.* pp. 120f) shows a tower and a portico which may reflect
earlier Etruscan features of the city. It is not unlikely that the
Roman practice of erecting columns with statues in public places
may have derived from Etruria as much as from any Greek
sources: the bells on chains which hung from the Columna
Minucia at Rome remind us of what Pliny said about the sepulchral monument of King Porsenna (*cf.* p. 155). Further, we know
that inscriptions, proclaiming the careers and achievements of
famous men, were erected not only in Rome but also at Roman
Tarquinii (*cf.* pp. 90f); they may have been accompanied by statues
and the practice may well go back to Etruscan times. Also in the
olden days at Rome gladiatorial shows were staged in the Forum
(Vitruvius, *de arch.* 5, 1): a wall-painting (sixth to fifth century)
from Tarquinii and a relief from Clusium depict wooden
scaffolding which was erected for spectators at Games.

For houses excavations have shown the stone foundations for
superstructures of mud-brick, sometimes laced with timber, at
Veii and Vetulonia, while at Marzabotto there are pebble foundations (*cf.* p. 206): further indirect evidence is provided by the
chamber-tombs, while cinerary urns sometimes reproduce the
appearance of houses. At San Giovenale (*cf. Pl. 17*) the early houses
in the eastern part are a confused jumble, but those on the slope
on the north of the acropolis, which are not later than 550 BC,
were terraced houses on high foundations of tufa ashlar work; like
the houses at Marzabotto, they are rectangular and some eleven
yards in width: they run along narrow alleys some eight yards
wide. At Vetulonia houses with porches face an irregular winding
main street (*cf. Pl. 61*). Larger houses might have upper storeys,
with flat or gabled roofs: the ridge-poles of the latter were often
brightly painted. These gabled houses and their doors are illustrated from the rock-cut tomb faces of the Blera district (*cf.
Pls. 19, 20*). Some of the larger tombs at Caere reveal the lay-out
of the interior of the larger houses: an entrance, a central hall, and
at the back a transverse passage which gave access to one, two or
three rooms. These may well have been the ancestors of the Italic
or 'Pompeian' house, while Vitruvius assigned the invention of the

10 Gorge of the Fiora, near Vulci, showing how the wild countryside is cut by deep ravines. The bridge of Ponte dell'Abbadia may rest on Etruscan foundations. See p.60. 11 Air view of the territory of Veii. The city is in the bottom left-hand corner, the Tiber at the top. The smoother ground in the centre results from Etruscan drainage-channels. See p.69.

12 Air view of Tarquinii. It lies just below, and stretches to the right of, the dark patch near centre; the rectangular Ara della Regina is on the extreme right. Modern Tarquinia is on the left, with Monte Rozzi just off the bottom of the picture. See Fig. 7, and p.86. 13 Part of south wall of Tarquinii; taken from near Ara della Regina, looking westwards. See p.89. 14 Remains of the Ara della Regina temple. See pp.79, 89.

15 Painted terracotta figures of winged horses from the temple of Ara della Regina at Tarquinii, of the fourth and third centuries BC. See p.90. 16 Part of wall painting from the Tomb of the Leopards at Tarquinii, fourth or third centuries. It illustrates the Etruscans' love of music, and it flanks a central painting of a banquet scene. See p.89.

17 Sarcophagus of Velthur Partunus, chief magistrate (*zilath*) of Tarquinii who died aged 82 (for the inscription see *TLE*, No. 126) about 250 BC. The head of the lid is decorated with lions and sphinxes. The scene on the coffin is a battle of the Amazons. See p.90. 18 Foundations of Etruscan houses at San Giovenale. See p.96.

Fig. 5 Models of Etruscan houses, from Clusium. One is the cover of an urn, the other itself forms an urn and its elaborate columns may suggest a portico

atrium to the Etruscans: its prototype, if not its developed form, may well go back to their days, though we cannot here enter into details of this controversial problem. This transverse vestibule sometimes took the form of a portico with columns and pilasters. These might have capitals decorated with flowered volutes, like the 'Aeolian' capitals of the eastern Greeks. In practice this form seems to have been more common in the sixth century than the plainer 'Tuscan' columns to which Vitruvius refers as an architectural order distinct from the three Greek orders. Thus we can see something of the considerable variety of detail both in the interior arrangements and the external appearance between the blocks of middle- and working-class houses and the larger mansions of the rich (Fig. 5). [67a]

FOUNDATION LEGENDS

Before reviewing the cities one by one, we must glance at some of their foundation legends. Many were known to the Romans, and in the second century BC Cato wrote a history entitled *Origines*, which in the early books dealt with the foundation not only of Rome but also of other cities in Italy; this was in the tradition of the Hellenistic historians who developed an interest in Foundations (κτίσεις). Dionysius praised this work of Cato, who 'compiled with the greatest care the 'genealogies' of the

Italian cities' (I, 11). How far Cato consulted and preserved genuine Etruscan local traditions when telling of the foundation of Etruscan cities we do not know, but he used many Greek legends. With the arrival of Greek colonists in Sicily and Italy the Greeks created many stories to explain the foundation of the new cities. The easiest way to do this was to elaborate and extend the adventures of the Greek heroes on their way home after the Trojan War. Of these journeys that of Odysseus, enshrined in the *Odyssey*, is the most famous, but other poems told of the Returns (*Nostoi*) of other Greeks, and these could be extended to Italy. Thus Philoctetes and Epeius were brought to southern Italy to found cities. Now the Etruscans borrowed so much from Greece, including their myths and legends, that when they heard the legends of Greek heroes in the west, they might think of attributing the foundation of some of their own cities to Greeks; this would be particularly attractive to small cities which lacked fine local traditions of their own, as it would add to their prestige.

That the legend of Aeneas was known in Etruria by about 500 BC is demonstrated by a sixth-century Etruscan scarab, showing Aeneas and Anchises, some early fifth-century statues from Veii and some vases from Vulci (*Pl. 117*).[68] The Greeks linked Aeneas with Odysseus, whose contacts with Italy were developed in legend.[69] According to Hesiod (*Theog.* 1011f: eighth century? *cf.* note 14) Odysseus was the father of Agrius and Latinus who ruled over the Etruscans, while the fifth-century historian Hellanicus says (*cf.* Dion. Hal. I, 72) that Aeneas came to Italy with Odysseus and founded Rome; this link between the two heroes is found later in Lycophron (1242ff). Hellanicus also recorded, as we have seen (p. 35), that the Tyrrhenians, once called Pelasgians, were led to Italy by the Pelasgian king Nanas who founded Cortona. The king may well be identified with Nanos whom Lycophron equated with Odysseus. Whether or not such an identification was made by the Etruscans, Nanas appears to belong to early Etruscan tradition which reached Hellanicus in the fifth century, and another part of the story is reflected by Lycophron who after saying that a former enemy, the Dwarf (νάνος, *i.e.* Odysseus), would join Aeneas, adds 'and

with him the two sons of the king of Mysia [Telephon] . . .
Tarchon and Tyrsenus, fiery wolves, sprung from the blood of
Heracles'. The many problems that these passages provoke cannot
be discussed here (*cf.* p. 157), but it is clear that intertwined with
some of the numerous stories of Greek heroes as founders of
cities in Italy were threads of Etruscan tradition. Most of these
Greek legends, however, have little worth as historical evidence,
and it is difficult to try to isolate any Etruscan elements of real
value; a few stories, however, will be mentioned later.

CHAPTER IV

THE SOUTHERN CITIES

TARQUINII[70]

TARCHUNA (OR TARCHNA), perhaps the oldest Etruscan city, was certainly among the richest and one of those which, thanks to the paintings in its tombs, throws most light on the life of the Etruscans. Its early days are reflected in three legends. First, it was traditionally founded by Tarchon, the brother or son of Tyrrhenus, the eponymous hero of the Etruscan peoples, who commissioned him to found twelve cities, one of which was named after him. Secondly, the legend of Tages tells how an Etruscan peasant was ploughing at Tarquinii when the figure of a youth emerged from a deep furrow: before long the whole of Etruria had gathered at the spot, and the mysterious boy, Tages, revealed to them the science of divination from the flight of birds and by the inspection of the entrails of animals. Many sacred books were later attributed to him (*libri Tagetici*), and these continued to be read during the Roman Empire. According to one version (Johannes Lydus, *de ostent.* 2) the ploughman was Tarchon himself, who then learnt this religious lore from Tages. A mirror from Tuscania shows Tarchies (Tages?) dressed as a *haruspex* teaching Tarchon the art of divination (Fig. 6). These stories might be mere local inventions designed to glorify the early days of the city, but in view of the undoubted antiquity of the settlement, they more probably reflect the real importance of early Tarquinii, and their implication that the city exercised some kind of leadership in Etruria may be justified. Further, the kings of Tarquinii, in their function as priests, may well have been the acknowledged authorities on divination, and Tarchon's claim to be the founder could reflect the prominence of one or more members of a *gens Tarchuna* in the city's early days.[71]

Fig. 6 A mirror from Tuscania shows Tarchies (Tages?) in the dress of a haruspex *inspecting the liver of a sacrificial animal, and thus teaching Tarchon the art of divination by hepatoscopy.* Cf. also Pl. 52

The third legend, which refers to a later period (seventh century), was known as early as Polybius (second century) and his sources. Demaratus, a member of the Bacchiad aristocracy at Corinth, had prospered through his trade with Etruria, so that when the Bacchiads were overthrown by Cypselus, who became tyrant at Corinth, Demaratus migrated to Etruria, taking with him many workmen, potters and painters. Settling at Tarquinii, he married an Etruscan wife of noble birth; later the younger of their two sons, Lucumo or Lucius, migrated to Rome where he became king, reigning as Lucius Tarquinius Priscus (616–579). Archaeology confirms the general background to this story and attests much trade between Tarquinii and Greece, including Corinth, as well as strong Greek influences on Etruscan art. Corinthian vases of the second half of the seventh century are found in large numbers at Tarquinii. True, they appear to be even more numerous at Caere and Vulci, but this slight difference of emphasis from the legend is scarcely a sufficient reason to discredit it entirely; if it over-emphasizes the role of Tarquinii at a given point of time, at least the general picture is true.[72]

Tarquinii lay on a hill some five miles from the sea. This hill (the Colle della Città) runs east and west, and is bounded to north and south by two streams that unite to the west of the hill and run into the river Marta (*Pl. 12*). Across the valley about a mile to the south another hill (Monterozzi) runs roughly parallel (strictly more north-west/south-east); here lay the chief necropolis with its hundreds of surviving tombs—well known to crowds of visitors, few of whom go on to the lonely site of the city. At the north-west end of Monterozzi lies the medieval and modern town (formerly Corneto, now called Tarquinia); for a long time it was erroneously considered the site of the Etruscan city. Villanovan settlement of the site is clearly revealed from a number of cemeteries, chiefly on the hills to the east (Poggio Selciatello, Poggio Impiccato, Poggio Quarto degli Archi, etc.), but some also on Monterozzi and even under modern Tarquinia, near the Via Aurelia. Unfortunately none of the villages or huts associated with these cemeteries have yet been found, either near the graves or on the hill of the city. By analogy with the early Iron Age settlers at Veii, we might expect a number of independent village groups rather than a scattered settlement over the whole hill-top, which only later became the centre of a united group. (Fig. 7).[73]

The archaic period at Tarquinii (*c.* 800–*c.* 550 BC) has been divided by Professor Pallottino into four phases: I to before 700; II to 675; III to before 600; IV to 550. The *tomba a pozzo* cremation burials were supplemented and superseded (*c.* 750–700) by inhumation in trenches (*a fossa*) or sometimes in crude stone coffins (*a cassa*), with an increasing richness of the buried objects; this impression of great prosperity culminates in the contents of the Tomb of the Warrior. Then there follows the full flowering of the orientalizing movement. Inhumation becomes normal; chamber-tombs, cut in the rock, develop and become increasingly rich. Painting, sculpture and ceramics (including *bucchero* ware) flourish, and imported Greek and Oriental objects and the motifs greatly increase. At last a few inscriptions appear: the city is by now, in language at any rate, Etruscan. Further, the nature of the tombs, designed for

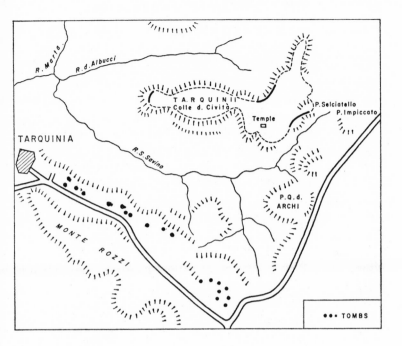

Fig. 7 Plan of Tarquinii

two or more occupants, suggests that the earlier days of the individual had merged into a more settled community in which family life flourished and the possessors of wealth and power were more sharply marked off from the less fortunate.

Thus we find continuous growth from early Villanovan villages to a rich city, which drew much of its cultural ideas from outside. Change there had been, and that on a grand scale, and yet without any cataclysmic break. Here then appears a splendid field to test the 'origin' of the Etruscans, or so it would seem. To one distinguished archaeologist the matter was settled by the change in burial rites: in 1924 D. Randall-MacIver wrote of the inhumation graves, 'it is obvious from the burial rite that they belong to a new and alien people, and . . . there need be no hesitation in identifying this new people with the Etruscans'.[74]

Many, however, now dismiss the change as of little significance (p. 48), but the question must remain open. Much important evidence derives from the so-called Bocchoris Tomb, in which was found a faience vase inscribed with the cartouche of the Egyptian king Boken-ranf, whom the Greeks called Bocchoris (c. 718–712 BC) which provided a firm *terminus post quem*. Further, the tomb contained other vases, figurines and pottery which show a remarkable mixture of oriental, Greek and Villanovan features. The continuation of Villanovan aspects into the seventh century is also illustrated by another tomb (number 66); its contents show that although it was roughly contemporary with the Bocchoris Tomb, it still preserved a strong Villanovan character.[75]

The 'classical' period of the life of Tarquinii after the orientalizing phase, is marked by an increasing flood of imported Attic vases in place of the earlier Corinthian wares, by the painted chamber tombs (the oldest not before 550 BC), and by the renewal of cremation. This revived funeral rite, which apparently did not continue beyond c. 500 BC, was an alternative to inhumation, particularly for the poorer class; the ashes were deposited in painted amphoras, either imported from Greece or local products, and then buried (*tomba a buca*), thus harking back to the older type of *tomba a pozzo*. Although in this period around 550 the city reached its greatest cultural and artistic height, in some respects it had passed its zenith. Until about 650 it had been the chief centre of the bronze industry, exporting its wares to Caere and other southern Etruscan cities; thereafter, however, Caere began to take the lead, especially with its more refined *bucchero* ware, while both Caere and Vulci began to surpass it in the number of Greek vases which they imported. A more marked decline set in from c. 500 when Vulci became a stronger commercial rival; it was accelerated in the early fifth century when the Etruscans were defeated at Cumae (see p. 196) and Etruscan Campania was isolated from Etruria itself. The earlier flowering of Tarquinii must have been matched by its political influence, although no details survive. To what extent it overshadowed the other cities of southern Etruria is not known, though the story that it provided Rome with her Etruscan dynasty is at least symbolic of its greatness.

Life in the city at this period is revealed with striking brilliance from the tomb paintings. These paintings are found in chamber-tombs which were cut into the sloping hillside, and where the slope did not allow adequate access they were approached through a corridor (*dromos*); inside they generally consisted of a single chamber, unlike the more complex structures at Caere, although the very late ones of the fourth century were larger and con-tained many burials. The paintings, some of which are later than the original tombs, portray scenes of banquets, dancing, music, athletics of various kinds, chariot racing, hunting and fishing (*Pls. 9, 16*); of the early tombs only one (Tomba dei Tori) shows a mythological scene, namely Achilles lying in ambush for Troilus. The series is interrupted in the fourth century, when Tarquinii was engaged in war against Rome, but the paintings of the later tombs are more concerned with the underworld and its terrifying demons: the *joie de vivre* of the earlier age had been quenched. Some fifty of these painted tombs are now preserved, nearly double the number known only a few years ago. The recovery of so many more, such as the Tomba delle Olimpiadi and Tomba della Nave, is due to new archaeological techniques. But even so, these are only a tiny fraction of the thousands of tombs that cover Monterozzi.

On the hill opposite, where the city was built, almost all the surviving remains belong to the later Etrusco-Roman period; its earlier monuments have long since perished. Most significant is the date of the walls, which were built in the fourth century, at the time of the wars with Rome. They do not form an unbroken circuit but were constructed only where the natural rock did not provide an adequate defence (*Pl. 13*). They are made of squared blocks of local stone; one of the best preserved stretches is on the north side. Gateways have been found, and a section of wall follows the line of a re-entrant angle to give the best defence in relation to the slope of the ground at this point. The chief surviving monument in the city is a fourth-century temple of impressive proportions, the so-called Ara della Regina

(*Pl. 14*). From it come the two famous terracotta winged horses (*Pl. 15*). Of the earlier glories of the city nothing remains, although fragments of *bucchero* ware and vases of the seventh to fifth centuries are found on the site. The life of the city is reflected for us, paradoxically, in its monuments to the dead, although the wall-paintings of the later tombs were more concerned with death and the grimmer aspects of the future life. Burial prevailed absolutely over cremation; there are no cinerary urns, like those which northern cities, such as Volaterrae, Clusium or Perusia, were producing. A new feature appeared *c.* 300 BC: the extensive use of sarcophagi, which preserved individual bodies in the large collective tombs. Some had lids on which lay the sculptured body of the deceased; since facial features were often formed with great care, many impressive portraits of individual Etruscans of this period survive (*Pl. 17*). The increasing number of inscriptions reveals the names of many of these Tarquinians, and a few family genealogies can be traced for short periods. Well over one hundred names of families or *gentes* survive, the most important of whom were the Velcha, the Partunu, the Ciclnie, the Pulena, the Curana, the Pompu, and the Ceisinie. Some of the links between the leading families can be made out, as well as the names of some lesser families dependent upon them, while the men who held magistracies naturally recorded the fact on their sarcophagi. Thus, despite difficulties of interpreting the evidence with any degree of certainty, we get some glimpses of the aristocratic administration of the city in this late phase of its history.[76]

These forms of government continued into Roman times, but the independent authority of the city declined and finally ceased in 90 BC when Tarquinii, with the rest of Italy, received Roman citizenship and became a Roman *municipium*, administered by a board of four (*quattuorviri iure dicundo*). Roman Tarquinii has thrown one beam of chequered light on earlier days. Some fragmentary inscriptions were found in 1948. Written in Latin and of early imperial date, they are *elogia*, brief statements of a man's career inscribed on the base of statues or monuments erected in honour of a magistrate or general. Many such *elogia* have been found in Rome, Pompeii and Arretium; thus Tarquinii too wished to remind its citizens of their past. The interesting point is that they drew on the traditions of their own city and thus we can get a glimpse at purely Etruscan history. On one of these *Elogia Tarquiniensia* the name of the legendary founder, Tarchon, can probably be read, together with the words Etruria and Tarquinii; another mentions the city of Falerii. A third records the exploits of a certain S . . . Orgolaniensis; his name, which started with S, is missing, and he came from the neighbouring town of Norchia (Orcle in the Middle Ages). He is said to have conquered a king of Caere, defeated Arretium in war and captured nine strongholds (either of the Arretines or perhaps of the Latins). This tiny fragment of lost history vividly illustrates the disunity of the various Etruscan cities; they were often at war with one another, despite any formal bonds that may have linked the Twelve Cities. Another *elogium* tells of a man whose name is scarcely preserved (Vel X, son of Lars?): 'As praetor he led an army against C(aere). He led another to Sicily. He was the first of the Etruscan generals (or of all the Etruscans) to cross the sea with an army. He was decorated with an eagle and a golden crown because of his victory.' Many questions arise from this inscription. What was the Etruscan equivalent of praetor? Was he the head of the Etruscan League (and thus a war by the League against one city would be implied), or the chief magistrate of Tarquinii? Were his honours the insignia of a triumph? And above all, when did he go to Sicily? Many answers have been offered to the last question: the original Etruscan invasion of Italy, with a call at Sicily en route; the early fifth century, when the Etruscans were engaged in naval operations against Syracuse; when the Athenians in 414 were besieging Syracuse and asked Etruria for help; or was the man the leader of mercenary troops in the wars in Sicily between Greeks and Carthaginians at the end of the fourth century? Perhaps the early fifth century has the strongest claim, but even more important than the precise date is the fact that here we have a piece of Tarquinian history, otherwise unknown, preserved until the days of the Roman Empire. Thus when the emperor Claudius came to write his history of the

Etruscans, he had local Etruscan traditions to draw upon to counterbalance the official Roman version of the relations of the two peoples.[77]

THE ROCK-TOMB CITIES

All the great Etruscan cities controlled large areas beyond their city walls. The extent of this *territorium* no doubt varied from time to time with the city's fluctuating fortunes, and our evidence for boundaries refers mainly to the Etrusco-Roman period from the fourth century onwards. However, if this limitation of application is recognized, the territories can be fairly clearly marked (see Fig. 26).

Tarquinii lay between Vulci in the north and Caere in the south. Its boundary with Vulci was the river Arrone, that with Caere was (roughly) the Mignone, and it controlled only about ten miles of coast. Its port was probably Martanum at the mouth of the Marta, on which Tarquinii lay, rather than at the insalubrious Graviscae (Porto Clementino), where in 181 BC the Romans established a colony (*cf.* p. 277). The eastern frontier ran from the south-west of Lake Bolsena starting north of Visentium (modern Bisenzo) via Viterbo past Lake Vico to a point north of Lake Bracciano where it turned westwards along the Mignone to reach the sea. We may now glance at the larger settlements in this area.

At Visentium (its Etruscan name is unknown), on the south-west shore of Lake Bolsena, was an early Villanovan settlement (*c.* 750) and an Etruscan cemetery of the sixth century. It imported some bronzes from Tarquinii and probably traded with Clusium in the north, but it also produced its own metal work; a recently discovered biconical vase has on its lid figures that are performing some kind of magical dance; they have been compared with the Salii, the dancing priests at Rome.[78] But the settlement apparently declined fairly soon (after the appearance of some Attic black-figure vases of the second half of the sixth century), until after the Roman conquest of the third century. Tuscana (now Tuscania), the other city in northern Tarquinian territory, developed so late that it might even have been a successor to Visentium. Apart from a small foundation, perhaps a sanctuary, of the late sixth century, little is known before the third century, to which some of its tombs belong. Sarcophagi like those of Tarquinii have been found, some perhaps imported, which give the names of some of the chief families who held magistracies (the Ceise, the Vibinana, the Atina, and the Statlane); in view of the apparent smallness of Tuscana, these magistrates possibly held office in Tarquinii rather than locally. Its importance increased in the Middle Ages.

A more interesting area of settlement lay in the east in a wild, rugged and romantic landscape. In the valleys formed by the tributaries of the Marta are many precipitous ravines where the streams have furrowed out veritable canyons. Often torrents run close to one another before joining, and high ground towers up between them; these almost impregnable and isolated hills formed ideal strongholds for early settlers, just as later they attracted castles and towns in the Middle Ages. On the precipitous faces of the cliffs opposite these citadels the Etruscans carved out tombs for their dead. These they decorated with architectural façades, thus giving to the cliffs the appearance of cities, with houses, temple-fronts, steps and streets (*Pls. 19, 20*). Such rock tombs are found at Bieda, Norchia, Castel d'Asso, San Giovenale, San Giuliano, and many smaller centres. They take three main forms. The tumulus, which is common to other parts of Etruria (*e.g.* Caere), need not be described here. The two others are cube tombs (*dadi*) and gabled tombs. The former present an almost isolated square block which projects from the rock behind; the façade represents the main side of a house with a false door. Often there is a plain lower part and an upper decorated one, but their forms vary. The gabled tombs represent another type of Etruscan house, that with a gable-roof; they jut out from the cliff-face and have false doors. More elaborate forms with porticos and with pediments were devised, the latter filled with sculptured figures, showing mythological scenes. The burial within the tomb was occasionally reached through a real door, but more commonly through a corridor; in these cases a false door of varied designs and proportion was carved in relief on the façade. All these tombs were grouped in vast cemeteries; many must have been washed away and destroyed, but those at Bieda have been reckoned at two to three thousand. They were arranged in rows, cut in the hill-side, and, where the slope was not sufficiently steep, terraces were cut; drains and canals helped to prevent erosion. Access was by stairways running up from the roads below; these might be special cemetery roads but more often the cliff façades were ranged along the main roads running through the valleys.

Despite the variety, the basic forms of the rock façades seem to show little essential change from the seventh until the third century. There is some evidence for Villanovan settlement, especially at Vetralla. The population does not seem to have achieved any great artistic level, perhaps because the area was essentially agricultural rather than urban. Some artistic influences from Caere have been detected, and some of the southern towns such as Blera and San Giuliano may possibly have been dominated by Caere for some time. Other known settlements in this area include Musarna near Castel d'Asso, where the family tomb of the Alethna of the third and second centuries has been found. Its ancient name is not known, but it provided at least one *zilath* (magistrate) for Tarquinii (*TLE*, 174).[79]

In the wild country in the south of this region, where deep ravines, cut in the tufa, may suddenly yawn at the feet of a walker who is crossing what appears to be a plain, two important Etruscan settlements have recently been investigated. One is at San Giovenale on the Vesca, a tributary of the Mignone; it is some fifteen miles from Tarquinii, and eighteen from Caere and from Bolsena, lying on a rocky plateau between two streams, a typical site. Since 1956 it has been excavated by members of the Swedish Institute in Rome under the patronage and with the personal participation of the King of Sweden. An interesting aspects of investigations on the site and in this area to the north of the Tolfa Mountains in the valley of the Mignone is the discovery of some Bronze Age settlements of the Apennine culture, at Luni, Sant' Andrea, San Pietro, La Mola and San Giovenale itself. Whereas that at Luni corresponds to a fairly early phase,

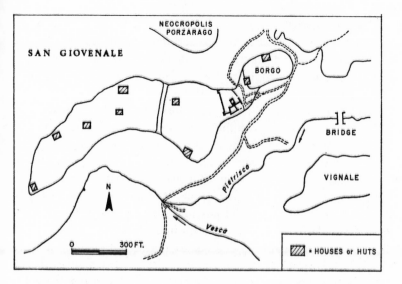

Fig. 8 Plan of San Giovenale

that at San Giovenale is later, perhaps about 1000 BC, and did not last more than a few generations. It lay on the eastern end of the plateau and it was succeeded, perhaps after an interval of time, by an Iron Age settlement on the western end. No Bronze Age burials, and only a few early Iron Age ones have yet been found. These were not on the acropolis, the site of the village, but round about it; they were followed later by a series of Etruscan tombs of various types, tumulus, cube and a third kind cut out of the sides of the hills, the last being late, in the third century; they contain imported Greek pottery from Protocorinthian to Attic black-figure. The Iron Age village apparently began in the eighth century but flourished in the seventh when it spread to the eastern end of the site (Fig. 8).

Towards 600 BC the oval huts of the farmers gave place to rectangular houses of squared tufa blocks, first at the east end and then the west (Pl. 18). Here clearly we have the Etruscans, indicated by pottery sherds, one inscribed with an Etruscan name, and by the corresponding tombs outside the settlement.

There are traces of Etruscan houses, (cf. Pl. 18) roads and wells, with a defensive fosse across the acropolis. Evidence of defensive structures is found on the east, but not on the west end; these structures may well belong to a late phase, when Tarquinii and San Giovenale on its southern boundary were facing the attacks of the Romans in the fourth century. Thereafter an Etruscan settlement continued to exist but died out by the end of the third century, when the more concentrated population of the settlements began to be scattered in the large estates of the *villae rusticae*. Thus San Giovenale (its ancient name is unknown) provides a good example of a smaller Etruscan town, yet not so rural that it did not import its quota of Greek vases and provide its richer citizens with fine tombs.[80]

Luni, whose name goes back to the eighth century AD and may be classical, lay four miles to the west on a similar plateau surrounded by ravines, and has traces of occupation from the Bronze Age to the Middle Ages. Most interesting is the Bronze Age 'Apennine' settlement on the centre of the plateau, where the inhabitants lived in a village of large houses which were partly sunk into the tufa rock, in place of the more usual simple huts or caves. The largest house (45 × 4 yards) had walls of stone, with a straw roofing laid over wooden roof-beams: clearly such 'long-houses' will have sheltered many families. Even more surprising is the discovery of six Mycenaean sherds in the settlement: these date from *c.* 1400–1100 and reveal contact between central Italy and the Aegean. Hardly less striking is a feature of the Iron Age village whose huts spread over the acropolis and nearby hills: this is a large, well constructed rectangular building measuring $9\frac{1}{2}$ × 19 yards. Such a house is so far unique in Iron Age Italy and was probably the residence of the chief, until it was destroyed by fire *c.* 700 BC. An Etruscan settlement followed. A weak spot at the east end of the acropolis was strengthened by a massive mound of tufa rocks and earth, thirty feet high; in places there are impressive walls which probably belong to the later period when the territory of Tarquinii was threatened by Rome after the fall of Veii. Remains of a sixth-century house underlie a fifth-century one. Luni

19 Rock-cut tombs at Norchia. Reconstruction by L. Canina (1846). On the right are tombs of the cube type (*dadi*), whose facades represent Etruscan houses with false doors. Gabled tombs might represent houses with gable-roofs, but those shown here are more elaborate, with porticos and temple-like pediments. See p.93. 20 Present state of such tombs.

21 Air view of Caere. In the lower half is the cemetery of Banditaccia, where many large tumulus tombs are visible. Above this (in fact to the south-east) across the Manganello valley is the site of Etruscan Caere, with modern Cerveteri occupying its right-hand end. See Fig. 10 and p.97f. 22 View looking south-west along the Manganello valley, with Banditaccia on right and Caere on left, with Cerveteri in distance.

23 Funeral Way (Via degli Inferi) at Caere. This leads down from the northern end of Banditaccia and then across the valley to the city. Along it came the great funeral processions. See p.99. 24 One of the largest of the great tumulus tombs. See p.98.

25 Interior of Tomba della Cornice at Caere. The back wall of the main chamber resembles the facade of an Etruscan house with doors and windows, leading to smaller burial chambers. See p.98.   26   Tomb of the Reliefs, also at Caere. On the walls and pillars domestic objects and animals are sculptured in relief; they are brightly painted. Cerberus is also included. See p.98.

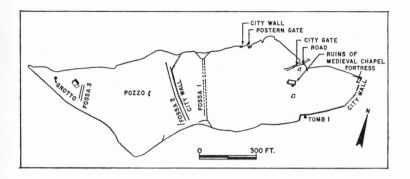

Fig. 9 Plan of Luni

also had a protective fosse, with subsidiary ones across the plateau, while a curious cult-cave had channels in its roof which led to the cliff above, perhaps for the blood of sacrifices to reach the cave below. The cult persisted until the site was converted into a Christian church.[81] (Fig. 9).

Thus this wild area in Tarquinii's southern territory, which even today is not easy of access with its rough maquis of bramble and bush and tracks which a sudden storm can render impassable, has preserved some interesting sites. Most significant is the construction of Etruscan houses over Villanovan huts: the excavators refer freely to the 'coming of the Etruscans': a new people—or merely fresh customs?

CAERE[82]

Caere, Tarquinii's great neighbour to the south, occupied a not dissimilar site, lying on the edge of some bare downland and looking across a plain to the sea some three to four miles away. Built on a tufa hill (running north-east/south-west) between two streams (Fossa della Mola and Fossa del Manganello), it was flanked by two parallel hills on which were the chief cemeteries: Banditaccia on the north-west and Monte Abatone on the south-east. These burials covered a vast area of more than 1000 acres, while the city-site occupied 375 (*Pls. 21, 22*). The hills were much closer together than the corresponding hills of La Cività and Monterozzi at Tarquinii, and whereas the city-site of Tarquinii has been uninhabited since Roman times, that of Caere has been partly covered by a village (Cerveteri-Caere vetus). It was called Cisra or Chaire by the Etruscans, Agylla by the Greeks, and Caere by the Romans. (Fig. 10.)

Its earliest settlement is marked by cremation graves of the eighth century (*a pozzo*) and some contemporary inhumations (*a fossa*). Many of these were at the south-west foot of the city hill in a locality called Il Sorbo, where the famous Regolini-Galassi tomb of the orientalizing period (seventh century) was excavated in 1836, thus revealing the great wealth of the city. Of the cemeteries on the two hills, that of Banditaccia is the better known to visitors and has much more impressive monuments. The form of the early trench burials was developed in the seventh century into a small chamber covered with stone slabs, and an earth mound above. These simple mounds of earth were later given a monumental appearance by the addition of a large circular base (there are a few giants of thirty yards in diameter), cut into the rock or built up, generally with a moulded cornice; inside were one or more groups of burials, which were sometimes approached through an ante-chamber (*Pl. 24*). The burial-chambers, which often had rooms opening out of them, were fashioned like the interior of houses, with central beams, chairs and beds, in contrast with the rock-tombs described in the last section which imitated the exterior of houses, but had very irregular and rough interiors (*Pl. 25*). During the seventh to fourth centuries these tumuli tombs became increasingly varied. There were also plain chamber-tombs, either cut into the side of the rock, or underground with ante-chambers. The later burials were not covered with mounds, but consisted of single underground rooms like the inside of houses, sometimes with pillars, niches and benches, and some with paintings or reliefs (*Pl. 26*). In general, paintings, apart from some early and late examples, are rare, unlike neighbouring Tarquinii. All these tombs lay in a great cemetery into which some form of planning was gradually introduced. A main road ran through it over the

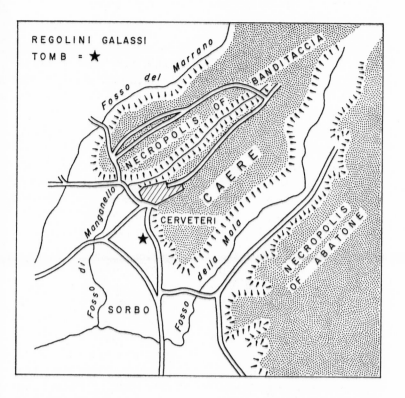

Fig. 10 Plan of Caere

hill for more than a mile and finally descended in the north-east through a cleft in the rock, and then turned across the little valley to the ancient city: along this funeral way (Via degli Inferi) the chief citizens of Caere were carried to their last resting-places (*Pl. 23*). The lay-out of the cemetery, with its elaborate system of lesser tomb-lined roads, has been strikingly revealed by air-photography, which has also disclosed a very large number of unknown tombs, some 400 in this cemetery and 600 in the still larger necropolis on the plateau of Monte Abatone, much of which is still rough pasture or cornland.[83]

Of the city itself little survives, although only a small part of its 375 acres was covered by the small medieval and modern village. From an examination of two sectors of the Banditaccia cemetery the population of Caere has been estimated at some 25,000 inhabitants.[84] Where the rocky cliffs were not steep enough to provide adequate defence, they were strengthened by stretches of walls of squared stone; a section cut out of the rock, with a ditch in front, is to be seen along the Manganello, and the remains of a gate survive at the northern end of the city; these walls are presumably late (*Pl. 22*). There is evidence for some eight temples, including those of Hera and of the 'Manganello', with rich terracottas and votive offerings. But the city of the living is barely known to us and all our evidence comes from the rich contents of the tombs, which show a continuous development of life on the site from Villanovan to Roman times, though without providing a clue to the question: at what point in its early days have we the right to call the city Etruscan?

Caere owed much of its early prosperity to the metals of the Tolfa region in the north and to the skill and enterprise with which the citizens exploited the possibilities of overseas trade. In the eighth century it lagged behind Tarquinii in its bronze work, but began to overtake and surpass its rival in the seventh, when the period of its greatest prosperity began and contacts were developed with the eastern Mediterranean. Caere imported on a vast scale. From Asia Minor and Greece came large bronze cauldrons decorated with griffins and lions (*Pl. 28*), pottery and vases and perfume from Corinth (from *c.* 675), and later Attic wares in the last quarter of the century, gold and silver ware and ivory from Cyprus, Syria and the East (*Pl. 27*). Caere also often acted as middleman for the distribution of goods in Etruria (thus the cauldrons were sometimes sent on to Vetulonia or Praeneste), and her own artists began to imitate imported wares: thus the Caerite goldworkers soon reached a high standard of excellence and were able to export their jewellery to other Etruscan and Latin cities (*Pls. 29, 30*). Often the impetus would come from Greek or oriental merchants or artists who settled in Caere, as Demaratus had in Tarquinii, and this policy of opening the door to resident aliens (whatever the legal status accorded to them) quickly paid dividends: it was to this, for instance, that the great Caeretan *hydriae* (waterpots, often painted by a master artist) owed their origin (*Pl. 32*). Caere's geographical position helps to explain her numerous contacts with the Greek world, including the Greek colonies in Italy. Alone of the Etruscan cities Caere maintained a Treasury at Delphi. These Treasuries were small buildings like temples, set up by leading Greek states, and contained offerings to Apollo. Such contacts are reflected in the legend that before the Etruscans arrived, the city had been founded by Pelasgians from Thessaly by whom it was named Agylla. For some two centuries her output of terracotta statues, which reflect Ionian influence (*Pl. 31*), her bronzes, her *bucchero* pottery (*Pl. 33*), her gold and ivory work enriched the city's life, but by *c.* 450 artistic activity declined, and Caere turned more to agriculture. This was due partly to a slackening in overseas trade after the defeat of an Etruscan navy by the Greeks off Cumae in 474 robbed the Etruscans of their previous control of the Tyrrhenian Sea.[85]

At a time when deep-ploughing is threatening to destroy the buried remains of some of the Etruscan cities, and swarms of visitors flock to the cemeteries of Caere and Tarquinii, it is good to be reminded of the peace and great natural beauty of many of these sites. One of the most sympathetic early travellers was George Dennis, to whose keen and appreciative eye we owe many an excellent picture; a few sentences from his description of Caere over a hundred years ago may tempt the reader to turn to his classic *Cities and Cemeteries of Etruria.* Any artist's eye would be delighted, he wrote, 'either on the site of the city itself, with its wide-sweeping prospect of plain and sea on the one hand, and of the dark many-peaked hills on the other, or in the ravines around, where one meets with combinations of rock and wood, such as for form and colour are rarely surpassed. The cliffs of the city, here rising boldly at one spring from the slope, there broken away into many angular forms, with huge masses of rock scattered at their feet, are naturally of the liveliest red that tufa can assume, yet are brightened still further by encrusting lichens into the warmest orange or amber, or are gilt with the most brilliant yellow—thrown out more prominently by an occasional sombering of grey, while the dark ilex or oak feathers and crests the whole.'

The territory of Caere stretched from roughly the river Mignone in the north, which formed its frontier with Tarquinii, to another stream named Arrone (*cf.* p. 92) in the south, and inland to embrace Lake Bracciano. In the north lay the Tolfa area, rich in metals, the treasure-house of Caere. Here are found traces of proto-Villanovan culture as well as small Etruscan settlements, few of which have been carefully explored. A start has been made at Monterano on the Mignone west of Lake Bracciano, a site later known as Manturanum; this name could mean the territory of Mantura, which in turn might hide an Etruscan name perhaps derived from Mantus, a god of the underworld. Many tombs have been found in the neighbourhood and the settlement appears to date from *c.* 700. Its links were with Caere, on which it doubtless depended; it seems to have declined when the larger city did. At first it probably shared in the exploitation of the minerals of La Tolfa but gradually became an agricultural community. The cemetery of another small settlement, revealed by air-photography, near the coast at Colle Pantano, has soil-marks which indicate at least forty ploughed-out tumuli. Caere's nearest port was Alsium (Palo), where tombs of *c.* 600 BC have been found.

Another little port, Punicum, now Santa Marinella, lay farther north, while at the southern end of Caere's territory was Fregenae, a Roman centre, but perhaps of Etruscan origin. The most important port, however, was at Pyrgi (Santa Severa), where the polygonal walls under the medieval castle are of early Roman date, though there are traces of Etruscan walls by the sea (*Pl. 34*). It was famed for its temple to Leucothea, which was sacked in a piratical raid in 384 by Dionysius of Syracuse who carried off no less than 1000 talents.[86]

Pyrgi's fame today, however, rests upon the excavations started in 1957. These uncovered the foundations of two temples side by side. The slightly larger one (A) comprised a colonnaded *pronaos* and three *cellae* and was built *c.* 480–470 BC. Terracotta fragments of a gigantomachy, showing strong Greek influence,

were found (Pl. 36), and an inscription (*unial*) indicates that one
of the temples was dedicated to Uni (Juno), whom the Greeks
possibly identified with Leucothea. Temple B is peripteral and
slightly older (c. 500). But the most exciting discovery of all
was made in 1964 between the two temples: three thin rectangular sheets of gold-leaf, one inscribed in Phoenician, the
others in Etruscan; holes and gilt nail-heads show that they were
once fixed to the temple walls or doors. Here at last a bilingual
inscription, a Rosetta stone for Etruscan, seemed to be emerging.
However, it falls just short of this, in that the Phoenician is not a
translation of the Etruscan, but the general meaning is similar and
so the find has greatly enriched our knowledge of the language.
The historical implications are equally important (Pl. 35).[87]

The general sense of the inscriptions is clear, even if accurate
translation is not attainable. The Phoenician text says: 'To the
Lady Astarte. This is the sacred place made and given by Thefarie
Velianas, king over Caere, in the month of the Sacrifice of the
Sun as a gift within the temple and the sanctuary (?), because
Astarte has chosen by means of him in the three years of his
reign. . . .' etc. The longer Etruscan one says roughly: 'This is
the temple (shrine?) and this the place of the statue dedicated to
Uni-Astarte . . . Thefarie Velianas has given them . . . three
years . . . of the *zilath* (chief magistrate?)'. The second Etruscan
inscription reads: 'Thus has Thefarie Velianas dedicated (the
temple?): he established the *cleva* offering in the month of
Masan and there was the annual (or anniversary) sacrifice of
the temple . . .'

Briefly what we have is Thefarie Velianas, ruler of Caere,
making a dedication at Pyrgi to Uni-Astarte, a foreign goddess
whose favour he apparently enjoyed, The date is generally
agreed to be about 500 BC. Innumerable questions are raised by
these new documents; but only a few points can be mentioned.
First, we have a new ruler at Caere. The Phoenician text calls
him MLK'L, 'king over' KYSRY (Cisra-Caere), in place of the
more usual 'king of', while the Etruscan version appears to have
named him *zilath*, the title of the chief magistrates in later times
in Etruscan cities; he had been in power for three years. Was

Caere at this time a monarchy or Republic, had it a king (*melek*) or a chief magistrate (*zilath*), or how are these titles to be understood? Professor Pallottino, to whose interpretation so much is owed, suggests that Caere, like many other cities at this time (*cf.* pp. 224f), was in a state of transition between established monarchy and emerging oligarchy: if so, Thefarie might have been in a position not dissimilar from that of a Greek tyrant. There had been kings at Caere—one of the Elogia Tarquiniensia attests a 'Caeritum regem'—but Thefarie may belong rather to the age of the condottieri like Vibenna, Mastarna and Lars Porsenna (see p. 226).

The international aspect is no less important: a Punic element has been revealed at Pyrgi. This indicates trade between Carthage and Caere (Punicum, quite close to Pyrgi, may have gained its name from a settlement of Punic merchants) and this at a time when the power of the Etruscans in central Italy was being threatened by the Greeks and Latins and they were relying on Carthage for help in the struggle. Further, it provides an appropriate setting for the first treaty which Carthage is said by Polybius to have made with Rome in 509: the Polybian date for this, often questioned, will now seem more firmly anchored. Thus the inscriptions give us a hint of the position of one Etruscan city in the wider world as well as of the internal condition of Caere, where we should now perhaps picture a stronger Punic element mingling with the Greeks and Etruscans.

VEII[88]

Veii was the eastern neighbour of Caere, but more significant for the future was the fact that it was only some twelve miles north of Rome and its territory reached to the Tiber; eventually this proximity led to hostilities, until in 396 BC Veii was sacked and destroyed by Rome. The city was built on a rocky tufa plateau, with steep cliffs, at the southern end of which was the citadel (Piazza d'Armi); at the foot of this height the river Cremera (Valchetta), which flowed around the eastern and part of the northern sides of the city, was joined by a tributary (Fosso dei due Fossi), which ran along the western side. The

27 Silver bowl
with Oriental scenes
from the Regolini-
Galassi tomb at Caere.
See p.100. 28 Bronze
cauldron decorated
with winged animals
in repoussé and with
griffin-heads attached
to the rim, from the
same tomb. See p.100.

29 Large gold fibula (the pin is hidden) ornamented with rows of birds in the round and figures of animals in repoussé with details in granulation. About 650 BC. From the Regolini-Galassi tomb at Caere. See p.29.

30 Large gold pectoral with repoussé figures in zones. It was composed of a thin gold sheet hammered round a bronze plate, now lost. The top four rows of the escutcheon depict men and lions, winged genii and winged sphinxes. From the Regolini-Galassi tomb at Caere. See p.30.

31 Terracotta sarcophagus from Caere. Husband and wife shown on banqueting couch. Although the artistic inspiration may be Ionian, the conception is completely Etruscan: Greek women did not dine thus with their husbands. The date is *c.* 510-500 BC. See p.101.

32 One of the Caeretan *hydriae* (water-pots) depicting a griffin and Arimaspian. These *hydriae* were made between 530 and 510 BC by an artist, perhaps an Ionian Greek (from Phocaea?) who settled in Etruscan Caere. See p.101.   33 A *bucchero* shiny blackish vase from Caere. On the body is an engraved syllabary and on the base an alphabet. See p.101.

34 Air view of Pyrgi (Santa Severa). The site of the Etruscan city lies on the coast. The Roman colony was further along the coast, off the picture to the left. See p.102.

35 Two of the three inscribed sheets of gold-leaf, recently found at Pyrgi: that on the left is in Phoenician, that on the right in Etruscan. *c.* 500 BC. See p.103.

36 Fragments of a terracotta group of the battle of Athene and the Giants from the pediment of a temple at Pyrgi. *c.* 475 BC. See p.102.

37   Air view of Veii. Piazza d'Armi is on the bottom left
(the south), Isola Farnese nearer the top, with the temple of
Apollo just above to the right. The isolated nature of the
site, on a rocky tufa plateau, with steep cliffs, and almost
surrounded by streams, is clearly revealed. See Fig. 11
and p.104f.   38   Foundations of the temple of Apollo, the
Portonaccio temple. See p.107.

39 The Ponte Sodo at Veii, a drainage tunnel, still over 70 yards long. See p.108.
40 The north-east (Capena) gate. See p.106. 41 Section of the city wall west of
the north-east gate, of the later fifth century BC. The four lowest courses remained
undressed because they were covered by an earthen glacis. See p.108.

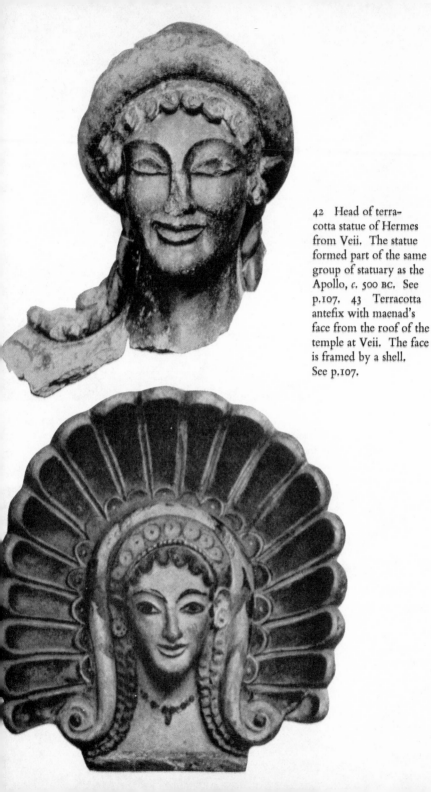

42   Head of terra-
cotta statue of Hermes
from Veii. The statue
formed part of the same
group of statuary as the
Apollo, *c.* 500 BC. See
p.107.   43   Terracotta
antefix with maenad's
face from the roof of the
temple at Veii. The face
is framed by a shell.
See p.107.

44 Terracotta statue of Apollo from Veii, the work of the artist Vulca or his school *c*. 500 BC. One of the most renowned of Etruscan works of art. See p.107.

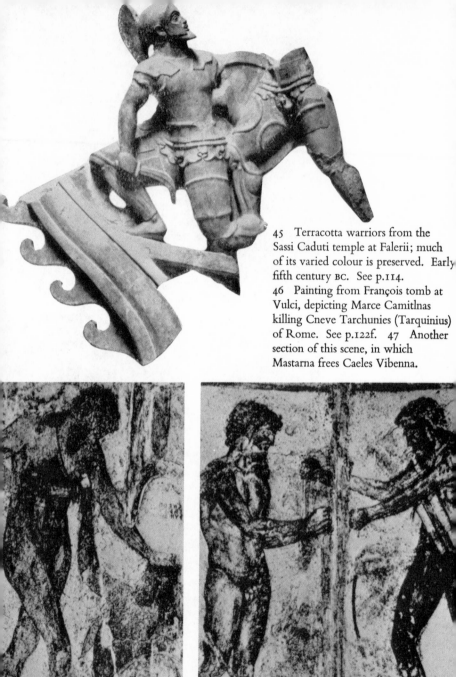

45 Terracotta warriors from the Sassi Caduti temple at Falerii; much of its varied colour is preserved. Early fifth century BC. See p.114.
46 Painting from François tomb at Vulci, depicting Marce Camitlnas killing Cneve Tarchunies (Tarquinius) of Rome. See p.122f. 47 Another section of this scene, in which Mastarna frees Caeles Vibenna.

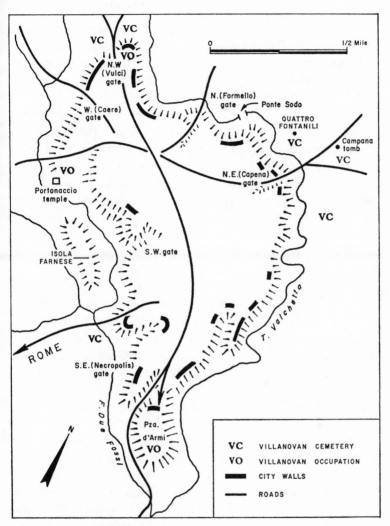

Fig. 11 Plan of Veii

city was thus surrounded by water apart from a small area in
the north-west, while its towering cliffs made it virtually impregnable (*Pl. 37*). Despite the nearness to Rome, the site still
retains something of its earlier wild and romantic appearance.
The hill is desolate, since a small medieval village grew up
around the castle on an adjacent height (Isola Farnese) (*Fig. 11*).

Villanovan occupation is revealed by remains of settlements and cemeteries. The development of the graves shows the same continuity from Villanovan to Etruscan as at Caere and Tarquinii. Cremations (*a pozzo*) are followed by trench-graves (*a fossa*), with a period when both were used; the trench-graves then became more elaborate, with recesses for grave furniture (*loculi*) which developed into virtual chambers; then came the proper chamber-tombs (*a camera*), the use of which lasted until after 396. Tumuli are comparatively rare in the seventh century; they are probably the burials of nobles and lie some distance from the city. The early Villanovan settlements appear to represent small independent villages, each with its own cemetery, grouped around the central area, rather than a closely knit community. The cemeteries lay beside the tracks which later developed into the roads that led from Veii to the countryside. Several of them have recently been destroyed by deep-ploughing, but swift action by the British School at Rome and Italian archaeologists has salvaged much from the wreckage, and further excavations have added to our knowledge. The chief sites are just outside the north of the city at Grotta Gramiccia (huts and cemeteries), Casale del Fosso and Quattro Fontanili (cemeteries), some huts on the west, and a cemetery at Valle la Fata; there is also a settlement on the Piazza d'Armi (the associated cemetery has not yet been found), and a scatter of Villanovan sherds on the rest of the city plateau. One striking result of the excavation of the huts outside the north-west gate shows that pottery of typical Villanovan type was less in ordinary domestic use than pottery of a distinctively 'Latian' type. Thus the co-existence of Villanovan and Latian elements at Veii suggests links with Rome, where the first settlement on the Palatine hill appears to be earlier than this Veientine village.

Little of Etruscan Veii remains. The streets were laid out radially from a centre that lay towards the north. One road passed out through the north-west gate and then forked, one branch to Nepet, the other to Tarquinii and Vulci. A road from the north-west gate led to Capena (*Pl. 40*), another from the south-west gate to Rome; from the west (by the Portonaccio temple) one started for the Tiber mouth and between this and the north-west gate another led to Caere. Foundations of a few houses have been found, both on the Piazza d'Armi and near the Capena Gate, and in 1958 two successive houses were excavated near the north-west gate; the first, dated to the sixth century, was rectangular with a timber framework and wattle-and-daub walls; it was rebuilt with a masonry socle which supported mud-brick or clay and timber walls. The existence of temples in several places is indicated by the survival of votive terracottas. The Campetti deposit (sixth and fifth centuries) contained warriors, youths, women's heads and seated couples, while that near the entrance to the Piazza consisted of some two thousand pieces, many representing organs of the human body. Traces of a large building, found in 1889 over against the Piazza d'Armi, may be a temple, while in the Piazza a small temple (*c. 600–550 BC*) was built over Iron Age huts; it has two cisterns associated with it. But the most famous temple lies on a platform just outside the western walls, the so-called temple of Apollo or Portonaccio temple (*Pl. 38*). It is uncertain whether it has a triple or a single *cella*, and the deity worshipped is not known: a cult of Minerva was established there in the days of the Roman Republic. Beside traces of the temple itself there survive a precinct wall, an altar, a road, and an elaborate system of tanks, suggesting that water played an important part in the ritual. In 1916 the famous statues of Apollo and other deities were found here (*Pl. 44*). It is usually thought that the figures of Apollo and Hercules, who were contending for the body of a stag, came from the temple roof, but some of the figures, including a goddess with a child and a head of Hermes (*Pl. 42*), may belong to other buildings within the sanctuary. These statues must date from about 500 BC, and a *bucchero* cup dedicated by Velthur Tulumne belongs to the sixth century.

For a long time Veii did not need the protection of walls. The citadel (Piazza d'Armi) may have been fortified separately at an early date, but the cliffs sufficed for the rest of the city until the struggle with Rome. The surviving traces of walls are uniform in character and were built as a single system, at a date not earlier than *c.* 450. Half-way along the east side sixteen courses of masonry are preserved to a height of some seventeen feet (*Pl. 41*). Elsewhere for the most part only the undressed base of the wall survives; this must have been below ground in Etruscan times. Little remains to be seen of the gates associated with this wall.

Finally, Veii provides many examples of Etruscan engineering skill. For several miles to the north of the city the valleys are honeycombed by an elaborate system of channels (*cuniculi*) to drain the fields (*cf.* p. 68, *Pl. 11*). Near the city itself a tunnel, over six hundred yards long and twenty-five feet deep at the lowest point, diverted water from the Fosso di Fornello under a ridge to the Fosso Piordo, thereby ensuring a regular flow round the west and south of the town throughout the year; from medieval times this has been used to drive a water-mill, and may have been so used by the Etruscans if the water-mill was invented by these hydraulic experts (it is usually credited to the Romans of the first century BC). A better-known tunnel is the Ponte Sodo, still over seventy yards long, which carries the Valchetta through a low cliff on the northern side of the city plateau in order to eliminate a bend at a point that was liable to flooding (*Pl. 39*). But *cuniculi* were needed for collecting as well as dispersing water; thus the city itself was supplied with water from cisterns which had lateral shafts leading into water-bearing strata of the rock. At Portonaccio below, *cuniculi* were driven into the hillside to conduct water seepage out, while one channel brought water to the cistern beside the temple. Whether these numerous channels gave rise to the famous story of how the Romans tunnelled into the rock when they were besieging the city, and burst out into the temple of Juno Regina on the citadel above when the king was in the act of sacrifice must remain in doubt (see p. 269).

Veii reached its most flourishing period somewhat later than Caere about the middle of the sixth century, when it was an important artistic centre. It specialized in the production of terracottas. One of its artists, Vulca, was summoned to Rome by Tarquinius to make a terracotta statue of Jupiter for the

Capitoline temple; the chariots (*quadrigae*) which served as acroteria on its roof were also made by Veientine artists (see p. 252). While he was in Rome, Vulca also made a statue of Hercules. The statues found at Portonaccio, if not from Vulca's own hand, presumably belong to his school. Other terracottas are represented by surviving votive offerings, some of which were dedicated by visitors to the temple from other cities. Thus Avele Vipiiennas, who offered a *bucchero* vase in the sixth century, may be from Vulci, while if it is accepted that Tolonios is a Faliscan name (-onios is an ending found at Falerii), then the L. Tolonius who dedicated vases in the third century may have been a visitor rather than a descendant of the two Veientine Tolumnes whose vases belong to the sixth century. In general the plastic work of Veii was more tense and harsh than that of Caere or Vulci, and it does not seem to have had much influence on her northern neighbours. Painting is represented by a single example in the famous Campana tomb outside the city on the east. This depicts multicoloured animals, both real and fabulous, possibly a hunting scene. Though under Corinthian influence, it is full of Etruscan exuberance; it has been variously dated between *c.* 675 and 550, a fairly late date being perhaps most likely. The *bucchero* pottery is good but comparatively plain and Veii appears to have imported fewer Greek vases than her neighbours, partly perhaps because she had no harbour and therefore little direct trade with the East.

The Roman sack of Veii in 396 ended its independence, but it did not revert to mere desolation and complete neglect, as is suggested by the romantic picture of flocks pasturing within its walls drawn by the poet Propertius nearly four hundred years later. We now know that its sanctuaries, except those on the citadel (Piazza d'Armi), continued to be maintained and visited. Further, its position on the main road from Rome to Nepet and Sutri (Via Veientana) gave it some importance as a small market town until early in the second century another route (the Via Cassia) was laid out and became the chief highway.

The territory of Veii extended south-west to the coast, where it was delimited by the Arrone and the Tiber. Its western limits were along the Arrone and then probably round the eastern side of Lake Bracciano and northwards to Lake Vico. Its eastern frontier ran along the Tiber from its mouth and then perhaps turned north-westwards from near Lucus Feroniae until it passed Nepet and reached Lake Vico. On this definition the area of Falerii and Capena would have been beyond its territory. This was a partly Etruscanized area of Italic-speaking peoples which reached as far as the Tiber. Since the extent, if any, of Veii's control over it is uncertain, it may be described as a separate, if partly dependent, unit.

ETRURIA TIBERINA AND FALISCAN TERRITORY

The country on the west bank of the Tiber, reaching westwards to Monti Sabatini and Monti Cimini, from south of Capena to north of Falerii, constituted a peripheral area of the Etruscan world. Inhabited by men who spoke an Indo-European dialect akin to Latin, it was penetrated by Etruscan cultural elements. Thus these peoples are regarded as either Etruscanized Latins or an Etruscan population that was progressively Latinized. In general the area was of secondary importance in the eyes of the great Etruscan cities.

The Ager Capenas is a wild country of deep gullies, which drain south-eastwards into the Tiber. It was limited by two roads, that ran north and south: on the east was a primitive route on the west bank of the Tiber (later the Via Tiberina), and on the west a road on the line of the later Via Flaminia, part of which has recently been shown to go back to Etruscan days. Capena itself, which lies south of Mt Soracte, was perched like a promontory-fort on cliffs with streams on three sides; this hill, known as Civitucola or Castellaccio, was at the north-eastern end of a depression called Lago Vecchio. The surrounding cemeteries do not attest settlement before the eighth century: a single *a pozzo* burial is followed by tombs *a fossa* and then *a camera*. Cato (Servius, *ad Aen.* 7, 697) records that Capena was founded by young men sent there by Propertius, a king of Veii, otherwise unknown. This story accords with the Italic practice of the Sacred Spring (*Ver Sacrum*), whereby the children born at a certain time were marked out to be sent to a new settlement when they grew up, but it receives no support from archaeology since both in language and pottery Capena's links seem to have been with Falerii in the north rather than with Veii. Its inhabitants spoke the Faliscan dialect which is closely akin to Latin (ninety-eight brief Faliscan inscriptions survive in the district of Capena), and its early pottery from the trench-graves resembles that from Falerii. Later pottery from the chamber-tombs includes imported Protocorinthian vases, but (unlike Falerii) Attic vases are very rare. On the locally-made incised *impasto* ware animals were favourite subjects; they include winged horses (not found at Veii), a man between two horses, goats (winged and unwinged), fish and birds. Since according to Cato (Varro, *RR*, 2, 3) the goats of Mt Soracte could leap sixty feet, they might well need wings! This ware, which was popular also at Falerii, is found also in both Umbrian and Sabine territory; so too belt plaques from Capena are widely distributed in the central Apennines. Some of the bronze ware and jewellery made at Capena and Falerii imitates Etruscan work, but the general cultural links of this area seem closer to Latium and Sabine territory. On the site of the city itself a few traces of a city-wall survive, together with a lower rampart and annexe; these suggest measures taken to strengthen the city in anticipation of Roman attack after the fall of Veii had opened Rome's path to the north (see pp. 268ff). The whole area has recently been thoroughly surveyed and many traces of Etruscan as well as Roman occupation have been found, *e.g.* an Etruscan settlement at Monte Palombo, south of Capena.[89]

To the south-east towards the Tiber lay Lucus Feroniae, a cult-centre of Feronia, a native goddess of central Italy, protectress of flocks and harvests. The site of the settlement, though not of the sacred grove itself, was found in 1953 at Scorano, near the modern Autostrada. Since it is not a naturally strong position it possibly started as a religious centre and fair which attracted worshippers and traders. These included Etruscans, Latins, Faliscans and Sabines. According to Livy (1, 30, 5) it was frequented in the seventh century, when according to

Dionysius (3, 32) it had the most celebrated fair in Italy. In 211 Hannibal thought it worth his while to cross from the other side of the Tiber in order to sack the sanctuary, and archaeologists have found traces of his attack: some of the objects that escaped his plundering troops were placed in a pit that can be dated to the end of the third century.[90]

In the north the chief Faliscan city was Falerii Veteres. The site is now occupied by Civita Castellana (*Pl. 48*). When the Romans destroyed the ancient city in 241 BC, they removed the population to a more open site in a plain three miles to the west, Falerii Novi. This new settlement, stretches of whose walls still stand, remained the chief centre in Roman times, but with the return of unsettled conditions in the Middle Ages the population returned to the safety of the old hill fortress. The choice of the site of Falerii Veteres, and indeed the pattern of human settlement in this whole area, was determined by geographical factors. The site lies on the Treia which runs into the Tiber some five miles to the east. The whole district to the south and west is intersected by numerous streams and valleys, which form a fan-shaped pattern, all converging near Civita Castellana. The streams have cut deep ravines, steep and cliff-bound, through the soft volcanic rock, while between these wild and gloomy gorges are stretches of rolling fields. In such country even small streams may present formidable barriers to communication; early tracks tended to avoid the deep and difficult valleys, which often might be blocked by flood-water or by thick vegetation, and to develop as ridgeways that followed the level ground between the gorges, at least where progress was not barred by uncleared forest. Civita Castellana was the natural centre of this area of radiating gullies and the high tufa promontories between them. It stands on a narrow stretch of land nearly three hundred feet high, surrounded on three sides by rivers and precipices. Only from the west can it be approached with any ease; access from the north over the ravine of the Rio Maggiore remained very difficult until Pope Clement XI built the Ponte Clementino in 1709. The Maggiore makes a loop just north-east of the city before it joins the Treia and thus

48 General view of Falerii Veteres (Civita Castellana) on its rocky plateau. See p.112.

49 Air view of Vulci (in lower half of picture). The plateau of the city is bounded on the right by the winding course of the Fiora. The tumulus tomb called La Cucumella can be seen on the right and the Ponte dell' Abbadia (*Pl.10*) is at the top. See Fig. 14 and p.120.

50 Sarcophagus lid of peperino stone from Vulci, of the first half of the third century BC. Husband and wife are asleep in death. An inscription gives the name of the woman: Ramtha Visnai, wife of Arnth Tetnie. See p.124.

51 Centaur in nenfro, a local stone, from Vulci, of c. 575 BC. The frontal view shows the influence of the Greek *kouros* type, but the whole is much heavier. See p.124.

52 Engraved bronze back of mirror, depicting the winged figure of the seer
Calchas scrutinizing a sacrificial liver (*hepatoscopy*): *cf.* the Tarchon mirror Fig. 6.
It comes from Vulci and belongs to the end of the fifth century BC. A fine
example of Etruscan metal engraving. See p.124.

53 General view of Orvieto, an Etruscan city; whether it is to be identified with Etruscan Volsinii remains uncertain. Its fine position on rocky cliffs made it almost impregnable, but the general lie of the land is less harsh than that around some of the southern cities. See p.127. 54 Etruscan tombs at Orvieto. They are arranged in parallel streets. Note the name over the entrance. See p.131.

55 Bolsena. The hill-site of the Etruscan city, which *may* be Volsinii, runs down to the medieval town (in centre of picture) which in turn runs down to the lake. See p.127. 56 Wall of the Etruscan city above Bolsena. Note the masons' marks on some of the blocks. See p.128.

57 Head of warrior from the cemetery of Crocifisso del Tufo at Orvieto; *c.* 525 BC. See p.131. 58 Terracotta head of a god (Tinia, Zeus?) from the Belvedere Temple, Orvieto; *c.* 450–400 BC. See p.131. 59 Gateway of the small Etruscan city of Saturnia. See p.125.

60 General view of
Rusellae, looking up
over part of the site. See
p.133. 61 Road leading
up to the citadel of
Vetulonia. There are
remains of Etruscan
houses on the left. See
p.141. 62 View of
Populonia, seen from
across the bay. The
medieval castle marks the
Etruscan citadel; the
cemeteries lie along the
shore. See p.141.

63 Small bronze statue from Populonia. Ajax falling on his sword. A fine bronze of the early decades of the fifth century BC. See p.144.

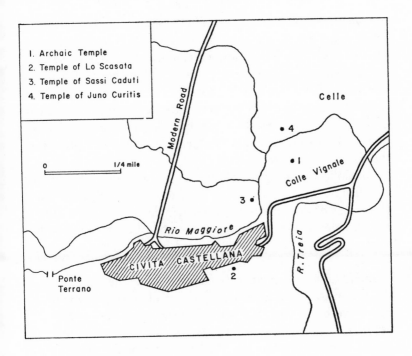

Fig. 12 Plan of Civita Castellana Falerii

encloses another hill, the Colle Vignale. Here probably was the site of the earliest Iron Age settlement, though settlers soon spread to the site of Civita Castellana itself (Fig. 12).

Cato ascribes the foundation of Falerii to Argos in Greece, and Dionysius records that even in his day many Greek customs survived at Falerii: the shields and spears were like those of Argos, and the temple of Juno Curitis, both the building itself and some ceremonies, resembled that of Argive Hera. Though not to be taken very seriously, this tradition reflects early Greek influences in this as in other parts of Etruria, and archaeological evidence suggests that at least one Greek potter was working at Falerii in the first half of the seventh century. The surrounding cemeteries show the customary development of cremation *pozzi* in the ninth to eighth centuries, inhumations *a fossa* in the eighth to seventh centuries and *a camera* in the seventh to sixth centuries which remained in use until the second century. Some stretches of the city walls of almost rectangular tufa blocks survive, together with a gateway cut in the rock (in the garden of the Convent of S. Maria del Carmine). Unlike the town itself, some of its temples continued in use into Roman times; fragments of their rich terracotta statues, antefixes, tiles and other decorations now make a striking display in the galleries and store-rooms of the Villa Giulia Museum in Rome.[91]

On Colle Vignale, probably the original acropolis, two temples date from at least *c.* 500 BC and continued into Hellenistic times. In the area of the ancient city is the temple of Lo Scasato, named that of Apollo from the statue of the god of *c.* 300 BC; this, like many of the terracottas, was inspired by the work of the great Greek sculptors of the fourth century, Scopas, Praxiteles and Lysippus. These associated terracottas date the temple from the fourth to first centuries and a layer of ashes suggests that it may have been burnt when the Romans took the town in 241 BC. In the area of Sassi Caduti is a temple called that of Mercury from the discovery there of the lower part of the statue of this god. Part of the acroterion of a fifth century building survives in the famous group of struggling warriors on which much of the varied colour is preserved (*Pl. 45*). The figure of one who has fallen on his knee is almost complete, while only the lower part of the man who has forced him down remains. Both are fully armed and details of the equipment, breast-plate, greaves, shield and sword, are clearly to be seen; Dionysius drew attention to the similarities of Greek arms to Faliscan. This acroterion was replaced by another, to which the figure of Mercury belongs, in the Hellenistic period, while many votive inscriptions survive from this temple. Lastly in the district called Celle beyond the Maggiore are the foundations of another temple of the fourth or third century; but many of the associated objects are very much older—some even of the Bronze Age—and it may be the temple of Juno Curritis. Juno was probably regarded as the presiding deity of the city; in the third century AD a colony at Falerii Novi was called Colonia Junonia, and it was her cult and its alleged analogies with that of Argive Hera that may well be at the bottom of the tradition that Falerii was a colony of Argos. The meaning of her title Curitis (or Curritis) has been much discussed; a Sabine origin is doubtful. The annual festival of the goddess was described by Ovid (*Amores* 3, 13) who once attended it with his wife who came from Falerii. He marked the hard approach to the sacred grove:

> Difficilis clivis huc via praebet iter.
> Stat vetus et densa praenubilis arbore lucus;
> Adspice: concedes numen inesse loco.

and he goes on to mention an 'ara per antiquas facta sine arte manus': some 500 yards upstream from the temple a rough altar of tufa blocks was found in 1873; it has since been destroyed.

Falerii is first mentioned in the Roman tradition in connection with Rome's wars with Veii: thus during the Roman siege of Veii, both Falerii and Capena tried to persuade the Etruscan League to help Veii. Later (357–1) Falerii fought alongside Tarquinii against Rome. But alliance with Etruscan cities, whether achieved or merely sought, does not involve kinship. When Rome's power was increasing, the Faliscan cities had a common interest with Veii, but Veii was not popular with the other great Etruscan cities; they did not help her, not would they bestir themselves on behalf of so peripheral an area as Etruria Tiberina. Though Livy may speak of the people of Falerii and Capena as two Etruscan peoples ('hi duo Etruriae populi': 5, 8, 5), he also called Nepet and Sutrium, which lay to the west of Falerii, 'loca opposita Etruriae et velut claustra inde portaeque' (6, 9, 4, referring to 386 BC): clearly the land near the Tiber was Etruscanized rather than an integral part of Etruria.

Many other small Faliscan sites are known, some perhaps in the territory of Falerii rather than independent, *e.g.* at Narce, Vignanello and Corchiano. The last, some five miles to the north, occupied some twenty-four acres on a promontory above precipitous gorges; cemeteries and numerous tombs lie around it, and there is a spectacular stretch of road-cutting (on the route to Falerii Veteres) and another on a westward-leading road, on the hillside face of which are carved in Etruscan characters the name Larth Vel Arnies, perhaps the maker of the road. Another site was at Ponte Nepesino, less than two miles south of Nepi. While such sites remain nameless, one famous Faliscan town, Fescennium, cannot be identified, though Corchiano is a possibility. It were here that the ribald Roman marriage songs (*versus Fescennini*) originated, which according to ancient commentators played a considerable role in the development of Roman drama. The foundation for further discoveries has been well and truly laid by the devoted labours in the field of many members of the British School of Rome, who have established the history of the successive road systems of the country, as well as recording many items that are the likely victims of agricultural development. Besides the ridgeway roads, cross-country roads were built; where possible these followed natural valley crossings, but in default of such help Faliscan engineers could bridge streams (probably timber structures on stone piers; one such is the foundation of Ponte Terrano just west of Civita Castellana) and cut through the tufa rock of steep cliffs, or even carry a road up through a cliff by means of a cutting. Some of these cuttings are over thirty-five feet deep and were equipped with either open or tunnelled drains. This impressive work must owe much to Etruscan skill. Later this early road system was fundamentally adapted and altered to meet new conditions by the Romans who drove two great arterial roads through Faliscan territory, the Via Amerina in the west and the Flaminia in the east.[92]

Some five miles south-west of Falerii Veteres lay Nepet or Nepete (modern Nepi), and some seven miles west of Nepete was Sutrium (Sutri). In later times these two towns formed a link between Faliscan territory and the Etruscan cities in the west such as Tarquinii. A traveller from the east to west would pass their sites to reach a narrow natural saddle or gap between the Monti Cimini and the Monti Sabatini, which would lead him on towards the coast. But in early times there was little need for strategic outposts: the great Ciminian forest presented a forbidding barrier. Neither settlement appears to have been very early.

Nepet was founded not later than during the seventh century: the archaeological material from the cemeteries in the neighbourhood resembles that from other Faliscan sites. Sutri may have been slightly later; apart from a single cremation burial of the eighth century, there are some Etruscan chamber-tombs of the seventh to fourth centuries which resemble tombs at Cerveteri except that the bodies were placed in *loculi* cut out of the side walls of the tomb. These, together with traces of the defences and some drainage *cuniculi*, are all that remain of pre-Roman Sutrium. There are traces of an ancient road linking the town with Nepet, but any continuation westwards beyond Sutrium, apart from a mere forest track, is likely to have been late. The Sutrium gap route may have been developed only when Veii began to press into Faliscan territory in order to reach the hinterland of Tarquinii and Vulci. Early in the fourth century Rome appeared upon the scene, established a Latin colony at Nepet against the Faliscans, and another at Sutrium against the Etruscans, and opened up the gap by building the Via Cassia and fortifying Sutrium to guard it.

But the new Roman road system was not built *in vacuo*: wherever it was feasible it adapted the earlier Etruscan system, but where strategic needs could not be thus met, new routes were devised (Fig. 13). In Etruscan days a road linked Veii with Nepet (it has been traced where it left the north-west gate of Veii), and Rome made use of it in the fourth century. But with the substitution of Falerii Novi for Falerii Veteres in 241 BC, the old local network of roads was thrown out of joint, and the Romans laid out a new road, the Via Amerina. This followed the old road from near Veii (Veii itself was bypassed: it was no longer of importance) to Nepet and then to Falerii Novi and the north. When in 220 the Via Flaminia was driven along the eastern side of Faliscan territory, the old site of Civita Castellana was left high and dry between the two new main roads. To lead through the Sutri gap and develop communications with Clusium and Arretium, the Romans constructed the Via Cassia some decades after the Via Amerina: in the southern stretch the same route was used, but the Cassia diverged from the

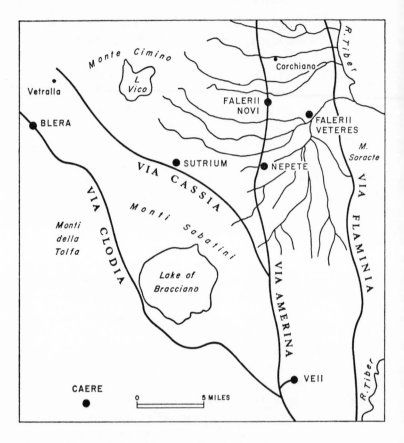

Fig. 13 Faliscan territory and the surrounding road-systems

Amerina about half-way between Veii and Nepet, and then swung north-west through the gap to Sutrium. A slightly earlier road, the Via Clodia, had been built to lead to southern Etruria. It probably followed the same line as the later Cassia from Rome to near Veii but it then turned north-west, skirting the south and west of Lake Bracciano, to reach Etruscan Blera, Norchia and Tuscania. But like the Amerina, the Clodia also in part made use of earlier Etruscan roads. Indeed, there is a striking difference between those Roman roads which used older routes and served the countryside, conforming to the existing pattern of settlement, and those which were built purely for strategic reasons and disregarded local needs, going straight to their objectives. By means of masonry arches Roman engineers might be able to span deep gorges with viaducts and bridges, and therefore drive a more direct line for their trunk roads, but the Etruscans had pointed the way.[93]

VULCI

Few of the great Etruscan cities have left less traces in the literary traditions and a greater wealth of Greek vases than Tarquinii's northern neighbour, Vulci (Etruscan Velch-). In 280 BC it was conquered by Rome, and T. Coruncanius celebrated a triumph over the peoples of Volsinii and Vulci; before that, silence. Visitors to the site even today may feel that this silence of ignorance is matched by the remoteness of the setting. How much more desolate the site appeared over a century ago to George Dennis, who approached it past the medieval castle and the Ponte dell' Abbadia (*Pl. 10*) which rests on what may be Etruscan foundations: the bridge 'is verily a magnificent structure, bestriding the rocky abyss like a colossus, with the Fiora fretting and foaming at a vast depth beneath . . . then the solemn castle, high on the cliff by its side, rearing its dark-red tower against the sky—the slopes clothed with the ilex and shrubs—the huge masses of rocks in the hollow—the stream struggling and boiling through the narrow cleft—the steep frowning cliff seen through the arch'. Then of the whole setting he wrote, 'the wide, wide moor, a drear melancholy waste, stretches around you, no human being seen on its expanse . . . deep is the dreariness of that moor . . . the sun gilds but brightens it not'. Even in 1927 D. Randall-MacIver could warn off all but the hardy traveller from a place that 'is extremely difficult of access and desolate beyond description'. Today the visitor may arrive in reasonable comfort, though his car may take a shaking.

The city lay on a hill of no great height, and was not defended by steep cliffs except on the river side; it was some eight miles from the coast on the left bank of the Fiora, and two small tributaries flowed along the northern and southern sides of the city (*Pl. 49*). It was inhabited throughout antiquity, and the Etruscan city is overlaid with many Roman buildings, but thereafter it was deserted and still remains so, although the area has been expropriated by the Ente Maremma for agricultural development, and deep ploughing now threatens some of the surrounding cemeteries. Its peace was first broken when a tomb was disturbed by a plough in 1828. This led to a feverish outburst of digging by Lucien Bonaparte, Prince of Canino, and neighbouring landowners; despite wanton damage and clandestine robbery at least five thousand Greek vases have been found; many are now among the treasures of the Vatican Museum, the Louvre and the British Museum. Further investigations included the opening of the tomb with paintings named after its discoverer, G. François (1857). In 1956 new systematic excavations were started on the site of the city and are already producing most promising results (Fig. 14).

Villanovan material of the ninth to eighth centuries comes from three cemeteries, Osteria in the north, Cavalupo in the north-east, and near Ponte Rotto in the east; it includes biconical cinerary urns (there is one fine one of bronze), hut-urns and weapons. A recent find from one of the ossuaries is of great interest: a bronze statuette of the *nurrhagi* type of Sardinian bronzes (*c.* 750). The small Villanovan settlements must gradually have fused into a single village, as the example at Veii has made clear, and the development of the tombs follows a normal pattern of *pozzo*, *fossa* and *camera*. The general line of the city wall is clear: a stretch dating to the fourth century survives at the east gate. Two main roads crossed the city: the later Roman *decumanus* from the west to the east gate and a north-south street which in the north led on eastwards to the acropolis. When the new excavations reach this older part, rich results may be expected. Already a temple, perhaps of the sixth century, on the north of the *decumanus* has come to light. Its external walls are some 37 × 25 yards. Further, a votive deposit near the north gate contains models of three buildings: a tower which recalls those of medieval Bologna or San Gimignano, a portico

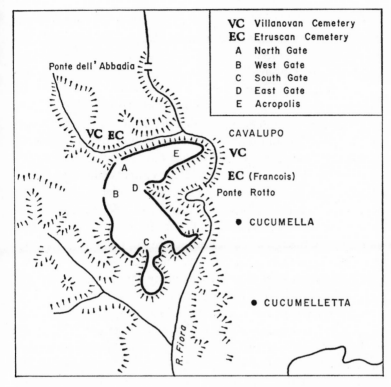

Fig. 14 Plan of Vulci

with seven columns, and a small pseudo-peripteral temple *in antis* (Corinthian order) with two figures in the tympanum, which, by analogy with the figures on a more elaborate tympanum from the necropolis of Montelupo, may be Liber and Libera, or Fufluns and Turan. Although these models date from the late Roman Republic, they represent three buildings in a public square that could well have preserved earlier similar features. The deposit also contained a bearded Janus head and two seated figures of bearded gods, one perhaps Jupiter (Etruscan Tinia), the other Hercules; with these more august offerings are many pleasant models of children and infants in swaddling-bands (*putti in fasce*). Another exciting discovery of the Roman age is a milestone near the intersection of the *decumanus* and *cardo*, inscribed 'Aur(elio) (C)otta co(s) m(ilia) a Rvma↓xx' thus marking the distance, 70 miles, from Rome. The form RVMA is interesting: it is found on an earlier inscription in the François tomb, where Gnaeus Tarquinius is described as 'Cneve Tarchunies Rumach', *i.e.* of Rome. The milestone, which must be later than Vulci's loss of independence in 280 but probably not much later than *c.* 150 BC, shows that the spelling *Rvma* continued in use. The identification of Aurelius Cotta presents another problem: a milestone of L. Aurelius Cotta, consul of 252, was found in Sicily in 1954, but one of the Cottas who were consuls in 200, 144, and 119 could have been the builder of this Roman reconstruction of what doubtless had been an Etruscan road.

The tombs were not very different from those at Tarquinii and Caere, although in general more simple; one type (*a cassone*), especially in the sixth and fifth centuries, had an unroofed antechamber open to the sky. Perhaps many tombs had tumuli, but only three of the mounds survive: La Cucumella ('the little coffee-pot') which was excavated in 1829 and has a complicated plan, the Cucumelletta and La Rotonda. There are, however, two tombs with paintings. One, which is very late, was opened up by Campanari in 1835; the paintings soon perished, but a copy, now in the British Museum, survived which shows the Underworld with Charon and perhaps the judgement of the dead. The other is the famous François tomb in the necropolis near the Ponte Rotto. One panel shows a mythological scene: Achilles sacrificing the Trojan prisoners to the shade of Patroclus. The theme was popular and this representation, like others, may have been copied from a famous original painting.

The second painting, probably of *c.* 300 BC, is of first-class historical importance. It depicts several warriors fighting, including two brothers from Vulci, Caelius and Aulus Vibenna (the names of all the men are painted in). Caile Vipinas is being freed by Macstrna (Mastarna) who cuts the cords that bound his hands (*Pl. 47*); three groups of single combat show Larth Ulthese (Lars Voltius) killing Laris Papathnas Velznach (Lars Papatius of Volsinii), Rasce (Rascius) killing Pesna Arcmsnas Sveamach (Pesius Arcumnius of Sovana) and Aule Vipines

(Aulus Vibenna) killing Venthical . . . plsachs (perhaps a man from Falerii); lastly Marce Camitlnas (Marcus Camitilius) is killing Cneve Tarchunies Rumach (Gnaeus Tarquinius of Rome) (*Pl. 46*). The cities from which the vanquished came are named, but not those of the victors because presumably they were all local heroes, men of Vulci. We clearly have here an episode of Etruscan history, showing with local pride the rescue of Caelius Vibenna in a struggle in which Vulci was engaged against Volsinii, Sovana, Rome, and perhaps Falerii. We cannot tell whether a full-scale war between the cities is implied or only a struggle between condottieri operating on a smaller scale. But a point of great interest is that according to one ancient tradition Mastarna was identified with Servius Tullius, the penultimate king of Rome, who was installed there as the successor to Tarquinius Priscus with the help of an army of his friend Caelius Vibenna (*cf.* p. 257). Here it is sufficient to note the proud claim of Vulci to have imposed a king on Rome.

Vulci's position as one of the great cities of Etruria is thus reflected in her local traditions: it is also shown by her wealth, attested by the prodigious number of Greek vases that she could afford to import. The three thousand or more discovered in 1828–9 presented a problem to scholars and antiquaries, who were only beginning to realize that not every vase found in Etruria must be Etruscan. Here now were Attic black-figure and red-figure, Corinthian, 'Pontic' and 'Chalcidian' vases, and this abundant new evidence played an important part in helping to unravel the history of ancient vase-painting.[94]

Imported ware has now been distinguished from the products of local schools, which imitated Greek vases and also later produced red-figure local ware. Only Caere imported more Corinthian ware than did Vulci, which seems to have surpassed all other Etruscan cities in the quantity of imported Attic ware in the sixth and first half of the fifth centuries. When the Etruscans suffered defeat at sea off Cumae in 474, imports, though not local production, were naturally affected; Vulci then drew her supply of Greek vases from the north, via Spina, at the head of the Adriatic, and Bologna. During the sixth century Vulci was a major artistic centre. Not only did she produce vases, including perhaps the black-figure 'Pontic' vases (which might however have been made at Tarquinii), but her bronzes (tripods, candelabra, etc.) were widely exported during the sixth century, not only to different parts of Italy but also to central Europe and to Greece (*Pl. 52*).

Vulci's early sculpture in stone shows strong Greek influence: thus the human part of a centaur (*c.* 575 BC) resembles a Greek *kouros* (youth) statue (*Pl. 51*), and an alabaster female statue has been considered to be 'Daedalic'. Sarcophagi of the third century show *e.g.* husband and wife in a chariot on the way to the Underworld, and in one example (a unique motif) husband and wife lying side by side on the sarcophagus lid in the sleep of death (*Pl. 50*). A fine example of *c.* 300 BC comes from the Tomba delle Iscrizioni discovered in 1959 in the cemetery of the Ponte Rotto; its four side-panels show scenes of fighting between Greeks and Amazons, though at the ends of the two long sides winged figures of infernal deities have been added, and at the centre of one of them a winged *lasa* (female goddess of death) looks on as if from a cloud. The tomb itself is entered by a passage leading to a central chamber from which no less than six rooms open; on the walls seventeen Etruscan funerary inscriptions name at least five families (Pruslnas, Murai, Visnei, Zimarus and Ceisatrui) together with six Latin inscriptions, naming two Sempronii and one Postumia.[95]

The territory of Vulci stretched from Telamon in the north to the river Arrone in the south. This river, which formed Vulci's border with Tarquinii, ran northwards to Lake Bolsena, and the whole area from the Lake westwards to Telamon, including Suana (Sovana), Aurinia (later Saturnia), Statonia, Heba (Magliano) and Cosa came within Vulci's sphere. One problem is to identify the port through which her imports and exports passed. This cannot have been Cosa, which was not an Etruscan foundation (its splendid walls belong to the Latin colony of 273). Orbetello, where Etruscan tombs and walls survive, is rather far away; perhaps there was a harbour at the mouth of the Fiora on which Vulci lay.

The settlements in or near the upper Fiora valley include Sovana, which belongs rather to the area of the rock-tombs discussed above (pp. 93ff), and Statonia. The latter is perhaps to be identified with a small city site near a necropolis at Poggio Buco; some sling-bullets inscribed *Statnes* have been found here, but it is of course possible that they belong to an enemy who attacked the city rather than to the inhabitants; if that were so, Statonia must be sought nearer Lago di Mezzano or Lake Bolsena, one of which must have been the Lacus Statoniensis mentioned by Pliny. At any rate the settlement of Poggio Buco flourished from the seventh century to about 500 and was then apparently deserted for two centuries until Roman times.

A similar early development and premature decline is characteristic of two settlements in the Albegna valley. Geologically this is an area which forms a bridge between south and north Etruria; the rocks are harder than the soft tufa of the south, which is broken up by numerous gorges, and the settlements were built on rocky, but not very steep, hills. This change is reflected in the construction of the tombs, which are seldom entirely cut into the ground, but are built up, in part or whole, by the use of cut stones. The change is seen in the chamber tombs at Saturnia, where there was a settlement from late Villanovan times, as shown by *a pozzetto* and contemporary trench burials; some of the ossuaries are interesting in that they are covered by a sphere like a human head and recall the canopic urns of Clusium, with which Saturnia may have had contacts (see *Pl. 59*). Saturnia seems to have been a small settlement that died out somewhat suddenly in the early sixth century, until Rome founded a colony there in 183 BC. Even in its palmiest days it was overshadowed by a city at Marsiliana farther down the Albegna, possibly ancient Caletra. The settlement is known less through its centre, which is possibly located at the castle of Marsiliana on the Elsa, a tributary of the Albegna, than through its tombs. These show great riches in ivories, gold jewellery and bronzes, and they resemble in form the tombs of Vetulonia; they are trenches surrounded by circles of upright stone slabs; probably originally earth tumuli were heaped above. Of the pottery and metal-work found in the tombs, some must be local work, some imported, *e.g.* some bronzes from Vetulonia, and perhaps from farther afield.[96] One famous object must be mentioned: the waxed writing-tablet of ivory inscribed with the archaic Etruscan alphabet (see Fig. 3 and pp. 46f) which reflects the literacy of the inhabitants of this inland settlement and perhaps their desire to gain a means to promote trade with the more literate peoples of the Near East.[97] The wealth of the city derived partly from agriculture, and partly from bronze. But like its neighbour Saturnia (*Pl. 59*), it came to an abrupt end about 600 BC, presumably as the result of war. The inhabitants possibly moved a few miles to the north to Magliano and its iron-mines, since an Etruscan settlement appears here at about this date and continued until the Romans established the colony of Heba on the site. Two famous inscriptions come from here: a long Etruscan inscription on two sides of a lead plate, and the Tabula Hebana referring to electoral reform in the early Roman Empire. Thus these early Etruscan settlements in the interior may have flourished at first as centres of agricultural districts and their disappearance at the end of the archaic period may be attributed to the increasing power of the great coastal cities.[98]

VOLSINII

Volsinii is described as one of the oldest (Zonaras 8, 7), richest (Pliny, *NH* 2, 139) and most flourishing (Orosius 4, 5) of Etruscan cities, and even as *Etruriae caput* (Val. Max. 9, 1). It first appears in the literary tradition in 392 BC when its army invaded Roman territory; it later suffered defeats by Rome in 310, 295, and 280. In 265 its citizens appealed to Rome for help against the slaves or serfs whom they had allowed to usurp power. Rome responded, destroyed the city and settled the survivors in another place. The story that the Romans took two thousand statues from the captured city to Rome illustrates its richness. Its Etruscan name is known to have been Velzna, but its exact location has given rise to acute controversies.

The city refounded by Rome in 264 was undoubtedly at Bolsena, at the foot and on the lower slopes of the hills that rise up from the north-east corner of the Lake, 'the great Volsinian Mere'. But where was the Etruscan city? The two main claimants have been Bolsena itself (some Etruscan remains were discovered in its vicinity by Gamurrini in 1896, and long before that Dennis had supported the identification) and Orvieto about nine miles distant (*Pls. 53, 55*). The name Orvieto (*Urbs Vetus*) suggests that this was the original city and its rich sixth- and fifth-century tombs show that the site was occupied by an important Etruscan settlement. One difficulty arises from the nature of the two sites; while Procopius says that Ourbibentos (a corruption of Urbs Vetus) had no walls because of its naturally impregnable position, Zonaras records that Volsinii had very strong walls. If the latter be followed this would point to Bolsena as the site of Volsinii, since here on the more open hills above the later settlement defensive walls would be needed, whereas Orvieto is perched on an isolated truncated cone of rock, one of the most impressive and strongest sites in all Etruria.[99] Further, the distance between the two towns militates against Orvieto, since the Romans would scarcely have established the new settlement so far off: Falerii Novi was less than three miles from Falerii Veteres. Since the excavations which were started in 1946 in the neighbourhood of Bolsena, the claims of this site have been greatly strengthened, and some archaeologists, including the chief excavator, R. Bloch, would regard the matter as now settled, but lingering doubts persist, since the Etruscan site at Orvieto appears to be the older and richer.

The new excavations above Bolsena have revealed late Bronze Age, Villanovan and Etruscan settlements. On an isolated hill called La Capriola some two and a half miles south of Bolsena traces of a Late Bronze Age village with typical tenth-century hand-made 'Apennine' pottery were found in 1956: the dwellings were cut out of the rock. A late Villanovan cemetery (700–675) was discovered farther down the hill. Some thirty tombs show a contemporary mixture of *a pozzo* and *a fossa*, with the latter largely predominating; the pottery includes two vases which resemble a type found at Vulci. Many of the graves are those of warriors: beside the heads of iron spears, javelins, and arrows, the usage of an earlier age is continued in bronze weapons such as sword-hilts, a breastplate and a small shield together with bronze fibulae, bowls and razors. An imported Protocorinthian skyphos, a rare object in a Villanovan context, was also found. Traces of another Villanovan settlement have been discovered under water on the east side of Lake Bolsena, whose level appears to have risen some thirty feet since early times (Fig. 15).

Some few hundred yards to the south-west of La Capriola, on the hills of La Città, Etruscan remains came to light. Besides traces of an early wall of the sixth century, there is a temple, comprising one room and a *pronaos*; it is wider than deep (12 × 11 yards) and contains a stone slab, perhaps for a cult statue; pottery shows that it cannot have been later than the fifth century and suggests that it was abandoned in the fourth. An Etruscan inscription was found. This settlement, in the view of its excavators, was only an outpost of Volsinii, which was abandoned when Volsinii itself was walled: others would regard it rather as a continuation of the nearby La Capriola settlement.

In any case, Etruscan Volsinii, it is claimed, lay on the hills above Bolsena itself, between the Fosso Brutto and the Fosso del Capretto with its acropolis on the height of Mozzetta (2380 feet). Here long stretches of wall have been found; the circuit is reckoned at some three miles and several of the tufa blocks are inscribed with Etruscan letters or signs, presumably masons' marks (*Pl. 56*). The wall, which at a fortified angle is formed by a double curtain, is probably to be connected with Rome's first clash with Volsinii in 392; within its circuit lies a cistern. The most important of the cemeteries is at Poggio Pesce, just east of Fosso del Capretto; it was used from *c.* 600 until late times. Near this was a temple or shrine, which was burnt, perhaps in 265. Another temple was found at Poggio Casetta near Mozzetta. It consists of a single *cella* and surrounding walls, some 18 yards broad and 14 yards deep (the *cella* is 23 × 28 feet) and is built on the rock without a podium. It may date from the sixth–fifth century and was not used after the second century. Nearly two miles north of Bolsena at Pozzarello remains of

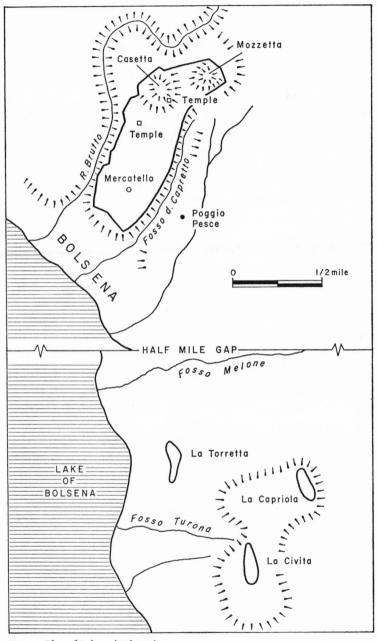

Fig. 15 Plan of Bolsena (Volsinii?)

another temple measuring 40 × 46½ yards were found in 1904; the walls of nenfro blocks were dated by the excavators to the early third century BC. Within it were two troughs and a well which served as *favissae* into which votive offerings were thrown; these objects can now be seen in the garden of the Archaeological Museum in Florence. The temple has often been identified with that of a Volsinian goddess named Nortia, but this is very uncertain. Nortia's temple at Volsinii is mentioned by the Roman annalist Cincius of late third century BC, who says that a nail was driven into it each year to record the passage of time, as was also done in the *cella* of Minerva in the Capitoline temple in Rome. Tertullian tells us (*Apol.* 24) that Nortia had no place in the official Roman cult, while Juvenal (10, 74) refers to her as the protecting deity of Tiberius' friend and betrayer, Sejanus, who came from Volsinii. Another deity associated with Volsinii, by Propertius (4, 2, 3), is the god Vortumnus, whom the antiquarian Varro called 'deus Etruriae princeps' (*LL* 5, 46). Unlike Nortia, Vortumnus was transplanted to Rome where he received a temple on the Aventine which was dedicated by M. Fulvius Flaccus, who destroyed Volsinii in 264. A bronze statue of Vortumnus also stood in the Vicus Tuscus in Rome: it may have been part of the spoils of 264, re-erected in a spot appropriate to a god of Etruscan origin.

If little is known about the last days of Etruscan Volsinii, less can be said about the days of its greatness. Pliny records that it was once completely burnt up by a thunderbolt (*NH* 2, 53) and also that its king Porsenna called down lightning from heaven to destroy a monster called Volta (or Olta) which was devastating its territory. The invention of the hand-mill is attributed to Volsinii on the authority of Varro, but even here the record is embroidered with the supernatural: according to Pliny (*NH* 36, 18), some of the mills turned themselves. As already mentioned (p. 122), the painting in the François tomb at Vulci shows the death of a Volsinian leader, Lars Papathnas. Lastly, local pottery includes the so-called Volsinian vases, with reliefs which are often gilded or silvered; they belong to a late period, perhaps just before the Roman conquest.

Such are the meagre scraps of information that can be recovered about one of the great cities of Etruria.

If, in fact, Etruscan Volsinii was near Bolsena, the Etruscan city at Orvieto must remain anonymous, unless it was Sappinum which Livy says (5, 31) helped Volsinii against Rome in 391 and was apparently a militarily strong city. Whatever its name, the city occupied a magnificent position on its rocky plateau, with good lines of communication towards Clusium, Falerii, Vulci and Tarquinii. It imported Greek pottery, a few Corinthian and numerous Attic vases from *c.* 575, besides producing local imitations of both types. There is not sufficient Villanovan material to suggest an early settlement, but the oldest tombs in the Cannicella cemetery belong to the late seventh century. In the necropolis of Crocifisso del Tufo, the most famous cemetery, the tombs are built of squared blocks and are ranged along three streets; the chambers are small and designed normally for two bodies, while Etruscan inscriptions are found on both the outer and inner walls (*Pl. 54*). Terracottas (*Pls. 57, 58*) attest several temples, but none of the cults can be located, apart from that of Tinia (Jupiter) which is attested by votive inscriptions: an altar inscribed *tinia tinscvil* was found in a pit near the Church of San Giovenale, which may represent a temple of Jupiter; another altar was found under the Duomo (*TLE* 258, 259). A temple was discovered near the famous Well of St Patrick (Pozzo di San Patrizio) at the site called Il Belvedere. It had three *cellae*, and some figures survive—the heads of an old man and of a Gorgon, both probably fourth century. Finally, some fourth-century painted tombs, found in 1863 at Poggio Settecamini, south of Orvieto, show scenes of banquets and of the kitchen, where the carcasses of an ox, a doe, a hare and some birds hang on the walls, and servants are preparing and cooking the meal.[100]

The centre where all Etruscans met for religious celebrations was Fanum Voltumnae (see p. 231). In the fourth century AD, this League meeting was held 'apud Volsinios', and so the Fanum has usually been assumed to have been near Volsinii. It is unlikely, but just possible, that the meeting place was changed and that the imperial meeting has no connection with Fanum Voltumnae.

Various sites such as Orvieto, Montefiascone, or even in Volsinii itself, *i.e.* around Bolsena, have been suggested but this is only guesswork.

The territory of the Volsinian state lay to the east of Lake Bolsena. On the west it bordered on that of Tarquinii and Vulci, in the north the Paglia divided it from that of Clusium, on the east the Tiber separated it from Umbria, and on its southern frontier lay Faliscan territory. It was thus well protected by rivers in the north and east, by mountains and thick forests in the south and west. Important centres were Viterbo (Surrina?), Ferentium (Ferento), Polimartium (Bomarzo), Horta (Orte), Montefiascone and Aquapendente. Of these it may be sufficient to refer to Bomarzo, which was described by Dennis soon after the excavations of the 1830s. Here a late painted tomb showed demons; other finds included the sarcophagus of a haruspex Vel Urinates, the arms and armour of a warrior, and a cup with the Etruscan alphabet on its foot.[101]

CHAPTER V

THE NORTHERN CITIES

RUSELLAE

WE NOW TURN to northern Etruria, and first to the territory of Rusellae, which lay between the Ombrone and the Bruna farther north. Of all the major Etruscan cities, Rusellae was for long perhaps the least known, but excavations started in 1959 are beginning to reveal something of its development. In its unspoilt remoteness the site (modern Roselle) resembles that of Vulci. The hill on which the city lay, although only six miles distant from Grosseto, rises up in rural isolation, some fourteen miles from the coast. The surviving walls are in part made difficult of access by the bramble thickets of thorny marruca shrub. The hill is a truncated cone, less impressive but not unlike that of Orvieto, and its shape is a reminder that this is border country between the deeply seamed south and the more open rolling north. The hill consists of two heights divided by a small depression in which lay the forum of the later Roman settlement; on the northern slope a Roman amphitheatre was built (*Pl. 60*). There is evidence for occupation from later Villanovan times (early seventh century). An early defence wall of sun-dried bricks (end of the seventh century) on the northern hill was succeeded in the sixth century by a two-mile circuit of limestone blocks, stretches of which, fifteen feet high in places, survive. If this dating is correct, the walls of Rusellae are much earlier than those of Veii and other cities. At one point there is a gate, with a vantage-court, set at an angle to the course of the wall; this is a new feature in Etruscan territory. Terracottas of local manufacture, which indicate the richness of the temple decorations, and imported vases suggest that the city reached its most flourishing days towards the end of the sixth century. It may well have been a rival to its neighbour Vetulonia, which lay less than ten miles to the north-west, and have begun to flourish as Vetulonia declined. Similarity between some of its terracottas of the fourth century and those of Orvieto may indicate some connections. On the southern hill a section of the late Etruscan city is represented by buildings, streets and drains, superimposed on a similar occupation of the fifth to fourth centuries (Fig. 16).

Of Rusellae's history before its first defeat by advancing Roman armies in 301, nothing is known apart from an isolated mention of the fact that it joined Vetulonia, Clusium and Volaterrae in declaring war on Tarquinius Priscus of Rome (Dionysius Hal. 3, 51). When captured by Rome in 294 BC, it lost, according to Livy (10, 37), two thousand men captured, and less than two thousand killed. When many centuries later the Roman Empire collapsed in the west, Rusellae continued as an episcopal see until 1138 when this and the inhabitants were transferred to Grosseto. Since then it has remained, in the words of Dennis, 'a wilderness of rocks and thickets—the haunt of the fox and wild boar, of the serpent and lizard—visited by none but the herdsman or shepherd, who lies the livelong day stretched in vacancy on the sward, or turning a wondering gaze on the stupendous ruins around him, of whose origin and history he has not a conception'. The long sleep of Rusellae, like that of Vulci, is now interrupted by the intruding spade and shovel of the archaeologist but not yet by the car-loads of visitors that flock to Caere or Tarquinii.[102]

VETULONIA

North-west of Rusellae across the Bruna was Vetulonia (Etruscan Vetluna or Vatluna), one of the earliest Etruscan cities. The site, which has been sought in a great many places, was at Poggio Colonna which changed its name officially to Vetulonia in 1888. It lies on a hill 1132 feet high which has steep cliffs on three sides and consists of three chief heights with numerous knolls between them (Fig. 17). It is some nine miles from the present coast-line, but in Etruscan times the sea may have come farther inland and formed a bay; thus the south-east slopes of the hill could have been marshy if not actually sea-girt. The ancient sources do not refer to Vetulonia as a maritime city, but they mention a Lacus

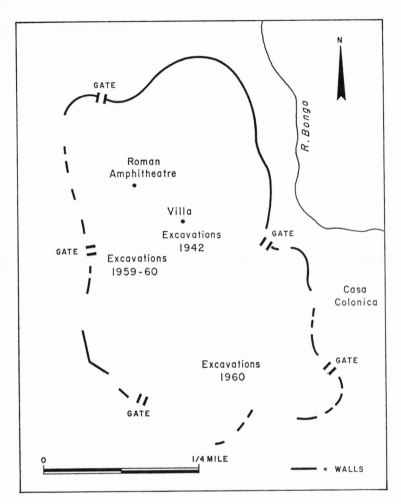

Fig. 16 Plan of Rusellae

Prilius; this lake may have been near the base of the hill, or indeed anywhere between Vetulonia and Rusellae, and it presumably developed into the marshes of Castiglioni in medieval times. It could have provided harbour facilities for one or both of the cities. In Roman tradition Vetulonia is best known as the city from which the Romans adopted the insignia of their magistrates

—the *fasces*, the curule chair, the purple toga and the trumpets. Some doubts have been raised on the score of the distance of Vetulonia from Rome, but these insignia were undoubtedly of Etruscan origin, and the fact that iron *fasces* were found in a tomb at Vetulonia (Fig. 25) certainly does nothing to weaken the tradition which specifically gives Vetulonia as the city of origin (see p. 223).

The settlement goes back to early Villanovan times and if originally there were two groups whose dead were disposed in the cemeteries in the east (Poggio alla Guardia and Poggio delle Birbe) and in the north-west (Colle Baroncio), they were united by the seventh century. One series of Villanovan *pozzetti* presents a peculiar feature: some fifteen interments are grouped together and surrounded by a ring of stones, thus foreshadowing the great circle-tombs that are a distinctive feature of Etruscan Vetulonia; further, they were associated with much richer objects than are usually found in Villanovan *pozzetti*: an amber scarab, a necklace of glass beads, a disc of gold, a gold-bound bronze fibula, and the engraved bronze-clad wooden sheath of an iron sword. This sudden influx of foreign influence marks a clear stage between the simple interments of the native Villanovans and Etruscan practice, although the graves may still be called Villanovan. Next, half-a-dozen graves were found, consisting of cylindrical holes containing black earth and no ossuaries; some were mixed up with the *pozzetti*, others were quite distinct. Typical of their contents are the objects in the so-called Tomba della Straniera: four silver fibulae, two silver bracelets and two silver necklaces, a silver buckle studded with amber, a silver plaque with two rows of ducks, two gold wire rings, amber and glass beads and two Egyptian scarabs. Nothing here can be called Villanovan, but all must rather be labelled early Etruscan. The foregoing description is based on I. Falci's account of the excavations of 1886 and D. Randall-MacIver's report, but some doubts have arisen; the foreign objects are assigned by some to *tombe a fossa* rather than to the *pozzetti*, (called 'ripostigli stranieri', with which some ossuaries are now claimed to have been associated). However that may be, the objects were found, the relative chronology

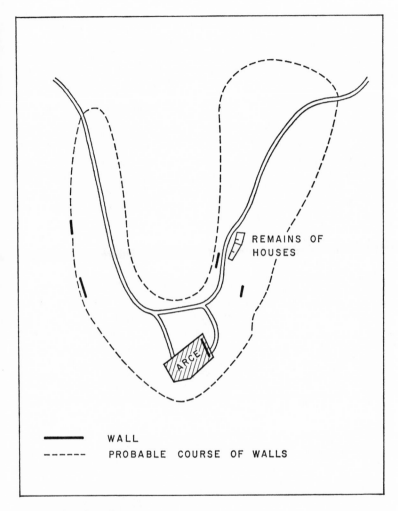

WALL

PROBABLE COURSE OF WALLS

Fig. 17 Plan of Vetulonia

does not seem to have been challenged, and they indicate an obvious transition from the poor equipment of the average Villanovan grave to the richness of the later Etruscan tombs.

Then comes the full flowering of the Etruscan tombs, which at Vetulonia take the form of circle-graves, averaging some fifteen to twenty yards in diameter. They are formed by stone slabs set vertically in the ground in a continuous line; within this circle are one or more oblong trenches. The contents are extraordinarily rich. Twenty-six are described in detail by Randall-MacIver, most of them being circle-graves, but a few of them lacked the enclosing stones, and two or three were tumuli. To the first half of the seventh century may be assigned the Circle of the Bracelets (Circolo dei Monili), which contained amber, gold and silver fibulae, bracelets of gold filigree, and the Circle of Bes (so-called from a green-glazed figure of the Egyptian god) which contained more horse-trappings than did the former. Other tombs are slightly later; the most famous is the Tomba del Duce, whose contents escaped later plunderers and have survived almost intact. The owner of the tomb was not necessarily an outstanding ruler or prince, but merely a wealthy noble, for many of the plundered tombs seem originally to have been no less richly equipped. Within the tomb were an ossuary of hammered bronze with repoussé designs in silver, containing purple linen, and the burned bones of the noble, a powerful man of about fifty, together with the remains of a chariot and harness, a circular bronze shield, a helmet, large numbers of bowls, basins, vases (bronze and pottery), buckets, early *bucchero* pottery, candelabra, and a cup with an inscription of forty-six letters. These witnesses to the wealth of Vetulonia are now housed in the Archaeological Museum at Florence. The Tomba del Guerriero, although plundered, contained a stone *stele* inscribed with the figure of a warrior and with his name, Avele Feluske (*cf.* p. 38). The Circle of the Trident, $18\frac{1}{2}$ yards in diameter, contained a long three-pronged fork, which was probably an instrument for winnowing. The Circle of the Cauldrons (Circolo dei Lebeti) had two pairs of bronze cauldrons; one vessel was decorated with the heads of lions, the other with heads of griffins. Finally, the Tomb of the Lictor, like so many other graves, contained parts of a chariot and many fine gold ornaments, but it also had the iron *fasces* and axe already mentioned:

'Vetulonia, once the pride of the Lydian race. This city first provided the twelve *fasces* to precede the magistrates and added to them twelve axes with their silent threat':

Maeoniaeque decus quondam Vetulonia gentis.
bissenos haec prima dedit praecedere fasces;
et iunxit totidem tacito terrore secures.

(Silius Italicus 8, 485)

The great quantity of metal found in the tombs testifies to the immense wealth of Vetulonia as well as to the exceptional skill of its metal-workers. Gold and silver must have been imported, the bronze must have come from the copper mines of Etruria, and the frequent use of iron, for instance for chariot wheels, shows that trade with Elba was lively. Indeed it is probably the exploitation of the mines of Massa Marittima that explains the dramatic transformation of a relatively poor Villanovan settlement into so rich and powerful a city. It is noteworthy that few Corinthian or early Attic vases were imported, and that a high proportion of the pottery is of local manufacture; the *bucchero* ware was not so fine as that produced by the southern cities (*Pl. 33*). The imported examples are found mainly in the very rich tombs. The same is true of the bronze work: much was of local manufacture, though some of the richer pieces, such as the cauldrons in the Circolo dei Lebeti, were imported. The bronzes have their own style, distinct from that of the southern cities, unpretentious but often pleasing, as exemplified in bowls with tripods, or candelabra with ends shaped into human figures. The only sculpture known consists of fragments of some very early work from the Tomba della Pietrera, a great mound of earth and stones, sixty-nine yards in diameter and fifteen high, which contained two massive masonry buildings; the upper chamber was decorated with statues of human figures, which are the earliest surviving examples of Etruscan sculpture. The bodies are in relief and only the heads in the round: some show women with their hands placed over their breast in a very Oriental manner. Although some of the heads combine Greek and Asiatic elements, they cannot be very closely associated with any particular school.

On a smaller scale Vetulonia produced much work both in amber and gold. In early times until about *c.* 600 BC amber was imported from the north and made up into brooches and necklaces. For jewellery, such as gold fibulae and bracelets, which were widely exported in Italy, her artists used the technique of granulation that was practised in the south, but they also developed filigree work of fine twisted wires separated by flat bands, and a tiny granulated gold dust which was formed into figures of sphinxes, lions or horses on strips of gold. This process is so difficult that modern goldsmiths have only recently been able to reproduce it: a similar process called 'colloid hard-soldering' was patented only in 1933. The general simplicity of style shown by this goldwork and by other aspects of the art of Vetulonia, is to be attributed not merely to its early emergence, but also to a continuing preference for geometric art over the more exuberant forms that some southern cities developed.

The general impression given by the art of Vetulonia accords well with its more northerly position, with its apparently rather weak contacts with the wider world, and with its early development and early decline. This decline may be explained by the rise of Rusellae, which quite possibly fought and destroyed Vetulonia in the sixth century. The population of Vetulonia may even have been moved to Poggio Castiglioni to the north, near Lago dell' Accesa and Massa Marittima, where traces of a late Etruscan settlement have been found. At any rate Vetulonia seems to have been relatively unpopulated in the fifth and fourth centuries, though it revived in the Roman period after c. 300 BC. Its former glory is reflected in a monument set up at Caere in the first century AD. This consists of statues personifying three Etruscan peoples, the Tarquinienses, the Vulcenses and the Vetulonenses, and was probably erected in honour of the emperor Claudius who revived the Etruscan League (see p. 283). Vetulonia is represented by a male figure standing by a pine-tree, with a rudder over his left shoulder; whether a personification of the city, or its guardian deity (scarcely Neptune), it remained to remind men of the Roman Empire of the Etruscan past, while the rudder may indicate that the Lacus Prilius gave Vetulonia easier access to the sea than present conditions might suggest. This aspect is also shown by coins of the Etrusco-Roman period, inscribed *Vatl*, with anchor or trident and two dolphins on the reverse, the obverse showing a head of Hercules; and incidentally a very large bronze club, now in the Florence Museum, was found at Vetulonia. But all that survives to be seen of ancient Vetulonia, apart from the remains of the tombs, are a few stretches of wall and a piece of road (the *decumanus*) with houses and buildings (perhaps shops) which were destroyed by fire during the Roman period; these belong to the late Etruscan or Etrusco-Roman period (*Pl. 61*).[103]

POPULONIA

In the days of Augustus the geographer Strabo visited Populonia and described it as 'situated on a high promontory that descends sharply into the sea and forms a peninsula . . . now although the town is entirely deserted except for the temples and a few dwellings, there are more people in the harbour-town, which has a small port and two docks at the foot of the mountain; and in my opinion this is the only one of the ancient Tyrrhenian cities that was established on the sea itself . . . beneath (or on) the promontory there is a tower for watching tunny-fish. When you look down from the city, you can see with difficulty the island of Sardinia in the distance.' This last statement misled Macaulay into writing of

> 'sea-girt Populonia,
> whose sentinels descry
> Sardinia's snowy mountain-tops
> Fringing the southern sky.'

In fact the island is too far to be seen, and even if it were not, the intervening mass of Elba would block the view. Strabo, however, has accurately described the old acropolis rising up from the sea, now crowned by its medieval castle, and he has distinguished the early settlement from the later town that developed at its foot along the coast (*Pl. 62*). This later town was in fact built partly over the cemeteries of the earlier inhabitants when the iron industry was developed. Thus the earlier tombs in the San Cerbone district, which became an industrial area, are now covered with quantities of iron slag, and many have been preserved. It has recently been shown that a wall was built from sea to sea across the neck of land at the base of the promontory, thus isolating the citadel and old city from the new industrial zone. This, as will be seen, occurred when Populonia evolved from a city whose prosperity was based on bronze to a centre of iron production (Fig. 18).

Servius, the commentator on Virgil, mentions some legends about the founding of Populonia, of which the Etruscan form was Pupluna or Fufluna. The wording of the passage is somewhat clumsy or corrupt, and may not represent precisely what Servius' source (Varro?) said, but it preserves a tradition that people from Corsica crossed to Italy and founded Populonia at a date later than the formation of the league of the twelve Etruscan peoples; others, however, reported that Populonia was a colony of Volaterrae, and yet others that Volaterrae seized it from the Corsicans. Neither the late date nor the Corsican origin can be accepted. Archaeology has shown an early Villanovan settlement on the site with no Corsican connections. Similarly any direct link with Volaterrae must be rejected: the early tombs there are later than, and differ from, those of Populonia, while in the seventh and sixth centuries Populonia was richer and stronger than Volaterrae. Behind the legends, however, may lurk some reflection of Populonia's commercial struggles at sea and the rivalry of the Phocaean Greeks in Corsica (see pp. 183f), and perhaps of the fact recorded by Strabo, that in early times the coast of Etruria was often raided by the Sardinian pirates—no doubt Corsica was equally enterprising.

The two main cemeteries were at San Cerbone, almost on the edge of the sea, and at Poggio delle Granate, a little to the north-east. If these represent two original settlements, they must soon have merged. Cremations *a pozzo* are intermingled with inhumations *a fossa*. Then come small chamber-tombs, covered with tumuli; some of the chambers are round with a false cupola. As has been seen, some very early objects (fibulae and swords) found in the tombs have suggested the probability of early settlement as well as of mere trade (see pp. 41f). Some larger and richer tombs consist of a square chamber, covered by a false cupola of overlapping rings of flat stones; this *cella* is surrounded,

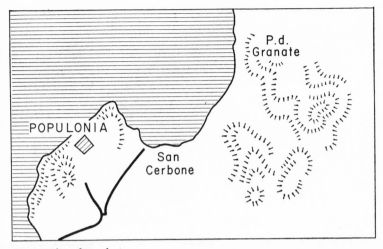

Fig. 18 Plan of Populonia

at a distance, by a circular stone-built wall, which forms the base for the heaped-up tumulus. One of these drum-like bases is thirty yards in diameter. They have a stone-laid path around them, while entrance to the central tomb is by a corridor (*dromos*), out of which two or three small chambers might open (*Pl. 65*). The surviving contents indicate power and riches. Thus tomb No. 2 of San Cerbone contained a gold brooch, an ivory trumpet bound with gold plate which was decorated with figures of men and animals, a bronze trumpet, fragments of a shield and other arms; and the remains of two chariots, the fittings of which were of bronze or iron. Two of the iron wheels survive almost intact, and some interesting bronze plates are inlaid with iron figures of animals and hunters; these clearly belong to a period in the history of Populonia when iron was still a valuable metal, more rare than bronze. From *c.* 550 BC, the tombs take the form of little rectangular shrines, built of blocks of stone. One, which was found under the iron slag in 1957, is unique in that its roof is preserved (*Pl. 64*). This was double, with an outer covering of large stone slabs, under which was a pitched stone roof whose triangular 'pediment' was visible above the door of the tomb, thus increasing the temple-like appearance of the whole. The tomb is some nine feet high, and the type persisted for about a century.

The tomb, named Tomba di un Offerente from a statuette of a man holding a plate of offering, was robbed by the Etruscans in the third century when they began to extract iron from this area, but the robbers carefully removed the skeletons in the sarcophagi from their resting-places within the tomb. The contents included some gold fibulae, a ram's head worked in amber, and a carved cornelian showing Hercules and Antaeus, as well as bronze, bone and iron work and pottery. Nearby the Tomba dei Colatoi (two bronze sieves were found in the tomb when excavated in 1960) is of a different type hitherto not certainly known at Populonia. Unlike the pseudo-cupola tomb, the rectangular *cella* was covered with a tumulus which lacks the usual drum base and is covered with a thick layer of clay to make it waterproof; the *cella* was reached by a short *dromos*. The contents, which included many *aryballoi*, show that the tomb was built *c*. 600 and the burials continued beyond 550 to the time to which the sieves belong; after a long interval, burials were resumed *c*. 300.

Many of the more valuable of the objects in the tombs were imported from southern Etruria or farther afield (*e.g.* the *Ajax*, *Pl. 63*). Although Protocorinthian vases are not very numerous, later Corinthian pottery and Attic vases, both black- and red-figure, reached Populonia in large quantities and trade with Athens must have been brisk in the fifth century; this was perhaps direct, although these goods could have reached Populonia through the hands of middlemen in southern Etruria. Further, Etruscan copies of Corinthian vases were imported. From Sardinia came a model of a boat in bronze, similar to one found in the Tomba del Duce at Vetulonia; it may have formed part of a lamp. In general Populonia did not produce much individual art of her own: no painting or sculpture survives and no fine terracottas. Her output of bronze-work was large, but not of outstanding artistic quality. And here lies the key to her prosperity and the means by which she could pay for her imports. She was an industrial city, using first bronze and later iron. Before *c*. 650 BC iron was rare, and it was by exploiting the neighbouring copper

64 *Aedicula* tomb at Populonia, of the second half of the sixth century BC.
The pediment emphasizes its temple-like appearance. It was found in 1957
under the iron slag in the San Cerbone cemetery. See p.143. 65 Circle grave
in the same cemetery. See p.143.

66 View from the extreme west end of Volaterrae, looking down over Badia and the eroded cliffs of Le Balze where an early cemetery has collapsed. See p.148. 67 Wall of the city, with polygonal masonry. The lower part here is medieval strengthening of the Etruscan work. See p.146.

68 The Porta all'Arco gate in the city wall of Volaterrae. Only the lower part belongs to the Etruscan period, but the three heads in the arch (guardian deities?) are also Etruscan. See p.147.

69 The tomb of the Atian family at Volaterrae. It was excavated by the Inghirami brothers and named after them. It contained 53 urns. It was removed *en masse* to the gardens of the Archaeological Museum in Florence. See p.148.

mines that Populonia developed from a Villanovan village to a wealthy city. Although some of the metal-work, such as the plates on the chariot mentioned above, might be quite attractive, and although it met local requirements, it seems to have sprung from commercial needs rather than original artistic impulses. Of this 'bronze' period of Populonia the ancient writers record no details: to them it was an 'iron' town, and they recount how iron ore, which the inhabitants of Elba were unable to work, was transported to Populonia where technical skill was greater (see p. 70). This work was done in the harbour area and, since slag covers some tombs of the late fifth century, this industry is not likely to have been developed on a large scale much before 400. Thus Populonia continued to flourish at a time when many cities in southern Etruria were suffering an industrial decline.

Its prosperity is reflected in the weight-standard of the coinage which is related not to that of southern Italy but to the Sicilian, *i.e.* Attic, system. If the rare gold coins are now considered later than the early silver and if they were issued at a time when silver was short and are to be related to the early gold coinage of Rome, the silver coinage may go back to the fourth century, if not to the fifth. The heads of Heracles, Hermes and Athena displayed on the bronze coins, may or may not have had much commercial or religious significance, but the type that showed the head of Vulcan on the obverse, and his hammer and tongs on the reverse, clearly advertised the main product of Populonia in later days. A third-century issue that bore the names of Pupluna, Vetalu (presumably Vetulonia) and Cha (probably Camars, *i.e.* Clusium) apparently indicates some kind of alliance, formed perhaps for commercial rather than political reasons.

The coins, the tombs and the iron slag remain to show Populonia's former wealth. Of the city itself nothing remains apart from traces of its walls. But the visitor to the site, if he turns from the tombs by the beach and climbs up to the old acropolis, will be rewarded with a fine view if the sun is shining on the bay and a fresh wind is driving the white sea-horses toward the shore.[104]

VOLATERRAE

Some thirty-four miles to the north-east of Populonia, and about twenty miles from the coast, a high hill dominates the valley of the Cecina; on it stood Volaterrae (Etruscan Velathri and modern Volterra) (*Pl. 66*). Strabo wrote: 'the walls of the city are built on the level summit of a lofty hill which is precipitous on all sides; from the base to the summit the ascent is fifteen stades long, and it is steep and difficult all the way'. In more romantic vein, Macaulay:

> From lordly Volaterrae
>   Where scowls the far-famed hold
> Piled by the hands of giants
>   For godlike kings of old.

Dennis, who lived before the motor-age, combined the romantic and practical: 'from whatever side Volaterrae may be approached it is a most commanding object, crowning the summit of a lofty, steep and sternly naked height, if not wholly isolated, yet independent of the neighbouring hills, reducing them by its towering supereminence to mere satellites; so lofty as to be conspicuous from many a league distant, and so steep that when the traveller has at length reached its foot, he finds that the fatigue he imagined had well nigh terminated, is then but about to begin'. Sulla's troops, who in 82 BC looked up at the battlements that were to defy their blockade for two long years, probably expressed themselves considerably more forcibly (Fig. 19).

The acropolis lay to the south-east, under the medieval fortress, and was probably surrounded by a wall of its own: two small pieces have been found, which appear to be earlier than the main city-wall. Some good stretches of the latter survive, especially near Santa Chiara in the west (*Pl. 67*). This wall was at least four miles in circumference, considerably more than twice as long as the medieval wall. The ancient population has been estimated at 25,000, compared with a modern population of some 11,000. The wall is made of blocks of sandstone called *panchina* in a technique that varies between polygonal and *opus quadratum*, which Lugli calls 'opus quasi quadratum'. Comparison

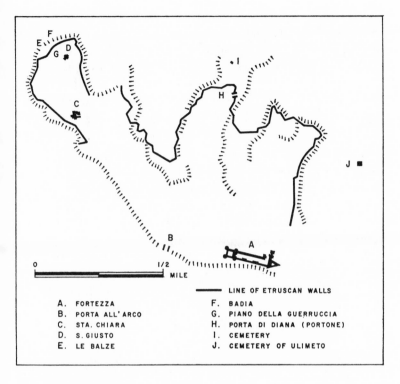

Fig. 19 Plan of Volaterrae

with the later wall at Rusellae suggests a date not before about
500, while the fact that the walls enclose the early cemetery of
Piano della Guerruccia in the north-west may suggest a century
later. Two gateways are preserved, the Porta Diana and the
famous Porta all'Arco (*Pl. 68*). Of the latter only the lower part
belongs to the Etruscan period, together with three weather-
worn stone heads which project from the arch and may be
guardian deities of the city. Although obviously replaced in their
present position, they were an early feature of the gateway
because they are shown in a representation of the gate on an
alabaster funerary urn of perhaps the third century BC; the artist
was in fact depicting the death of Capaneus as he was scaling

one of the gates of Thebes, but he has reproduced one of the gates of his own city (*Pl. 72*). Of Etruscan buildings in the city only one temple is known. It stood on the acropolis, under the Fortezza which is now a prison; the excavation, started in 1925, was never completed. Under the temple were traces of the podium of an earlier temple; small finds included a seventh-century bronze statuette of a man, together with some terracotta torsos of women (fourth to third or second to first centuries).

An early cemetery lay in the west at Piano della Guerruccia, though part has fallen into a ravine known as Le Balze (*Pl. 66*): it shows a normal Villanovan development with tombs *a pozzetti* mixed with *a fossa* inhumations, and then chamber-tombs. The early tombs are late Villanovan (seventh century) and their equipment is poor; the pottery shows some local peculiarities, and some ossuaries resemble those found at Bisenzio on Lake Bolsena. These burials are followed by small chamber-tombs of the sixth and fifth centuries, and such tombs are found also in the later cemetery in the north at Portone. But the main type of tomb both here and at Ulimento in the north-east is different. It consists of a large circular chamber carved out of the rock, with a central pillar, in which numerous cinerary urns were placed on a circular bench around the chamber, while others were grouped around the central pillar. These were large family vaults, which were used for several generations. Two tombs of the Caecina family were found in the eighteenth century, with forty urns. In the Ulimento cemetery the tomb of the gens Atia (the Tomba Inghirami: it was excavated by two Inghirami brothers) was found with fifty-three urns (*Pl. 69*). It has been removed en masse to the gardens of the Archaeological Museum in Florence, where it has been filled with other urns from Ulimento; the original fifty-three remain in the Museo Guarnacci at Volterra. These tombs belong to the fourth to first centuries and, although plundered, still contained bronze and terracotta vases, as well as the urns.

The evidence provided by the late tombs, combined with the rarity of bronze objects and Greek vases in the early tombs, suggests that Volaterrae did not become really prosperous until the fourth century. There was copper available in the Cecina valley, but the Volaterrans did not exploit it in early times, perhaps because they were primarily an agricultural community. The apparent poverty of the fifth century could possibly have been because the graves of that period remain undiscovered, but more probably Volaterrae's development was late. At any rate in the fourth century she built up a local industry of red-figure vases, including some large bowls of a type which has been found in other parts of northern Etruria. Since these closely resemble vases found at Clusium, they have been attributed to both cities, but recently Volaterrae has been regarded as the more likely source. Another marked feature was a funerary *stele*, consisting of a long rectangular slab of stone, rounded at the top, with the standing figure of the dead man carved in relief and framed by a border except on the right side, on which his name was inscribed. That of Avele Tite (Aulus Titus) is now in the Volterra museum, while that of Larth Atharnies (or Tharnies), now in Florence, came from Pomarance some fifteen miles to the south of Volaterrae (*Pl. 71*). They are usually dated to the sixth century, but although archaic in appearance are possibly not older than the fifth. They resemble other *stelai* from Fiesole (*stele fiesolane*), and thus attest the cultural links of Volaterrae with the north-east. They also have strong similarities with parallel sculptures in Lycia in Anatolia.

The most characteristic product of Volaterrae, however, was the cinerary urns, which must impress all visitors to the museum, if only by their sheer numbers—some six hundred; their artistic quality varies considerably (*Pls. 70, 72*). Some earlier ones are made of tufa, but the great mass from the third to first centuries BC are of alabaster, which still provides the raw material for the chief industry of the town. They are chests for the ashes of the dead and resemble small sarcophagi, seldom being more than two feet in length. On the lid is the recumbent figure of the dead man or woman; the body is often unnaturally shortened, and the main attention is given to the head which often reproduces the individual features. Around the sides of the chest a great variety of scenes is shown, the figures often having originally been coloured: these scenes include the descent of the dead to the Underworld, depicted in various ways; mythical scenes from Greek epic or tragedy; marine deities, dolphins and hippocamps; griffins; winged deities, including the grim figure of Charun; hunting scenes; circus games; triumphal processions of magistrates (see pp. 228ff); sacrifices, including human victims; banquets; a school scene and death-bed scenes of family separations. The chapter devoted by George Dennis to these urns should still be read, even if modern students of religion or art would give a somewhat different emphasis here and there. Lastly, the well-known terracotta figures of an old man and his wife must be mentioned: they are reclining on the lid of an urn and are executed with a sense of great intimacy and liveliness of expression, which owes something to Roman verism of the first century BC.[105]

It is not easy to assess the extent of Volaterrae's territory and influence. Although Strabo attributed to her a stretch of the coast, there is in fact no evidence that she took advantage of the natural highway of the valley of the Caecina to reach the sea. In later times, after the second century, she established a harbour at Vada, where similar urns have been found; it became known in Roman times as Vada Volaterrana. She may even have landed goods at the mouth of the Caecina, but in early days she imported little and the nearest settlement to the sea was on the hills at Casale Marittimo where two circular tombs with false cupolas of the sixth century have been found. There are many Villanovan settlements in the Caecina valley and in the general neighbourhood of Volaterrae, such as Cerrate, near Montecatini, Casaglia, Montescudaio and Pomarance, but they do not seem to have exploited the copper of the adjacent mountains, which would have provided means of exchange for imports; rather they remained agricultural settlements, some of which became prosperous. Thus Volaterrae followed a different policy from Populonia; so far from having had a hand in establishing Populonia, she even conceded the coast, since a settlement (c. 500 BC) at San Vincenzo di Campiglia was an outpost of industrial Populonia, not of agricultural Volaterrae. The line of Volaterrae's extending interest seems rather to have been north and north-eastwards, to which two tributaries of the Arno led—the Era and the Elsa. Her relations with Pisa are unknown, but she possibly made some efforts to overawe the Ligurians beyond the Arno, if, as is probable, settlements in which she had an interest grew up north of the Arno well inland between the Sieve and the Ombrone (which must not be confused with its homonym in the south near Rusellae). Etruscan expansion in this area around Florence is discussed later, but if Volaterrae in the days of her power in the fourth century could claim some control as far afield as this, she clearly became the centre of a very large agricultural zone.

CLUSIUM

We turn now to the inland cities of northern Etruria. Of the Twelve Cities of Etruria, Macaulay records,

> 'The banner of proud Clusium
> Was highest of them all'.

Clusium is first mentioned in the literary tradition as one of the five Etruscan cities that helped the Latins against Tarquinius Priscus of Rome, but it is best remembered as the city of Lars Porsenna who at the end of the sixth century championed the cause of the exiled Tarquinius Superbus and captured Rome or would have done so but for the bravery of Horatius who held the bridge (see pp. 261f). The Etruscan name of Latin Clusium (and modern Chiusi) was probably Clevsin. Camars was probably the Umbrian form of the city's name, although some scholars have postulated two Etruscan cities, Camars (= Chiusi) and Clevsin. The city lay on an isolated hill overlooking the fertile inland valley of the Clanis (Chiana) (Pl. 75), a tributary of the Tiber running northwards from near Orvieto towards Arezzo and the Arno; this valley forms one of the corridors of central Italy, where

> 'sweet Clanis wanders
> Through corn and vines, and flowers'.

Because the city has been inhabited through Roman and medieval until modern times little of the Etruscan settlement remains, apart from some walls of irregular construction and uncertain date, and several cemeteries. Other cemeteries, at neighbouring villages, attest the existence of small towns enjoying a fairly uniform culture and forming small agricultural centres which presumably regarded Clusium as their metropolis. The tombs were ransacked during the nineteenth century and their contents widely scattered, with the result that few museums in Europe lack objects from Clusium; there are substantial collections in the museums at Chiusi, Florence and Palermo.

Chiusi was a leading Villanovan settlement in this part of Etruria; the district that lies to the north-east appears not to have been settled by Villanovans. Another important settlement lay at Sarteano some five miles to the south-west but, whichever was the older, Chiusi had taken the lead by 700 BC. A peculiar feature of its development was the predominance and persistence of cremation; inhumation is not found much before the sixth century. The burials developed from a *pozzetto* to what are known as *tombe a ziro*; chamber-tombs begin to appear only at the end of the seventh century. A *ziro*, which elsewhere in Italy is generally referred to as a 'dolio', is a large burial jar which contained the ossuary and all the rest of the tomb-furniture; the oldest of these jars contain Villanovan urns. The practice of incineration stimulated the growth of a peculiar form of art which in origin should be regarded as Villanovan rather than Etruscan. Bronze or pottery masks were fixed on cinerary urns; later the whole head was moulded in pottery, and sometimes the bust and arms, but the lower part of the urn was never fashioned into human form (*Pl. 73*). Sometimes the urn was placed on a chair. The material varied: pottery seems to have been commoner, but bronze urns and heads are found, and in one example a pottery head on a bronze ossuary, placed on a bronze chair. Some of these heads are crude or even grotesque, but later ones are well modelled and show individual features which, if it were not for the fact that the same features appear in more than one example, would suggest actual portraits. The urns have been called 'Canopics' from the mistaken analogy with Egyptian jars which contained

70 Cinerary urn from Volaterrae, second century BC. The dead man is shown on horseback, followed by a servant, on his way to the Underworld. See p.149. 71 Funerary *stele* of Avele Tite of Volaterrae, of the sixth or fifth century BC. See p.149. 72 Sculpture showing the legendary siege of Thebes. The local artist has probably depicted a gateway of Volaterrae (*cf. Pl.70*). See p.148.

73 A Canopic cinerary urn from Clusium. A pottery head is placed on the urn which rests on a chair. See p.152.

74 Sarcophagus from Clusium, with funerary relief. See p.154.

75 View of Clusium. Though on a hill, the site is much more open than that of the cities of southern Etruria. See p.151. 76 View of Cortona. The Etruscan city ran down the hill-side, doubtless in much the same manner as the later settlements. The more gentle slopes are characteristic of some northern cities. See p.156.

77 The Porta Marzia gate at Perugia. The Etruscan arch and the upper part in the form of a loggia are incorporated in the Sangallo Renaissance bastion. See p.160. 78 Another gate of Perugia, the Arco di Augusto. The lower part is Etruscan, the upper is Roman, while the loggia on the left is Renaissance. See p.160.

79 The sepulchral monument
of Arnth Velimnes Aules
in the Tomb of the Volumnii,
near Perugia. Two winged
female figures frame and guard
the Gate to the Underworld.
Second century BC. See p.162.
80 Bronze lamp from Cor-
tona, of the second half of the
fifth century BC. See p.158.

81 The Chimera from Arretium, one of the most famous of Etruscan bronzes, of the middle or late fifth century BC. See p.166.

82 Bronze reliefs of a 'Loeb' tripod, found near Perugia, of *c.* 500 BC and possibly made at Caere. The middle panel shows Athene protecting Perseus as he escapes from the Gorgons with Medusa's head, which is covered. See p.163.

83 View of Arretium (Arezzo). Contrast the relatively low hill and more open position with the site of *e.g.* Cortona (*Pl. 76*) or still more with the southern cities. See p.165.

84–86 Chamber-tomb of the seventh century BC called La Montagnola, found at Quinto Fiorentino in 1959. It provides valuable evidence for Etruscan penetration northwards at this early period. 84 The *dromos* entrance. 85 The vault of the central chamber, seen from below. 86 The interior corridor. See p.168.

the viscera that were not embalmed with the corpse; Chiusine jars, however, contained only the ashes of the dead. From such anthropomorphic jars the step to statuary is a short one, and before long a school of sculpture developed; several full-sized pottery statues, made hollow to hold ashes, are known from the fifth century. These led on to stone or pottery sarcophagi, with recumbent figures.

The early prosperity of Clusium was based on agriculture and the fertility of the district, together with the advantages of its geographical position. The Clanis, which was navigable, gave access to the south, while not very difficult communications led westwards to Populonia, Vetulonia, Vulci and Tarquinii. Through these coastal cities artistic influences from overseas probably reached Clusium. Early Clusium gives the impression of a prosperous agricultural community, less sumptuous and 'fashionable' but more solid than the cities of the coast. During the seventh century contacts increased and Clusium imported bronze-work and pottery from some of these cities, and her own artists produced local copies. Her population increased; the old Villanovan cemetery at Poggio Renzo had to be supplemented by others. The centres at Sarteano and Castelluccio di Pienza flourished, while new ones grew up at Dolciano to the north and Cancelli to the south, and isolated tombs *a ziro* suggest the spread of agricultural settlements.

By the end of the seventh century, when chamber-tombs begin to appear, Clusium grew richer and her imports increased; examples include a fine gold fibula from Vetulonia, ivory boxes from Caere or Tarquinii and numerous Attic vases, both black- and red-figured, which perhaps reached her through Vulci. The last include the famous François vase (570–60 BC) which has been called 'a compendium mythological dictionary' (D. Randall-MacIver). Local sculptors and bronze-workers increased. A special feature which continued until the end of the fourth century consisted of seated figures of men and women, with detachable heads to allow the ashes to be placed within. The bases of stone cippi, cinerary urns and sarcophagi were decorated with reliefs from before 500 until after 400 BC; the scenes depict games, banquets and funerals (*Pl. 74*). One shows a gathering of men who have been regarded (probably wrongly) as magistrates (see p. 230); another magnificent panel found at Perugia, but of Clusine manufacture, pictures the return of an expedition from war. Of the sarcophagi with the figure of the dead resting on the lid the most famous is that of the woman Seianti Thanunia Tlesnase, who holds a mirror in her left hand and draws back her mantle from her head with the right (a late work: second century). Typical of the vases of Chiusi and district are the so-called *buccheri pesanti* which go back to at least the sixth century: the decoration was impressed by a cylinder in the form of a band around the vase. One sixth-century example shows two men seated at a table playing some game like chess. Another feature of Clusium was the painted tombs (the earliest is *c.* 600 BC) but unlike those of Tarquinii, all, except the Tomb of the Monkey, are now ruined and their paintings destroyed, apart from those in the local museum. The themes do not differ essentially from those at Tarquinii: banquets, games, chariot racing, athletics, wrestlers, dancers and musicians. For a description the reader may turn to the account by G. Dennis, who noted that the paintings were so powdery that they 'might be effaced by the touch of a finger or by the sweeping of a garment'. Thus the vanished paintings, the friezes on vase or sarcophagus, the strange faces on the urns, all reflect the life of Clusium which flourished when many another Etruscan city was on the decline, and extended its influence up the Clanis valley to settlements at Bettolle, San Francesco, Broglio and Marciano—and, if Roman tradition be accepted, as far south as Rome.

The prosperity of Clusium may be illustrated by listing some of the contents of two of the richer tombs and by reference to the 'tomb of Lars Porsenna'. A chamber-tomb, found in 1877 at Poggio alla Sala some four miles to the north-west, contained a bronze chair on which stood a simple bronze urn, similar to but plainer than vases found at Vetulonia. Over this ossuary was a linen cloth, perhaps purple in colour, covered with gold-leaf, traces of which remain. In front of the chair, as now arranged in the Florence Museum, is a bronze table about three feet long, together with a bronze basin and plate, pottery jugs and several unguent vases (Protocorinthian imports and local ware), small ornaments and dice, swords and shields. The Pania tomb, three miles south of Chiusi, is peculiar because in the inner chamber, which was partly divided into two by a small partition, part of the floor between this wall and a stone mortuary couch was paved with sheets of bronze. In the tomb were two interments, one a cremation in a bronze ossuary, the other a burial: on the floor amid numerous fragments of coloured glass lay a skeleton, doubtless thrown from its couch by tomb-robbers in ancient times. The ossuary, which contained much gold-leaf, was placed in a larger *situla* in which was the magnificent granulated gold fibula already mentioned. Besides iron spear-heads and axes, a bronze chair, *bucchero* vessels, including one with griffin-heads like those at Vetulonia, and twenty balsamries, there was a splendid ivory *situla* with four rows of carving: at the top a procession of men, animals and a boat, and below a chariot, a man on horseback and soldiers on foot. This *situla* links Clusium with Caere and Praeneste of the mid-seventh century, although a time-lag may be allowed for its arrival and that of associated objects so far inland. This ivory *situla* and other objects are now in Florence, but the gold fibula went to Berlin.

Varro, who is quoted by Pliny (*NH* 36, 19), described the 'tomb of Porsenna' who was buried below the city ('sub urbe' can mean in lower ground outside the city rather than 'beneath the city') in a vast mausoleum: the base was three hundred feet square and fifty feet high. Beneath it was an 'inextricable' labyrinth; on it stood five pyramids, each seventy-five feet wide and fifty feet high, on which rested a bronze circle with hanging bells. On this circle four other pyramids were based, each one hundred feet high, and above these five more, the height of which Varro was ashamed to mention: Etruscan accounts record ('fabulae Etruscae tradunt') that it was equal to that of the rest of the structure. Many modern scholars from Niebuhr onwards have not unnaturally rejected the account out of hand, and few would accept the figures and dimensions. But Varro, one of

Rome's greatest scholars, would scarcely have quoted this account unless he had thought that some such great monument could have existed, whether or not he himself had visited Clusium. Granted that Etruscan pride has inflated the monument to super-natural size, we should not necessarily go to the other extreme and transmute it into thin air. About three miles north-east of Chiusi a hill called Poggio Gajella, described by Dennis, con-tained a vast labyrinth of *cuniculi* and burial chambers. Though this may not have been the origin of Varro's account, such tombs as this and La Cucumella at Vulci may well lie behind a tradition which has been accepted by Sir John Myres, who found the nearest parallel to Varro's description in western Asia Minor.

The spread of the population of Clusium is illustrated by many inscriptions of the Etrusco-Roman period. Members of a score of families are buried beyond the urban cemeteries in those of the smaller centres, especially in the Val di Chiana as far as the shores of Lake Trasimene: the chief families included the Larciena, Apuna, Velethna, Hermana, Faunamena, Semusathni, and Spuriaza. The precise extent of its territory, which has been estimated at some eight hundred square miles, is naturally un-certain, but it probably ran from the north-west of Trasimene in an undulating line westward to Asciano, then turned southwards along the Ombrone, and then south-east along the Orcia, past Amiata to near Aquapendente, and then back north-east to the southern end of Trasimene. Thus Cortona lay beyond its borders in the north, Siena in the north-west, Roselle in the south-west, Orvieto in the south-east, and Perusia in the east.[106]

CORTONA

Cortona, probably Curtun in Etruscan, lay on a high hill stretch-ing from the top down a steep slope facing westwards (*Pl. 76*). Its walls, parts of which survive, are reckoned to have been some two miles in circumference; they have been dated to the sixth or fifth centuries but may be later, although traces of a double gate with voussoir arches, which are certainly not so early as this, need not have been contemporary with the original walls. Later occupation continuing into modern times, as at Clusium, has destroyed all but a few traces of Etruscan settlement. Although Livy links Cortona with Perusia and Arretium as one of the chief cities of Etruria in 310 BC ('ferme capita Etruriae populorum': 9, 37), little is recorded of its history in Etruscan or Roman times, apart from an incidental reference to the fact that its impregnable position saved it from direct attack by Hannibal who ravaged its territory as he swept through the broad and fertile valley beneath it in 217 BC.

If little firm history survives, the vacuum has been richly filled by legends. We have already seen (p. 36) Cortona's alleged Pelasgian origin and its role as the centre from which Etruria was colonized. According to Dionysius (1, 20) it was an Umbrian city which was later seized by the Pelasgians; after they had left Italy, it then passed to Etruscan control. According to another tradition Cortona was founded by Corythus, whose wife bore to Zeus a son named Dardanus; the city was called Corythus after its founder who was buried there. Thus Dardanus, the founder of Troy, came from Cortona, as Virgil recorded ('hinc illum Corythi Tyrrhena ab sede profectum': Aen. 7, 209) and in consequence the poet could make Trojan Aeneas say of Italy, 'hic domus, haec patria est' (VII, 122). We have also seen that according to Hellanicus the Pelasgians who took Cortona were led by Nanas, that he probably belongs to an early Etruscan tradition (pp. 82f), and that he may well be identified with Nanos, whom Lycophron equated with Odysseus. If Nanas, a native hero of Cortona, was adopted by other Etruscan towns, he may in Etruscan tradition have been something of a wanderer—Nanas meant 'wanderer' according to the scholiast Tzetzes on Lyco-phron—and thus the identification with Odysseus would be easier for the Greeks. Whether this identification was made by the Etruscans is uncertain: their knowledge of Odysseus was probably early, since the name is found on vases as Utuse or Utuste, which is derived from the epic form and not from those forms that led to the Latin Ulixes and Ulysses. Further, Lycophron wrote (Alex. 805) that when Odysseus 'is dead, Perge, a hill of the Tyrrhenians, shall receive his ashes in the land of Gortyn' (ἐν Γορτυναίᾳ). Gortyn here is not the city in Crete, but Cortona, and it is tempting to follow those scholars who identify Perge with Monte Pergo near Cortona. This non-epic tradition, that Odysseus left Penelope, sailed to Etruria and founded Gortyn where he died, is at least as old as the fourth century (Jacoby, *FGrH*, Theopompus, no. 354). The significant point of these varying traditions is their agreement about the importance of Cortona, which Stephanus of Byzantium summarized when he called it the metropolis of the Tyrrhenians, an importance that finds little direct support in the general historical tradition or in the archaeological remains.

Remains of Etruscan Cortona, within the walls, are negligible. The most famous relic is a bronze lamp, comprising a Medusa mask surrounded by two small friezes and a circle of alternating Sirens and Sileni (*Pl. 80*). This work, of the second half of the fifth century, was described by Dennis as 'of such surpassing beauty and elaboration of workmanship as to throw into the shade every toreutic work yet discovered in the soil of Etruria'. To some tastes it may appear too heavy and decorative, but there is much truth in his further observation that 'were there nothing else to be seen at Cortona, this alone would demand a visit', since few photographs adequately reveal its full magnificence. It was found in 1840 in a ditch, not a tomb, some two miles west of the city. Other bronzes which are said to come from Cortona may in part derive rather from the neighbourhood, so that the precise centre of this production cannot be fixed. It was on the northern bank of Lake Trasimene, south of Cortona, that the famous bronze statue of the Orator was found. Some of the bronzes are inscribed with dedications to deities. A bronze base, if correctly read (it no longer survives), names not only Juno but Cortona itself: 'mi unial curtun' means something like 'I belong to Juno of Cortona' (*TLE*, 644). Two statuettes were dedicated by the same man, one to Selans (Silvanus), and the other to Culsans (possibly Janus: see *TLE*, 640, 641). A bronze candelabrum and a statuette of a boy, found at Monrecchio near Cortona, are dedicated to Thuflthas (perhaps the Di Consentes: *TLE*, 652, 654); the deity Muantrns, who received a statuette of a boy holding an apple, is otherwise unknown (*TLE*, 653).

Tombs of the fourth and third centuries are found near the city; slightly farther away are three isolated tombs. The best known, the Tanella or Grotta di Pithagora (Cave of Pythagoras), misnamed from confusion with Croton in south Italy where the philosopher lived, is a stone-chamber on a circular base, surrounded by a wall that is broken only by the entrance gate; it belongs perhaps to the fourth century. At the village of Sodo, $1\frac{1}{2}$ miles west of the city, under a mound known as The Melon lies a chamber-tomb consisting of a vestibule, corridor and *cella*, with two other *cellae* on each side of the corridor; an inscription of the fourth century was carved on the architrave of the inner doorway (*TLE*, 630). The third tomb, the Melon of Camuscia (or Grotta Sergardi), was a great tumulus, sixty-seven yards in diameter and fifteen high, with two parallel oblong chambers each subdivided into an outer and inner *cella*, approached by a corridor fourteen yards in length; the plan is not dissimilar from that of the Regolini-Galassi tomb at Caere. Three small tombs, inserted in the upper part of the mound, are later than the main chamber which may belong to the seventh century rather than the eighth.[107]

PERUSIA

Perusia (modern Perugia) was situated on the irregular top of a hill, 1,620 feet above sea-level and nearly 1,000 feet above the Tiber, in a strong position commanding fine views over the hills and plain of Umbria (Fig. 20). Though it lay west of the Tiber and was considered part of Etruria, originally, as also in medieval and modern times, it belonged rather to Umbria. Servius (*ad Aen.* 10, 201) makes it a settlement of the Sarsinates, an Umbrian tribe. He also records another tradition, that Perusia was founded by Aulestes, a brother or father of Ocnus who later founded Felsina, Mantua and other cities in the Po valley—a story that reflects Perusine interest in the development of trans-Apennine Etruria. In general, the reference to a pre-Etruscan Umbrian period accords with the late appearance of Etruscan remains and with the pre-history of the neighbourhood. This provides much evidence for life in the Palaeolithic, Neolithic and Bronze Age periods, but finds of the early Iron Age are scarce. But although early Iron Age graves have not been found at Perusia this does not exclude inhabitants from Umbria, since the Sarsinates, unlike the majority of Umbrian peoples who buried their dead, appear to have used cremation. So commanding a height is likely to have attracted early settlers and to have been among the three hundred Umbrian *oppida* that Pliny said (*NH* 3, 113) were conquered by the Etruscans; whatever the ethnic affinities of these settlers, the oldest cemeteries do not suggest a date before *c.* 500 BC for the beginning of the Etruscan phase. In fact, although Perusia is surrounded by a dozen cemeteries, little is known about the early phase; from *c.* 450 the same cemetery may contain *fossa* and chamber burials, with the contemporary use of cremation and inhumation.

The Etruscan city, whose precise name is not known, was smaller than the medieval and modern town. The line of the walls suggests a circumference of under two miles, less than half that of Veii or Tarquinii. Stretches of the walls survive, especially in the north and south-west, and five gates are still used today. The finest are the magnificent Arco Etrusco or d'Augusto in the north and the superstructure of the Porta Marzia in the papal fortress, both well-known to the modern visitor (*Pls. 77, 78*). The walls and gates have been assigned to every century from the fifth to the first BC, but even if late they probably reproduce the pattern of the early Etruscan city, and are essentially Etruscan in inspiration even if not entirely in construction. Of the buildings in the city little remains. There are traces of a small temple with a fine fourth-century antefix in the south and of another outside the walls to the north-east, but the deities associated with them are unknown. Appian and Dio Cassius record temples to Juno and Vulcan. Since Juno was the tutelary deity of the city her temple was probably on the highest ground in the north-east on the acropolis on Monte Sole. Vulcan's temple, which escaped destruction when the city was burned in 40 BC, was outside the walls if the *Etrusca disciplina* had been properly observed: it prescribed that temples of Vulcan, Venus and Mars should be 'extra murum' (Vitruvius 1, 7).

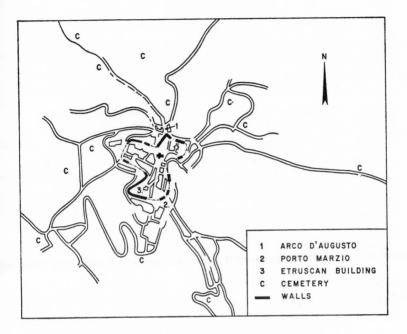

Fig. 20 Plan of modern Perugia, with remains of Etruscan Perusia

Although some isolated tombs have been found, the majority
of the population were buried in hundreds of tombs in the
numerous cemeteries around the city; a late cemetery (third to
first century) lay some three miles to the west at Palazzone. The
normal tomb was a square or rectangular chamber cut out from
the natural tufa rock, usually with a flat ceiling. Most are plain,
and none is decorated with paintings or columns. They suggest
that Perusia was less rich as well as smaller than many other
Etruscan cities, but there is also a considerable number of isolated
hypogaea, family tombs of different construction, some being
of considerable magnificence. The most famous is the Tomb of
the Volumnii, some three miles from the city, dating from 100 BC,
or possibly a little earlier. It has the form of a house, with atrium,
tablinum and two wings; the walls were decorated with stucco and
reliefs, and the ceiling has heads cut out of the rock. It is entered

by a *dromos*, and an inscription on the door proclaims, 'Arnth and Larth Velimna (Aruns and Lars Volumnius), children of Arznei, have founded this tomb'. In the central chamber six fine urns contain the ashes of four generations, but the similarity of their style suggests that Arnth and Larth transferred the ashes of their ancestors to new urns made at the same time as their own. Both the covers of the urns, which represent the dead reclining on couches, and the carving on the lower part that contained the ashes, are striking achievements. In particular the two female winged figures, who frame and guard the Gate to the Underworld on the base of one casket, have reminded many of the works of Michelangelo (*Pl. 79*). Other family tombs include that of the Precu family at San Manno, some two miles south of Perugia, and that of the family of Rafia in a cemetery to the east. The former was built underground of large travertine stones fitted beautifully together; it was entered by a *dromos*, and vaulted doorways led from the main chamber to two smaller rooms. On the front of one of the twenty-nine urns of the Rafia tomb the figure of Veli Rafi is shown, standing outside a gate, probably the Porta Marzia, his left arm wrapped in a white toga with a blue border; he wears gilded shoes and holds what may be a symbol of office (tables of law?) in his right hand—this elderly man may well be depicted as a city magistrate.

These cinerary urns were a characteristic product of Perusine industry. They are later than, and influenced by, the urns of Clusium and Volaterrae. Most are made from travertine from local quarries, and their artistic level varies considerably. A few are very good, but the general level is lower than that of Clusium and Volaterrae. Most are coloured, but the best were stuccoed before the colour was applied. Many show scenes of war, perhaps reflecting the 'struggle of life', often taken from mythology: the combat of Eteocles and Polynices, of Troilus and Achilles, the death of Iphigenia, the adventures of Odysseus and the Caly- donian boar-hunt are favourite subjects, together with scenes of the monster Scylla or Arimaspi and the griffins. The emphasis may, however, be not so much on the mythological aspect, as at Volaterrae, but rather on the scenes reflecting daily life. Local industry also produced a supply of unpainted vases made from the light-coloured clay of the district, for daily use. Some painted vases were also produced, but not on sufficient scale for export; rather, Perusia imported Attic vases through the coastal cities, some Campanian ware, and some Etruscan vases from Volaterrae in the fourth century. In one of the oldest cemeteries, that of Sperandio, just north of the city, a large sandstone sarcophagus (*c.* 500 BC?) was found, with reliefs that show banqueting scenes and a procession of men, women, prisoners and animals; this may be a funeral procession, but more likely is the return of a raiding party. There is no certainty that it was a local product: it may well have been made at Clusium.

Perusia developed a considerable bronze industry, but before local production is considered, the origin of some early bronzes must be mentioned. In 1812 a collection of bronze objects was found at Castel San Mariano some four miles south of Perugia; some of them are now in Munich and the British Museum. They include statuettes of mythical female figures, with mermaids, sphinxes, hippocampi and dogs. Many fragments of sheet metal were found: one group formed the decorations of a four-wheeled vehicle, perhaps a hearse, showing various mythological scenes, another of a battle chariot, depicting the combat of Heracles against Cycnus and Ares. There were also three silver pieces. They date from the middle to the end of the sixth century; although they resemble Ionian work, they were probably not imported from abroad or even made by Greeks in Etruria but are rather the product of native Etruscan metal workers. Yet the general evidence for the culture of Perusia in the sixth century does not suggest that they were made there, southern Etruria being a more likely source than northern. Another group of bronzes, which include the three so-called Loeb tripods, came from a chamber-tomb at San Valentino near Marsciano some eleven miles south-east of Perugia (*Pl. 82*). They have very similar bronze reliefs of slightly later date (the end of the sixth century) and could have been made at Caere. Many other bronze objects, including statuettes of warriors, have been found in Perusine territory, not least at Bettona in the south, where offerings representing parts of the human body were discovered. At first sight all these bronze objects might suggest a sixth-century Etruscan phase at Perusia: they certainly imply Etruscan influence, whether they are merely imported or were actually made in the district by artists who had come from the south (*e.g.* Caere). But we cannot properly call Perusia an Etruscan city until regular burials start in the oldest Etruscan cemetery in the fifth century. Thereafter a local bronze industry flourished at Perusia, producing a great variety of vases and household goods: specialities seem to include helmets, *kottaboi* which were used in a game played at banquets, when wine was tossed into them, and above all mirrors with engraved backs (mostly fourth and third centuries) decorated with scenes from Greek mythology. One of the finest shows Castor, Pollux, Helen and Laomedon, with their names inscribed: Castur, Pultuke, Elenei and Lamtun. Many small gold ornaments of fine workmanship, pins, rings, earrings, bracelets, beads and the like, have been found and may be of local manufacture. Thus Perusia gives the impression of considerable prosperity, being one of the smaller Etruscan centres in the fourth to first centuries BC but by no means unimportant.

The history of Perusia as a state cannot be recovered. The titles of the magistrates are not recorded on their funerary urns. One of the longest surviving Etruscan inscriptions, the Cippus Perusinus, of 46 lines and 151 words, is apparently a legal document which may deal with the conveyancing of property; even if it could be properly translated, it might not throw much light on the city's public life. Perusia's territory probably reached Lake Trasimene in the west, the Niccone (which joins the Tiber near Umbertide) in the north, and the Nestore in the south. She probably exercised some control beyond the Tiber in the east, for instance at Bettona (Roman Vettona) some ten miles to the south, and Arna eight miles to the north; these may indeed have been outposts of Etruscan Perusia against the Umbrians. Parts of the walls survive at both these places, and goldwork and other objects attest their prosperity in the fourth and third centuries. The quantity of military arms and armour found in Perusine territory suggests that she had to keep back the Umbrians of the foothills of the Apennines, if not rivals in other Etruscan cities, in order to protect her farmers who cultivated the land and produced the corn and timber, for which she was noted at the end of the third century (Livy 28, 45).[108]

ARRETIUM

Most of the area between the Chiana and Tiber, of which Lake Trasimene formed the centre, was controlled by Perusia, Clusium and Cortona. At the northern approaches to this 'land between the rivers' was Arretium, which commanded the northern end of the Clanis valley and also the small gap between the end of this river and the Arno flowing some four miles to the north. The city occupied the same site as modern Arezzo, although earlier scholars (*e.g.* Dennis) thought that it lay at San Cornelio (or Castelsecco) two or three miles to the south where there are remains of ancient walls. These, however, may well have belonged to an Umbrian settlement which was taken over by the Etruscans as an outpost to protect their new city when this was established on the ground where Arezzo now stands. This is a pleasant hillside less than a thousand feet above sea-level, which was more approachable than the forbidding heights of Perusia or Volaterrae (*Pl. 83*). It formed a centre for the agricultural population of the rich fields around, and Strabo called it the most inland city of Etruria.

Arretium is mentioned by Dionysius (3, 51) as one of the Etruscan cities that promised to help the Latins against Tarquinius Priscus, who was traditionally king at Rome from 616 to 579, but there is no archaeological evidence that it was a considerable independent city so early. The earliest tombs in the oldest Etruscan cemetery at Poggio del Sole to the west are not prior to the first half of the sixth century, while the majority are later (fourth to third centuries). Arretium probably began as a small centre, perhaps even as a dependency of Clusium: Etruscan remains are found only along the route which led thither. However, by the first half of the fifth century Arretium had at least one finely-decorated temple, from which three terracotta antefixes survive, with battle-scenes of men on horseback and on foot; the figures are in very deep relief and almost rounded. Numerous fragments of other terracottas attest later temples, *e.g.* an acroterion in the form of a man's head painted red, and a Nereid riding on the back of a sea-monster. According to Vitruvius and Pliny the city walls were excellently constructed of brick; apparently the reference is to the Etruscan rather than the Roman walls. A stretch of brick wall has been found in the north-east of the city, and there are remains of a stone wall. The latter is probably medieval, but the date of the former, whether Roman or Etruscan, is disputed.

If Arretium started primarily as an agricultural centre, it gradually developed some art and industries. Beside the terracottas already mentioned, there are several heads, *e.g.* of Minerva and of a young man wearing a Phrygian cap of *c.* 200 BC, which show very clearly the passionate and pathetic style which Hellenistic artists inherited from Scopas. Many bronzes have also been found at Arretium, including two very famous ones indeed: the Chimera, discovered in 1552, and the statue of Minerva, both now in Florence (*Pl. 81*). The Chimera is generally dated to the middle or late fifth century; although some attributed a Greek origin to it, it is more probably the work of an Etruscan artist but whether he came precisely from Arretium or not must remain uncertain. If it was made locally, the skill and reputation of the Arretine artists must stand very high, but even if it was imported it at least reflects the taste of its Arretine owner and indirectly the culture of his city. The bulk of the smaller bronzes at any rate may reasonably be attributed to local artists. But apart from works of art, Arretium became a large industrial centre. In 205 BC it was able to supply Scipio with great quantities of equipment for his struggle against Carthage: 3000 shields, 3000 helmets, 50,000 *pila*, short spears and lances, together with axes, shovels, sickles, baskets and hand-mills sufficient for forty warships, and 120,000 *modii* of wheat.

Apart from the dubious reference in Dionysius, Arretium does not appear in the written tradition until 311, after which some of its dealings with Rome are related. One episode gives a momentary glimpse into its internal affairs and class struggles.

In 302 the Arretines tried to drive out the powerful and wealthy family of the Cilnii, but this provoked such widespread disturbances in other parts of Etruria (the Cilnii must have had friends among the nobles in other Etruscan cities) that the Romans intervened to restore peace. Livy records that this was achieved either by a peaceful reconciliation between the plebs of Arretium and the Cilnian family, or else by a full-scale war in which the Roman forces defeated the Etruscans near Rusellae. Further, Maecenas, the friend of Augustus, was descended from the Cilnii on his maternal side, and the poets Horace and Propertius both harp on his royal ancestors, *e.g.* 'Tyrrhena regum progenies'; 'Maecenas atavis edite regibus'; 'eques Etrusco de sanguine regum'. If taken literally, this tradition would point to an early period of monarchy at Arretium before the Cilnii had to share their political power with other noble families. One other tantalizing glimpse of Arretium's early history is provided by one of the *elogia* from Tarquinii (see p. 91) which tells that 'S. Orgolaniensis' defeated Arretium. Professor Banti believes either that this tradition was invented to the greater glory of the man or his city, or else that, if it must be accepted, the episode cannot be earlier than about 300 BC because Arretium cannot have been politically independent of Clusium until then. But such scepticism seems unnecessary, and whatever the date, the success over Arretium would be a feather in Orgolaniensis' cap. However, even if this piece of local Tarquinian history is accepted, it unfortunately remains unanchored in time.

Arretium thus appears to be a late Etruscan city, developing from an agricultural to an industrial centre, whose great days did not begin much before the fourth or even the third century. Much later it became famous for its red-glazed ware, Arretine *terra sigillata* (so-called Samian ware) which was widely exported through the Roman Empire, even as far as India. The technical excellence of the potters had behind it the tradition of the Etruscan Arretines who made the fine temple terracottas in the fifth century and the brick city-walls which excited the admiration of Vitruvius: '(e latere) in Italia Arretio vetustum egregie factum murum'.[109]

FAESULAE AND NEIGHBOURHOOD

We finally come to the last part of Etruria proper, the north-eastern area, now dominated by Florence. This great city, however, scarcely comes into our picture except as a chronological frame: Villanovan tombs found in the centre of the modern city attest a pre-Etruscan settlement on the site, but there is no evidence for Etruscan occupation, so that its history begins only with the Roman city of Florentia, in either the second or first century.[110] The Iron Age settlement, however, suggests that many sites in the Arno valley may have received settlers who began to develop its agricultural resources. There is important recent evidence for the orientalizing period that succeeded the Villanovan. Between Quinto and Sesto Fiorentino, north of Florence, a large monumental tomb called La Montagnola was found in 1959 (*Pls. 84-86*). A *dromos* led to a corridor with false vaulting, from each side of which a burial chamber opened out; beyond this was a *tholos*, a dome with a central pillar. On the doorpost of the burial chamber was an early Etruscan inscription. Although robbed, the tomb contained fragments of ivory, gold, bronze and ostrich eggs. It must date at latest from the second half of the seventh century and provides important evidence for early Etruscan penetration into this area. The impulse may have come from the direction of Volaterrae, which as we have seen tried to probe north of the Arno. How far all Etruscan settlements in this area were due to her initiative is obviously uncertain and of less importance than the fact of the expansion itself. No doubt a tomb at Terricciola and a sixth-century *stele* at Laiatico, both in the valley of the Era, were not unconnected with Volaterrae, as also perhaps were a tomb near Monteriggioni which contained an inscribed *bucchero* cup, and four rich sixth-century chamber tombs at Castellina Chianti; perhaps even the Quinto Fiorentino tomb.

Throughout this area are found the 'Fiesole *stelae*' already mentioned (*Pl. 87*). One, that of Larth Aninie from Faesulae itself, now in Florence, seems to be linked with the *stelae* of Aviles Tites and Larth Atharnies from Volaterrae and Pomorance. A slightly later fifth-century type is illustrated by an example

87 One of the Fiesole
stelae, of the second
quarter of the fifth
century BC; provincial
work, but pleasing. From
Travignoli. These
monuments are named
'fiesolane' because the
stone comes from the
Fiesole quarries. See
p.169.

88 Sacred area at Faesulae. In background, a temple with steps leading to it; a small altar stands in front of it. In centre, the bases of two large altars. In foreground, a paved area. See Fig. 21 and p.170.

89 Air view of Capua. On the right, the Roman amphitheatre. In the central area in the lower part of the picture the Roman (and Etruscan?) rectangular city-planning is still partially preserved. See p.192.

90 Gold clasp from the Barberini tomb at Praeneste. See p.174.

91 Etruscan helmet, dedicated at Olympia by Hiero of Syracuse, to celebrate his naval victory over the Etruscans off Cumae in 474 BC. The inscription reads: 'Hieron, son of Deinomenes, and the Syracusans (dedicated) to Zeus the Etruscan spoils won at Cumae'. See p.196.

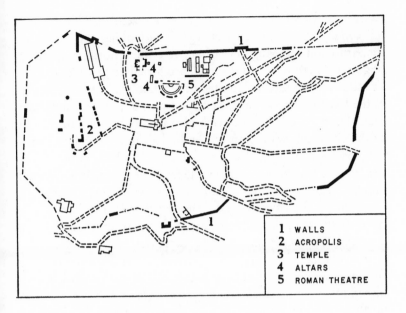

Fig. 21 Plan of Faesulae, with modern street-plan indicated

1	WALLS
2	ACROPOLIS
3	TEMPLE
4	ALTARS
5	ROMAN THEATRE

from Travignoli, east of Fiesole: it has three bands, the top one depicting a banquet, the middle a fluteplayer and dancers, the bottom a stag attacked by animals (*Pl. 87*). They were made of stone from the Faesulae quarries, but are not of very high artistic quality. They are found not only south of Fiesole, but scattered over the large area north of the Arno from the Ombrone to the Sieve. This suggests that they represent Etruscans who lived in relatively isolated small farming communities rather than in large settlements. These *stelae* also have their counterparts at Bologna, where two are inscribed 'mi suthi velus kaiknas', 'I am the tomb of Vel Kaikna': Kaikna or Caecina was a prominent Volaterran family, but the question of Etruscans north of the Apennines must be discussed later.[111]

The prosperity of this area apparently declined in the fourth century probably owing to increasing danger from Ligurian and Gallic tribes. In the third century the Gauls were checked by the

Romans and a strong new centre arose at Faesulae. This lay on a hill some eleven hundred feet high, overlooking the valleys of the Arno and the Mugnone, about five miles north of Florence (Fig. 21). There is not much evidence for an early settlement on this site: a cult centre and limited occupation may have developed in the fourth century, but the city as such was probably not older than about 300 BC. A fine stretch of wall survives, and the circuit of the city walls was about one and a half miles: the Gauls may have been the enemies that it was designed to keep at bay. Near the later Roman theatre is a temple (*c.* 300 BC) which has several unusual features, including only one *cella*. The external walls form three sides of a rectangle; the fourth side, *i.e.* the front, is open, with two columns and steps in front. Within this the *cella* abuts on the back wall, but it is narrower than this and thus leaves two lateral passages which run through from the back to the open front: in other words the *cella* is like a smaller box placed in and at the back of a bigger one (*Pl. 88*). In the area just north of the temple remains were found in 1961–2 of Etruscan walls, drains and fragments of pottery, some of which belong to the archaic period before the existing temple. In front of the temple are two altars, one of which is protected by a large stone cover and walls built around it by the Romans; it may correspond with the *mundus*, the sacred centre of the city.[112]

CHAPTER VI

ETRUSCAN EXPANSION INTO LATIUM AND CAMPANIA

ETRUSCAN CULTURE, and to some extent Etruscan political influence or even domination, soon spread beyond Etruria itself, thanks in part to increasing seapower. Some Etruscans advanced southwards over the Tiber into Latium, where they occupied Rome and other centres. They also thrust farther south into Campania, where they came into competition and ultimate conflict with the Greeks who had settled there. A parallel impingement of Etruscan and Greek interests developed at sea. Gradually, however, the tide began to turn against them, in Campania, at sea and finally in Latium, and they lost control of everything south of the Tiber. Meantime, while their hold on the south was loosening, they expanded northwards over the Apennines into the valley of the Po (*c.* 500 BC) where they exerted some political and still more commercial and economic influence for over a century. However, here also they were finally ejected, succumbing to attack by Celtic tribes who overran the northern plain of Italy. Thus they were confined to Etruria proper, over which soon fell the lengthening shadow of a Rome freed from its Etruscan overlords. We must now consider the rise and fall of Etruscan power in more detail.

LATIUM

In the Alban Hills, at the site of Rome, and elsewhere in Latium traces survive of early Iron Age culture; whether it is called southern-Villanovan or Latian, it was similar to that found in southern Etruria (p. 27). Since the latter area proved fertile soil for the growth of Etruscan culture, it might have been expected that northern Latium would have been equally receptive.

However, either early Etruscan adventurers did not attempt to penetrate into this land, or else, on the autochthonous theory, the 'spontaneous combustion' just did not occur. It was only when Etruscans or Etruscan influences spread southwards from an Etruscanized Tuscany itself that Latium was affected, and even then Etruscan culture never drove its roots down very deeply: the area remained essentially Latin-speaking and was never fully assimilated to Etruria, either culturally or politically. Nevertheless Etruscans did cross the Tiber and one of their most spectacular successes was the occupation of Rome. During the sixth century under strong Etruscan influences in all aspects of her life, political, religious, artistic and economic, Rome became an important centre (see pp. 247ff) and, since it commanded the chief ford over the Tiber, it formed the bridge-head from which the Etruscans could advance farther southwards.

This development at Rome, which can be traced in some detail, probably reflects the general story of much of Latium under Etruscan influence. On entering Latium in the seventh century the Etruscans found the Latins at various stages of development. Some of the population was still partly pastoral and semi-tribal, but some of the villages were beginning to coalesce into larger units, and these in turn perhaps to enter into alliances with some of their neighbours; but any such 'leagues' were unstable and fluctuating. It was the gift of the Etruscans to encourage agriculture in place of pastoral life, fostering industry and commerce, promoting synoecisms, founding cities, and thus sweeping the whole area into a wider world. It is difficult or even impossible to determine how much was due to their direct encouragement and example, or how much to the spontaneous consolidation and self-realization of the Latin peoples under the pressure of another culture, the more so since the pattern was complicated by the spread of Greek ideas in Latium, some of which may have come in with the Etruscans, while others came independently from the Greeks in Campania. The political aspect is equally difficult: where and when do Etruscan features represent definite Etruscan rule? But the extraordinary difference between the collection of villages that was Rome at the beginning of the sixth century, and the united city that emerged by the end of the century, with one of the largest and finest temples in Italy crowning its Capitoline hill, such an amazing metamorphosis, which we know was brought about under Etruscan rule, should make us chary of minimizing potential Etruscan influence elsewhere even if the evidence is slender.

One of the earliest Etruscan settlements in Latium was at Praeneste (modern Palestrina), whose ancient citadel (now Castel San Pietro) rises not less than 2400 feet above sea-level. The foundation of this Latin city was ascribed by legend to various figures: to Caeculus, a son of Vulcan, to Telegonus, the son of Odysseus, or to an eponymous Praenestus, son of Latinus; it was also said by Diodorus to be a colony of Alba Longa. The name is possibly of Illyrian derivation. The city may have been of somewhat mixed origin (Latins and Sabines), but there is no evidence for Etruscan participation at the beginning; that comes later. Contemporary with the Regolini-Galassi tomb at Caere are two tombs at Praeneste, the Bernardini (excavated unscientifically in 1876 by two Bernardini brothers) and the Barberini tomb. Their architecture is not known, but their rich contents include four silver-gilt bowls and dishes, engraved with pictorial scenes which are reminiscent of Egypt and Asia Minor; they very closely resemble five similar bowls from the Regolini-Galassi tomb (*Pl. 27*). Though one is inscribed with a Phoenician name, the work is more probably Syrian. They use stock themes inspired by Egypt or Assyria, but at second-hand. Thus one shows Pharaoh threatening a group of captives whom he has seized by the hair; around this central scene are Nile boats and figures of Isis and Horus. This, however, is not the real Egypt, but as Randall-MacIver wrote, 'the Egypt of the opera *Aida*, . . . conceived in precisely the same vein of romance'. Other bowls depict hunting scenes with lions seizing their prey, which are Assyrian in feeling. Another shows a long line of soldiers, an army on the march, while yet another picture is more peaceful: horses at pasture, a herdsman with his cattle, and a workman trimming a tree. The combination of country scenes and a procession of warriors significantly is found on an Etruscan bronze vessel from

Bologna, which is some two hundred years later in date (see p. 66). These silver bowls thus had a profound and lasting effect on Etruscan metal-workers, and they exemplify the 'orientalizing' movement that swept over Etruria. They are also important for purposes of dating; together with other contents, they show that these tombs at Praeneste and Caere belong to about 650. Other imported objects include carved ivories, but an ivory cup and wand are probably the products of local workmen. This is the case with the jewellery too, which native Etruscan goldsmiths began to produce, including a large clasp for a belt or pectoral, ornamented with rows of lions, horses and human-headed birds in the round, soldered on to an oblong plaque (*Pl. 90*). Equally striking are the cauldrons of hammered bronze and their stands, resembling those of Caere and Vetulonia.

But are these the tombs of Etruscan nobles rather than of Latin chiefs who had surrounded themselves with all this orientalizing art? An Etruscan origin is sometimes denied on the strength of the famous gold fibula which bears an early Latin inscription, 'Manios med fhefaked Numasioi', that is 'Manios made this for Numasios'. If this object really came from the Bernardini tomb, and if it was not only the property of the owner but was made specifically for him, then he must have been a Latin, but in fact none of these points is assured. On the question of provenance Randall-MacIver was outspoken: 'it is essential that the student should realize that there is no trustworthy evidence whatsoever to prove that this fibula belongs to the tomb'. Nor is the Manios fibula unique, in that another of the same class bears an Etruscan inscription. In view of these uncertainties and the fact that the contents of the tombs cannot be distinguished from those of the tomb at Etruscan Caere, it would not be unduly hazardous to attribute the tombs to Etruscans rather than merely to Etruscan influence, and to regard Praeneste as a key point in their advance into Latium. Among surviving architectural terracottas from the sixth to the first centuries is a sixth-century tile showing a procession of two charioteers with winged horses, guided by a soldier and a priest, which is reminiscent of Etruria, as also are some of the later *cippi* for tombs. Another survival from Etruscan days is no doubt the very flourishing industry in artistic bronzes, both ornamental toilet boxes (*cistae*) and decorated mirrors, which continued until the second century BC. The industry may have fallen into the hands of Campanian-Greek workmen, but a reminder of the Etruscan background survived in the influence of Etruscan pronunciation of the names (Alixentr, Casenter, etc.) of some of the Greek characters that figure in the mythological scenes with which the bronzes are engraved. Praeneste later took pride in its gladiatorial games, to which Cicero refers more than once, but since this was a 'sport' that was shared by so many other cities, it might be safer not to follow those who connect this specifically with her Etruscan past.[113]

At Tusculum little but the name remains to link the city with the Etruscans (Tusci). It shared in the life of the 'Villanovan' age in the Alban Hills, but no certain Etruscan traces survive: the roof of an archaic cistern is thought by some to resemble in construction the Regolini-Galassi tomb, but this connection is tenuous. Like Rome, it may have come under Etruscan control in the sixth century. At any rate Octavius Mamilius of Tusculum was the son-in-law of the Etruscan Tarquinius Superbus of Rome. Etruscan derivations have been suspected for other place names. Thus Velitrae (Veltri) may be compared with Velathri-Volaterrae, and Terracina (which was renamed Anxur when it was captured by the Volscians) may be linked with Tarkina, Tarchna (*cf.* Tarquinii). The name of the little river Melpis may be Etruscan: a later Etruscan foundation in north Italy was called Melpum (see p. 216). Turnus, the leader of Ardea, the chief city of the Rutuli, is sometimes credited with an Etruscan name, *i.e.* Turnus-Tursnus-Tyrrhenos, while Appian, and possibly Cato, thought that the Rutuli were Etruscans; the Aeneas legend makes them allies of the Etruscan Mezentius against the Trojans and Latins. But too much weight should not be given to such views: at any rate Ardea started as a Villanovan settlement, and so the Rutuli, if they were the earliest occupants, would then be Latins. To such meagre evidence can be added a single Etruscan inscription: it comes from a *bucchero* vase at Satricum and comprises only two words.[114]

In view of their sea-power the Etruscans might reasonably be expected to have tried to control the cities on or near the coast of Latium, and there is some evidence to suggest that Etruscan Rome gained some authority here. When the Etruscans were expelled from Rome, the new Republic made a treaty with Carthage, which was almost certainly a renewal of an earlier one between the two sea-powers in the west, the Carthaginians and the Etruscans. The date which Polybius assigns to the treaty has sometimes been questioned, but it has withstood criticism and should be accepted as evidence for conditions at the end of the reign of Tarquinius Superbus. In this treaty Rome spoke for, and protected the interests of, the peoples of Ardea, Antium, Circeii, Terracina, and perhaps Lavinium, and 'of any other of the Latins who are subject to Rome'. These 'subjects' were probably allies (*socii*) who had recognized Rome's military leadership in individual treaties. This obviously does not mean that these Latin cities were Etruscanized, but it does imply that the Etruscan rulers at Rome had been able to exercise some control over them. Although these cities have not preserved any material remains to link them with Etruria, the elder Pliny records (35, 17) seeing in ruined temples (*in aedibus sacris*) at Ardea paintings that were older than Rome itself. He mentions another painting at Lanuvium by the same artist, which the emperor Caligula would have removed to Rome if the plaster has been strong enough, and adds that there were even older paintings at Caere. These may well therefore have been Etruscan paintings, and Pliny, who did not use the word *templum*, may have mistaken the tombs for small ruined shrines.[115]

Rome, and as far as is known, Latium, had no temples before the Etruscan period: since it was the Etruscans who introduced this new form of architecture into Rome, their influence may be suspected in Latium also, although Greek influences were also active. Further, the scholar and antiquarian Varro, as reported by Pliny (*NH* 35, 154), stated that before the Greeks Damophilus and Gorgasus decorated the temple of Ceres in Rome in 493 BC, the Tuscan style of decoration was universal. In the temples in Latium, for instance at Satricum, Velitrae and Lanuvium, the coloured terracotta decorations are in fact virtually indistinguishable from those in Etruria and indeed resemble many in Campania. The clay of the antefixes from Etruria and Latium may not be so well purified as that from Campania but the finished article is often so standardized that the moulds must have been carried around by the workmen wherever their work took them. A worshipper who found himself in one of these temples might well be pardoned for wondering whether he was in Falerii, Caere, Velitrae, Satricum, or even Capua. The wealth of brightly-coloured gay decorations that would confront him may now best be appreciated by a visit to the Villa Giulia Museum, particularly, for instance, to the rich remains from the temple of Mater Matuta at Satricum; these decorations go back to the mid-sixth century, while votive offerings from a still earlier sanctuary on the site have been found in a pit. The sources of the impulse that created this expanding common culture are clearly Etruscan and Greek, but it is difficult to discern to what extent Greek ideas were modified by the Etruscans or how far they were transmitted direct from the Greeks in southern Italy. A recent discovery has given fresh importance to the direct channel. In 1959 a series of thirteen massive archaic stone altars was found at the Latin city of Lavinium (modern Pratica di Mare) some sixteen miles south of Rome: one of them had a bronze tablet inscribed in archaic Latin to Castor and Pollux. It has often been thought that the cult of the Dioscuri reached Rome from Etruria, but now it looks as if the route may have been Magna Graecia (Locri), Lavinium, Tusculum (the centre of the cult in Latium), and Rome. But even though the tide was sweeping in strongly from the south, the Etruscans should be regarded as the main agents and it can be maintained that 'the whole culture of Latium between the seventh and sixth centuries BC, was bound to Etruria.'[116]

ETRUSCANS AND GREEKS AT SEA

The Etruscans spread beyond Latium to Campania where they came into direct contact with Greeks. Whether their first advance there was by land or by sea, the sea provided a continuing channel of communication. It was essentially as a seafaring people that the Greeks first viewed them. In the Homeric *Hymn to Dionysus* (seventh century?) they appear as pirates: the young god, with his dark hair waving about him and a purple robe around his strong shoulders, was on a headland jutting into the sea, when 'there came swiftly over the sparkling sea Tyrsenian pirates on a well-decked ship'. During the epic age piracy was a recognized means of livelihood (*Odyssey* 3, 73) and as late as *c.* 450 BC the text of a treaty between two small Greek states on the Corinthian Gulf which arranged to protect their harbours and citizens, recognized that the high seas were open to acts of piracy (Tod, *Greek Historical Inscriptions* no. 34). But since we hear of Etruscan seafaring activities chiefly from the Greeks, who were their trade rivals, the stories told about them are not likely to be friendly. Thus Ephorus (see Strabo 6, 2, 2) said that before the earliest Greek colonies were founded in Sicily 'men were so afraid of the pirate vessels of the Tyrrhenians and the savagery of the barbarians in this region that they would not so much as sail there for trading'. Since it was Greek penetration in western waters that limited the spread of Etruscan interest, we must now see how the Etruscans reacted to the developing pattern of Greek trade and settlement.

That they reacted at all may at first sight seem surprising to those who accept the autochthonous view of Etruscan origins. It is remarkable that the Iron Age Villanovans in their villages should have been so attracted by the gradual inflow of foreign goods that they ventured on to the sea in order to increase this flow, which in any case Greek merchants would presumably have been only too willing to bring to their doorstep in return for the minerals of Etruria. Equally astonishing is their success in grappling with the dangers of this new element, so quickly and on such a scale that they were able not only to compete with the Greeks but also to terrify them. Even if the Greeks did not inherit any of the sea-faring skill of their Mycenaean predecessors, the indented nature of their coastline and the strings of islands in the Aegean soon tempted them to venture from the land. But the Villanovans had few such inducements: the coast of Etruria

was not very attractive for anchorage, and even their coastal
settlements were slightly inland. If a somewhat less rigid view of
the composition of Villanovan civilization is held, and the possibility of some early infiltration from the sea is postulated, then
the problem of the amazing growth of Etruscan sea-power
becomes slightly less acute. But it disappears altogether for those
who accept Herodotus and believe that the Etruscans arrived in
Italy by sea. In fact their later 'thalassocracy' is a very strong
argument in support of their eastern origin.

The basic cause of the great Greek colonizing movement
which started in the middle of the eighth century and led to the
transformation of the Greek world has been much debated. Since
trading was a form of private rather than civic enterprise, and
since the sites with the best harbours, *e.g.* Brundisium in the west
and Byzantium in the east, were not among the first chosen, the
earliest colonists were probably seeking land. But trade motives
were often not far behind. Indeed since there is some evidence
of a limited amount of trade immediately preceding the colonizing period, it may have been the local knowledge gained by very
early traders that led some of the colonists to the sites that they
chose.[117]

The earliest Greek colony in the west was on the island of
Pithecusae (Ischia). It is remarkable that so northerly and distant
a point was chosen, but the island was fertile, contained some
gold and was defensible. From it the colonists could trade with
the Etruscans, whose power prevented any Greeks from establishing themselves still farther north; or at any rate they could levy
transit-tolls on passing shipping. The colonists, who came from
Chalcis and Eretria in Euboea, have left traces of their occupation
from the mid-eighth to the sixth century when the site was
abandoned because of volcanic activity or perhaps because of
Etruscan pressure. Fragments of Geometric, Protocorinthian and
Corinthian pottery indicate that its trade was increasingly with
Corinth. But the most important relic is the cup with a scratched
verse on it written in the Chalcidian alphabet, saying that anyone
who drank from it would be inflamed by Aphrodite, and claiming that the cup was superior to that of Nestor (see p. 46).

Thus the owner of the cup knew about Nestor's cup in the *Iliad*, and these settlers probably brought with them legends about Odysseus. Further, a locally made late Geometric vase depicts a shipwreck which might represent a less happy incident of Greek voyaging in the west, or could even reflect a heroic story, such as that of Odysseus. When the Etruscans made contact with these Greek settlers they came across this Chalcidian alphabet and, according to the most widely accepted view, this was the area from which they adopted it for their own use (p. 46); it was soon in use in Rome and is found on the Manios *fibula* (*cf.* p. 174). Soon afterwards, more Greeks, mainly from Euboea, established a colony at Cumae on the mainland nearby (*c.* 750–725). Here too a *graffito* on an early seventh-century vase proclaims in the same letters, 'I am the vessel of Tataie; may anyone who steals me be struck blind.' Cumae quickly developed contacts with Etruria, and some Etruscan jewellery found there may not have been imported from Etruria but actually made at Cumae by Etruscan workmen.

After a short period of preliminary trade the Greeks started to send colonies to Sicily also: the earliest at Naxos was soon followed by the greatest of all, Syracuse. With these widening horizons the straits of Messina between Sicily and the toe of Italy soon became a key position. First some 'pirates' from Cumae and then colonists from Euboea established themselves at Zancle-Messene (modern Messina); they soon co-operated with more Euboeans who came and occupied Rhegium across the strait. The Etruscans must have watched with apprehension the Euboean colonies gaining this grip on a vital trade-route. Further, the Achaeans in the Peloponnese also sent a great number of colonists to south Italy: Sybaris (traditionally in 720) was soon followed by Croton, Metapontum and Caulonia. The importance of the new cities to the Etruscans was that they offered fresh markets for Etruscan goods. Chief among them was Sybaris, whose fertile soil and skill in acting as middleman soon increased her wealth until her name became a synonym for luxury. Her citizens were not given to shipping, but they attracted a great deal of trade both from Etruria and from the Ionian cities of Asia Minor, particularly Miletus, which reached the peak of its prosperity in the sixth century. Sybaris soon established a colony of its own at Poseidonia on the west coast (*c*. 700), half way to Cumae, and also some smaller settlements, such as Laos. When the Etruscans began to expand into Campania and their trade with Sybaris increased, Sybaris developed a new trade-route across the waist-like isthmus of southern Italy to Laos, thus by-passing the straits of Messina. Luxury goods, such as fine woollens and carpets, could now come by sea from Miletus, be humped by mule over the mountains from Sybaris to Laos; here, or at Poseidonia, they could be met by Etruscan merchants or ships. What the Etruscans offered in payment was probably mainly iron and copper (and perhaps slaves) rather than their own metalwork, since no Etruscan bronzework has yet been found in south Italy or Sicily. Etruscan imports also included vast quantities of Greek vases. In this trade Corinth at first held a virtual monopoly and Attic ware is not found in Etruria before *c*. 620–10, but by about 550 it had almost completely superseded the Corinthian. The political relations of Athens and Corinth, however, continued to be friendly, and the explanation may be that when the Corinthians realized that their own vases were becoming less popular in the west they started to carry Attic ware in their own ships; the geographical position of Corinth on the Corinthian Gulf made it much easier for her than for Athens to trade with the west, in the days before the Corinth Canal was cut. In fact some of these wares may have been carried by neither Corinthian nor Athenian ships, but by merchants from the eastern Aegean, such as Phocaeans and Chians, since marks scratched on the bases of some show Ionian hands. A certain number of 'Chalcidian' vases have also been found in Etruria; if this ware was made in Euboea, the distributing centre in the west was probably Rhegium but more probably it was manufactured there. Rhodes also contributed a small quota of painted vases to Etruscan markets.

Later a new phase started thanks to the initiative of the Phocaeans of Asia Minor who, says Herodotus (1, 162), 'were the first Greeks to make long voyages and it was they who first revealed the Adriatic, Etruria, Iberia and Tartessos, and they made these voyages not in merchant vessels but in fifty-oared galleys' (*i.e.* warships). About 620 BC a mariner from Samos, named Colaeus, was blown by an easterly gale beyond the Pillars of Hercules into the Atlantic where in southern Spain (Andalucia) he discovered the rich kingdom of Tartessos. After this pioneer had revealed this fabulously wealthy new source of silver, tin and lead, the Phocaeans began to take an interest in the Tartessian market, though it was separated from them by the length of the whole Mediterranean. The Rhodians may already have established a settlement at Rhode in north-eastern Spain (and have given the Rhone its name of Rhodanus), but the Phocaeans were the chief colonizers and gained an invaluable base when they established themselves at Massalia (Marseilles) about 600 BC. The arrival of these newcomers in the western Mediterranean was not to the liking of the Phoenician merchants, especially the Carthaginians who were seeking to establish a monopoly of trade in these waters, and Massalia was founded only after the Phocaeans had fought and defeated the Carthaginians in a naval battle recorded by Thucydides (1, 13). Some other small settlements were set up either directly by the Phocaeans or by Massalia: at Maenake near Malaga in southern Spain, at Emporion (= 'The Market', modern Ampurias) near Rhodes, at Nicaea (Nice) and Antipolis (Antibes). The result was a Phocaean thalassocracy in western waters, which would tend to limit Etruscan, no less than Carthaginian, commercial interests.

A new challenge to the Etruscans also soon arose in more southern waters. Led by Pentathlus, a group of Cnidians from south-west Asia Minor and Rhodians tried to establish themselves at Lilybaeum in western Sicily but were driven out by the native Elymians with Phoenician help (*c.* 580). They then settled in Lipara and the other islands and developed an interesting system of complete communism which was gradually somewhat modified. The alleged reason for the original system was to enable part of the community to cultivate the islands while the rest fought the Etruscan 'pirates' who were harassing them. The Etruscan point of view may have been different: the arrival of the Cnidians at Lipara threatened their communications with the

Straits and hostilities broke out. Recent excavations on the acropolis of Lipara have revealed traces of this early Greek settlement and a preceding Mycenaean one. Some Attic pottery has been found, but the prevailing import appears to have been Ionian ware.[118]

Massalia, with its good harbour and fertile land quickly flourished: from it hellenizing influences radiated out and Greek pottery, imported from Ionia or made locally, soon found its way to the native strongholds (*oppida*) of Languedoc (*e.g.* Ensérune), and to some extent eastwards also (*e.g.* at Sanary). The Etruscans soon turned to this new market, where Etruscan *bucchero* ware appears in the first half of the sixth century, although after the battle of Alalia (see below) political considerations led to these imports ceasing. Massalia also built up an inland trade with the Celtic kingdoms to the north: when this began to decline in the second half of the sixth century, the Etruscans again moved in by developing their trade in Greek pottery with the Celts by a different route, over the Alps of northern Italy (see p. 218).[119]

A new phase opened when the Phocaeans advanced nearer to the shores of Etruria by entering Corsica. About 560 BC, apparently with oracular support from Delphi, they settled at Alalia on the east coast over against the cities of southern Etruria, whose reactions are not recorded. But in Asia Minor Phocaea itself was soon threatened by the Persians, and many of the inhabitants sailed westwards to join their compatriots in Alalia. After five years during which, as Herodotus tells, 'they harried and plundered all their neighbours, the Etruscans and Carthaginians made common cause against them and sailed to attack them, each with sixty ships'. They met the sixty warships of the Phocaeans at the battle of Alalia (*c.* 535). The Phocaeans gained a 'Cadmean' victory from which the survivors escaped to Alalia; they ultimately settled at Elea, the home of the 'Eleatic' philosophers. The majority of the captured crews, for whom the Carthaginians and Etruscans drew lots, were taken to Agylla (Caere) and stoned to death. Herodotus then tells of the curse that fell on all who passed their grave and how the Caerites sent to Delphi and were ordered by the Pythian priestess to sacrifice to the Phocaeans as heroes and establish a gymnastic festival and a horse-race in their honour, a festival that was still celebrated in Herodotus' time. The setting up of such games would be little penalty for the sport-loving Etruscans: Caere's relations with Delphi were apparently good; they maintained a Treasury there, but whether it was established before, or as the result of, these events is not known. As the fruits of victory the Etruscans gained control of Corsica, by agreement with their Carthaginian allies who took over Sardinia. If Diodorus is to be trusted, they expelled Phocaeans from another Corsican settlement named Calaris, but this may be an error either for Alalia, which the Romans called Aleria, or possibly for Caralis in Sardinia; they also founded a 'city of Victory', Nicaea, but in view of its Greek name this may have been an earlier settlement of the Phocaeans (who had one thus named in southern Gaul, now Nice) which the Etruscans took over. From Corsica the Etruscans exacted as tribute resin, wax and honey; further, the slaves from Corsica were excellent according to Diodorus, though Strabo curiously says just the opposite. Corsica remained under Etruscan control for a considerable time, at least until 453 when we hear of Syracusan raids on the coast of Etruria and Corsica.[120]

The assertion of Etruscan supremacy in these waters and the growing power of Carthage did not put an abrupt end to all Phocaean trade, although by the time of Herodotus Phocaeans were no longer sailing to Tartessos for metals: the Carthaginians saw to that. But there is some slight evidence for their continuing commerce at Massalia and Velia in the fifth century: many coins found in Etruria, *e.g.* at Volaterrae, in Provence and in Spain, are Phocaean in type and mintage, while the earliest Etruscan coinage (that of Populonia) seems to be inspired by Phocaean types, *e.g.* a lion's head. It has even been suggested, on the ground that some of the Attic vases found in Etruria have been marked by merchants with letters of the Ionian alphabet, that they may have been transported there, at any rate for the last part of their journey, perhaps from the straits of Messina, by Phocaeans.[121]

Pressure by the Greeks led Etruria and Carthage to form an alliance. Aristotle says, 'it is not the end of the state to provide an alliance for mutual defence against all injury, or to ease exchange and promote economic intercourse. If that had been the end, the Etruscans and Carthaginians would be in the position of belonging to a single state; and the same would be true of all peoples who have commercial treaties with one another.' He unfortunately gives no hint of the date of this treaty; it fits best into the sixth century, but whether before or after the battle of Alalia is uncertain. It could have marked an early drawing-together; but it was more likely a sudden agreement as a basis for joint action against the common enemy; or indeed it might have been the formal result of such successful joint action. Again, little is known about its content, other than the decision to establish spheres of interest, the Carthaginians taking Sardinia, and the Etruscans Corsica. Its general form presumably resembled the treaty between Carthage and the new Roman Republic, which in turn is usually regarded as the renewal of a treaty between Carthage and Etruscan Rome. Aristotle unfortunately refers only to 'the Etruscans'. Who signed the treaty we do not know, whether the Etruscan League, or the Twelve Cities individually, or only those cities that were most interested, like Caere. Nor do we know how far its commercial clauses promoted trade between the two partners. An ivory tablet found at Carthage, with the figure of a boar, has an Etruscan inscription (*mi puinelkarthazie*) which may mean 'the property of Puina of Carthage'. If such is in fact the meaning, Puina may have been an Etruscan trader resident in Carthage, but whether he was merely an individual or the member of an Etruscan 'colony' of businessmen remains unknown.[122]

Over fifty years later, at the next major action at sea between Etruscans and Greeks, fought off Cumae in 474, the Etruscans were without help from their Carthaginian friends, since the latter had just suffered a resounding defeat at the hands of the Sicilian Greeks at Himera. But before this collapse of Etruscan sea-power is considered (see pp. 195f) we must look further at its origin and extent. If the passage of Strabo already quoted (p. 178) is to be taken literally, Etruscan 'pirates' were strong enough to frighten the Greeks away from seas so far distant from Etruria as the Straits of Messina soon after 750, that is, before the real start of the 'orientalizing' period in Etruria in the seventh century. This need create no problem for those who believe that a nucleus of Etruscans had come in their ships from Asia Minor, but the early date is generally rejected as anachronistic by those who believe in an essentially 'Italian' origin, even though Professor Pallattino tries to have the best of both worlds in accepting Strabo's evidence and rejecting that of Herodotus.[123]

The extent of direct Etruscan contacts overseas is difficult to assess. There may have been early contacts with Corsica before the arrival of the Phocaeans, but it would be hazardous to believe this on the strength of Servius' idea that Populonia was founded by Corsicans (see p. 142). At any rate the island passed into Etruscan hands after the battle of Alalia. Little weight should be given to Strabo's reference (5, 2, 7) to an Etruscan origin for the Sardinians, nor need the Greek name of Sardinia, Ichnusa, suggest Greek settlement there, although Olbia in the north-east might have been a Phocaean colony, as was Olbia in Gaul. The native 'Nuragic' culture of the island is now known to have started about 1000 BC, and not in the second millennium as was thought until recently; it reached its zenith in the eighth and seventh centuries. This Bronze Age civilization continued in the island at a time when the Iron Age was emerging on the Italian mainland, and is marked by the skill of its bronze-workers and by the cone-shaped towers (*nuraghi*), built of large polygonal blocks and each containing a large circular room with a dome-shaped roof, of the *tholos* type. The construction of these castles became more complex in time and several were grouped about a central keep, and huts were built around, thus forming villages. The tombs, the so-called 'Tombs of the Giants', were long narrow chambers each with an apse-like approach with seats where, perhaps, the living could meet to worship the dead; the entrance to the chamber was closed with a monolithic block. This culture had many contacts with Etruria. Not only do the *tholoi* resemble those of northern Etruria, and some rock-tombs at Sant' Andrea

Priu have architectural similarities with tombs at Caere, but Sardinian objects have been found in Etruria, for instance in eighth- and seventh-century tombs at Vetulonia, and recently at Vulci. These include an interesting bronze ship with animals from Vetulonia and an eighth-century bronze warrior from Villanovan Vulci (see pp. 144 and 120). Further, Etruscan *bucchero* ware is found in Sardinia, and the Sardinian tribe of the Aesaronenses on the east coast may have an Etruscan name (*cf.* Etruscan 'aisar', 'gods'). The island, however, gradually succumbed to the Carthaginians, although the Greeks still cast covetous eyes in its direction. In 540 after the Persian conquest of Ionia a proposal was made that the Ionians should all migrate and found a single city in Sardinia, while in 498 Histiaeus is said to have tried to tempt Darius with the prospect of conquering Sardinia. Whatever the situation was in 540 on the eve of Alalia, by 500 the island was firmly in the hands of the Carthaginians, who developed the early Phoenician trading stations on the plains of the south and west of the island.[124]

Etruscan wares reached southern Gaul and Spain, as already noted, during the period of the Phocaean thalassocracy. An attempt to trace any early Etruscan settlement in Spain by means of place-names has not proved very successful. When Diodorus, probably following Timaeus, says that the Phoenicians discovered a wonderful island in the Atlantic (perhaps Madeira), which the Etruscans would have colonized but for Carthaginian intervention, the story may be taken as an illustration of the boundless ambitions which the Greeks attributed to their Etruscan rivals. From the second half of the seventh century Etruscan *bucchero* kantharoi are found at Carthage, together with some 'Etrusco-Corinthian' aryballoi and alabastra made in Etruria following Corinthian models. Importation of *bucchero* continued in the sixth century, but most of the bronzes are later. Sixth century *bucchero* is also found in considerable quantities in eastern and southern Sicily, while some fragments dating back to 650–625 come from Megara Hyblaea. The route by which Etruscan merchants travelled is marked by finds of *bucchero* at Cumae and elsewhere in Campania, in Lucania (*e.g.* at Sala Consilina) and at

Rhegium. The absence of Etruscan metal-work in south Italy and Sicily may be explained by the probability that cities here preferred to import the unworked metal from Etruria. The ancient sources attest the export of Etruscan metal-work to Greece, but little has turned up apart from a Vulci tripod which was found on the Acropolis at Athens. On the other hand *bucchero* is distributed widely in the eastern Mediterranean: at Athens, Corinth, Delos, Naxos, Samos, Rhodes, Ionia, Cyprus, and even the Black Sea and Egypt. Thus in general Etruscan merchants, even if not Etruscan settlers, spread their contacts widely, especially during the sixth century.[125]

ETRUSCAN CAMPANIA

Less than a hundred years ago some historians doubted whether the literary tradition of an Etruscan occupation of Campania was true. Few could continue to be sceptical after the discovery in 1899 of one of the longest surviving Etruscan inscriptions at Capua, but individual statements, for instance Strabo's mention of an Etruscan phase at Pompeii, were still challenged. Archaeology, and especially the discovery of over fifty more Etruscan inscriptions, have resolved all doubts. Yet today the history of Etruscan Campania cannot be written nor even the general pattern of Etruscan settlement be established. By what route or routes did the Etruscans arrive? At what date? Which were the earlier and which the later settlements? Was the occupation primarily economic or military? Was its effect deep or transitory? Although new evidence is coming to light, as yet only tentative answers can be offered to such questions.

Strabo records that the Etruscans founded twelve cities in Campania, the chief of which was Capua, but this alleged 'dodecapolis' looks like an arbitrary repetition of the twelve cities of Etruria itself, and it is difficult to compile a list. The cities to which the ancient sources assign Etruscan foundation or occupation are Capua, Nola, Nuceria, Herculaneum, Pompeii, Sorrento and Marcina.[126] Others indicated by coin legends, but not identified are Velcha, Velsu, Irnthi, and Uri or Urina (perhaps Hyria). Acerrae and Atella are possible candidates (Fig. 22).

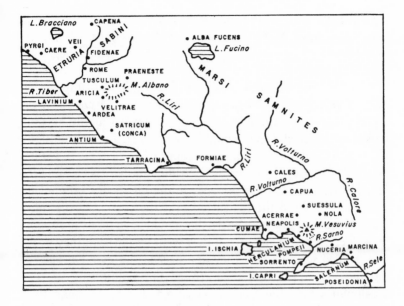

Fig. 22 Map of Latium and Campania

At Pompeii Etruscan occupation was confirmed by the discovery of fragments of *bucchero* with Etruscan inscriptions under the temple of Apollo near the Forum. The problem here is no longer the actual fact of occupation, but its date; the earlier Oscan settlement on the site was probably controlled by the Greeks, possibly from Cumae, during part of the sixth century, and they must have been responsible for the introduction of the cult of Apollo. The name of Herculaneum suggests a Greek origin but the Etruscans may have had a stronghold there first. The most southerly area occupied by the Etruscans was the 'ager Picentinus' in the neighbourhood of Salerno; this ran some thirty miles from around Sorrento to the mouth of the Sele near Poseidonia. Pliny specifically states that this area belonged to the Etruscans, and it may have been here that the colony of Marcina lay, probably at Fratte. At Pontecagnano (see p. 27) there is evidence for Villanovan occupation which merged into an orientalizing phase, marked by two scarabs, imitations of

Egyptian work, probably of Phoenician manufacture, found in an *a fossa* burial. Since life declined at Pontecagnano *c.* 550 BC, it may have been overshadowed by Fratte which began to flourish *c.* 600.[127]

How did the Etruscans reach the rich lands of Campania? If they advanced by land from Latium, they could have taken the route followed by the later Via Appia, that is roughly keeping to the coast, or else they could have gone farther inland along the Trerus and Liris valleys (the route of the later Via Latina) which is probably the older track. Although there is no archaeological evidence for their presence in the Liris valley, the inland route would avoid the marshland near the coast. On the other hand, if they kept nearer the sea they could have received support from their ships. At any rate, if they went by the coast they probably turned inland when they approached the '*ager Falernus*' as did the Via Appia, and then crossed the Volturnus near later Casilinum where the Via Latina joined the Appia. Here their base would be Capua, from which their further line of advance may have been close to the hills, to Nola (Cato recorded that Nola was founded after Capua), Nuceria and Salernum. They would thus avoid the marshy land of the river Clanis, which flowed from near Acerrae to the sea near Liternum. This area was later drained by canals, and Livy (28, 46, 5) mentions a *fossa graeca* which drained the lower Clanis. In view of their great engineering skill it may well have been the Etruscans who were responsible for this system, which made possible the development of Acerrae and Atella near the Clanis. Further, the river quite possibly owed to them its name which it shared with the tributary of the Tiber in Etruria—the Chiana. From these inland sites the Etruscans may then have gradually exerted pressure on the cities of the coast, finally getting control of Pompeii and Herculaneum, though not Cumae. But if the advance was made by sea, two possibilities are open. They may have sailed from the north and occupied as many coastal cities as they were able to master (*e.g.* Pompeii) and then have pushed inland to Capua, Nola and Nuceria. Alternatively as suggested by M. Pallottino they might have sailed directly southwards to the Salerno area and then moved north, first to the coastal cities and then ulti-mately to Capua. This view depends largely on the date of their occupation of Capua.[128]

The date given by the literary sources is varied. Velleius Paterculus puts it *c.* 800 BC, while Cato according to Velleius gave a date which works out at 471. Neither is generally accepted. The former is obviously too early in view of conditions in Etruria itself, while the latter falls in the period of the decline of Etruscan power: after their defeats at Cumae by land (524) and sea (474) the Etruscans are not likely to have founded a new city in this threatened area; and since they lost it to the Samnites before 420, this foundation date would give Etruscan Capua a life of less than fifty years. Various devices have been resorted to in order to save the reputation of Cato, whose authority is con-siderable, especially since Servius, the Virgilian commentator, says that 'Cato described the development of the Etruscan empire very fully'. Perhaps Velleius has misquoted him. On this assump-tion reasons can be adduced to suggest that Cato gave the date as either 693 or *c.* 600; the latter has been widely accepted. Recently Pallottino has tried to justify Cato's apparent date of 471 on the basis of his belief in the south-to-north direction of the Etruscan domination of Campania and his views about Aristodemus of Cumae. He points out that the anti-Etruscan oligarchs whom Aristodemus drove out of Cumae when he became tyrant, fled to Capua (see below); this would be curious if Capua was already in Etruscan hands. This fact, combined with the absence in the story of Aristodemus of any suggestion that Capua was in Etruscan hands, suggests that Cato's date should be accepted, despite the consequential short life that this would allow to Etruscan Capua.[129]

New evidence for the pattern of settlement in Campania is however coming to light. In addition to the Villanovan crema-tions, together with some *a fossa* inhumations in the Salerno area which have already been mentioned (pp. 27f), three phases of early settlement have now been found at Capua. Burials dating from at least *c.* 750 BC have been discovered, some of which are inhumations and others typical Villanovan cremations with material similar to that of central Etruria. This is also the period of the foundation of Cumae and the spread of Greek influences in Campania. Then by *c.* 650 imported Etruscan *bucchero leggero* and local imitations begin to appear; finally heavy *bucchero* is found. Similar material has been found near the temple of Diana Tifatina and at Cales, and indeed farther north between Cales and Teanum. Until all this new evidence is fully assessed it would be rash to build too much upon it, but it certainly suggests that the Etruscan phase at Capua may have begun by the mid-seventh century and that one route, if not the only route, by which the Etruscans reached Campania was by land.[130]

The later city of Capua (*Pl. 89*), which had a rectangular street-plan (*per strigas*), had two quarters named Albana and Seplasia (Cicero, *de leg. agr.* 2, 94). It is just possible that the latter was an Etruscan word and that Albana was the earlier, possibly Oscan, name. The name 'Capua' was variously explained by the ancients: it derived from *campus* (*cf.* Campania), from *caput* (as head of the Campanian colonies), from Capys (an eponymous hero who was nurtured by a hind, as Romulus and Remus were by the wolf), and from *capys*, the Etruscan word for falcon. The suggestion that the name comes from an Etruscan family, *cape* or *capna*, is attractive.[131] The 'Etruscanizing' of Capua and the other Campanian cities is seen most clearly in the language. Surviving Etruscan inscriptions, apart from the long one on the Capuan tile, are found on vases of which the earliest date to *c.* 500, and the latest *c.* 300. These show that the Etruscan language was not only spoken widely, but must also have taken fairly deep root since it continued to be used for some time after Capua had been overrun by the Samnites, as is shown by the later vases. The interrelationship of the two peoples is illustrated by an inscription in the Oscan language but written in Etruscan letters, which records that 'Venox Venilius gave the wine-vessel to Venilius Vinicius' (*vinuchs veneliis meraciam tetet venilei viniciiu*). Although the vase may have been made in the first half of the fifth century, the inscription may be a little later. An Etruscan workman has inscribed it for an Oscan purchaser, while the names suggest that a Samnite family, the Vinicii, were closely linked with bearers of Etruscan names, Venox and Venel.

The bronze industry of Capua, famous still in Roman times, was profoundly influenced by Greek work but it developed a speciality of its own in the bronze cauldrons, with lids decorated with figures, *e.g.* a Silenus and maenad surrounded by galloping horses; here the inspiration was Etruscan. There is a fine specimen in the British Museum, which owes much to Greece and dates from the end of the sixth century. Campania was also famous for its painted tombs, but these belong to the period after the Etruscan occupation, except one, of which now only a drawing survives: it shows two men wearing mantles, seated on folding chairs with a game-board between them, and dates to *c.* 470 BC. To what extent the later paintings of gaily-caparisoned cavaliers with plumed helmets and cloaks, and of gladiators fighting to the last gasp (*c.* 300 BC), drew their inspiration from earlier Etruscan paintings cannot, in the absence of any surviving originals, be assessed.[132]

Capua was a very rich centre for the production of terracotta roof-tiles, of the common type that spread from Greece to south Italy, Campania, Latium and Etruria; our ignorance of the precise artists may be disguised by calling them Etrusco-Campanian. These temple decorations provide some evidence for the early temples. In the fondo Patturelli on the east side of the city they attest the existence of a temple which goes back to *c.* 550. Here a vast hoard of over six thousand terracotta votive offerings to a mother-goddess was found; although nearly all of them belong to a later period of the temple's history, a few of the statuettes of women may be contemporary with the ante-fixes of the end of the sixth century. The more famous temple of Diana Tifatina outside Capua is also shown, by a few archi-tectural terracottas which resemble those of Cumae, to go back to 550–500. The inspiration of the terracotta decoration was Greek, but Capua added her own touch to this form of art which she helped to spread within the common culture of central Italy, with its complicated pattern of interacting influences from Magna Graecia to Etruria. Thus there is sufficient evidence to suggest that Capua was a prosperous and wealthy city under the

Etruscans. The luxurious life of the Capuan nobles later became a byword for bad influences among the moralists, who cited as an example the ennervating effect on Hannibal's troops of a winter spent amid its attractions. Something of this tradition may well antedate the Samnite period and reflect the habits of the Etruscan overlords.

If Capua was an Etruscan city by 524 it must have taken a prominent part in the attack which the Etruscans decided to launch upon Greek Cumae. Unfortunately our sources, as so often happens, speak merely of 'the Etruscans' without specifying the individual cities. The initiative could have come from the cities of Etruria proper in an attempt to establish or increase their hold on Campania, or from the cities of Campania who had got sufficient hold on the rest of the area to be able to try to squeeze out the chief Greek city: much depends on the uncertain chronology. Dionysius' account of the attack is embroidered with fictions: he records that the Etruscans, helped by Umbrians and Daunians, numbered more than half a million; and that the Cumaeans would not have resisted if they had not been encouraged by the miracle of the rivers Volturnus and Clanis starting to run backwards. The numbers he ascribes to the Cumaeans are more reasonable: a third of their force defended the city, a third guarded their ships (what, one wonders, was the 'Etruscan' navy doing?), while four thousand five hundred infantry and six hundred horsemen, the men of real military age, defeated the Etruscans in a narrow defile, probably to the north of the city. Of the Cumaeans the palm for bravery went to Aristodemus, who then proceeded to champion the people against the aristocrats, in a way that was normal in a Greek city.

When in 510 the Etruscan Tarquinius was driven from Rome, the other Latin cities were encouraged to seek freedom from the Etruscans. In resisting Etruscan counter-attacks they appealed to Cumae which sent a force by sea under Aristodemus. He routed the Etruscans under Arruns, the son of Lars Porsenna of Clusium (see p. 262), at Aricia in *c.* 506. The victorious Latins could now cut the land communications between Etruria and Campania. Aristodemus, however, used his popularity to seize power and

became tyrant of Cumae, employing some of the Etruscans captured in the battle as a bodyguard. Those aristocrats who escaped
found refuge in Capua, until some time after 490 when they
managed to regain Cumae and kill Aristodemus. Meanwhile
Aristodemus, who was nicknamed the Soft, *Malakos*, had tried
to eliminate all potential resistance to himself, especially among
the rising generation, by suppressing gymnastic and military
exercises and bringing up all the children as girls. The lurid picture
which Dionysius gives of this attempt to unman the youth of
Cumae has suggested that in fact Aristodemus was encouraging
a more luxurious way of life, such as flourished in Sybaris and
some Etruscan cities. The 'Etruscanization', however, need not
have been reflected in the political field though it is just con-
ceivable that it was chiefly the Cumaean nobles who had pursued
a hostile policy towards the Etruscans, which Aristodemus could
have relaxed after his victory at Aricia. But one need not go so
far as to postulate an active friendship on which to base the
hypothesis that if the Capuans did not kill, imprison or extradite
the Cumaean nobles, it must have been because Capua was not
an Etruscan city at this date. Capua might even have given
asylum to the refugees, thinking that one day they might prove
a useful weapon against Aristodemus.[133]

The days of the Etruscans in Campania were now numbered.
After their defeat at Aricia their land communications with the
north were at the mercy of the Latins: hence the maintenance of
their mastery of the sea-routes, demonstrated at Alalia, was vital.
Once again, Cumae, which had resisted the Etruscan attack in
524 and then took the offensive in helping at Aricia, was enabled
to play a crucial role. This was because of the changing fortunes
of the Greeks in Sicily, who had smashed a Carthaginian invasion
at Himera in 480. This resounding victory not only saved the
Sicilian Greeks from Carthage but also enhanced the rising
strength of Syracuse, which under its ruler Hiero a few years
later saved the Italiote Greeks from the Etruscans by responding
to an appeal for help from Cumae in 474. Two episodes, which
are unfortunately not dated, may perhaps belong here. Strabo
(6, 1, 5) records that Anaxilas, the tyrant of Rhegium, built a

naval station at the rock of Scylla (Scyllaion) in order to protect the straits of Messina against the Etruscans. This action has often been placed early in his reign which started in 494, but it fits in better after the Carthaginian defeat at Himera; before the battle Anaxilas had been friendly with the Carthaginians and would therefore be less likely to take action which would offend their allies, the Etruscans; it appears, too, that merchandise was passing freely through the straits without Etruscan interference in the early fifth century.[134] The second episode is recorded in the *elogium* from Tarquinii which tells of the exploit of the 'praetor' who was the first Etruscan general to lead an army overseas to Sicily (see p. 91). This undated episode could well refer to some action taken before Himera or some anticipatory action on the eve of the Syracusan attack in 474.

However that may be, when Hiero received the appeal from Cumae for help against the Etruscans, he responded in a way that would have been too risky before Himera. Whether Cumae was fearing another Etruscan attack or whether she took the initiative in an attempt to deliver a further blow against Etruscan power, the combined fleets of Syracuse and Cumae met and defeated the Etruscans off Cumae. Among the spoils which the victors dedicated at Olympia were at least two bronze helmets, inscribed with the words, 'Hieron, son of Deinomenes, and the Syracusans (dedicated) to Zeus the Etruscan spoils won at Cumae': one now rests in the British Museum (*Pl. 91*).[135] The victory was also celebrated in one of Pindar's Odes to Hieron (*Pyth.* 1, 71):

> 'Grant, I beseech thee, O son of Cronus, that the battle-shout of the Carthaginians and Etruscans may abide at home in peace and quiet, now that they have seen that their over-weening insolence off Cumae hath brought lamentation on their ships; such were their losses, when vanquished by the lord of the Syracusans,—a fate which flung their young warriors from their swift ships into the sea, delivering Hellas from grievous bondage.' (Transl. J. E. Sandys.)

Thus the earliest and most northerly of the Greek colonies in

Italy regained the freedom of the seas around Naples, and the Etruscan cities in Campania were isolated.

In the event neither victors nor vanquished in Italy enjoyed an independent existence in Campania for very long. Soon the Sabellian tribes were descending from the hills to the fertile plain below. Capua succumbed in 423 if not before, and Cumae in 421; virtually the whole of Campania from Cumae to Salerno became Sabellian. But the superior Greek and Etruscan civilization of the earlier inhabitants soon conquered the hardy Samnite mountaineers who adapted their mode of life to their new surroundings, and Capua and the other cities entered a new phase in their history.[136]

CHAPTER VII

ETRUSCAN EXPANSION IN NORTH ITALY

THE ETRUSCAN OCCUPATION of the valley of the Po, or what may be called Etruria Padana, was regarded by Livy (5, 33) and other ancient writers as a deliberate act of colonization by the twelve cities of Etruria, who sent out twelve colonies beyond the Apennines and 'took possession of all the region beyond the Po as far as the Alps, except the angle belonging to the Veneti'. Archaeological evidence, and the absence of it, has shown that Livy's statement is wildly exaggerated, but before the real extent of Etruscan penetration is examined, we should look at the three pivotal points which were established by the Etruscans, the development of which has been illuminated recently by archaeology: Felsina, Marzabotto and Spina. These were the first real cities ever to be formed in the Po valley; and each made its peculiar contribution to creating a firm basis for the political, economic and cultural life of Etruria Padana[137] (Fig. 23).

FELSINA (BOLOGNA)

The Etruscan city of Felsina retained its name until 196 BC (Livy 33, 37); shortly after this it received a Latin colony and was named Bononia, after the Gallic tribe of the Boii who had assailed it. Although Tarquinii claimed that the foundation of all the cities north of the Apennines was due to its own hero Tarchon, Perusia asserted that Ocnus, the brother of its own founder, had established Felsina: hence the poet Silius Italicus could call it 'Ocni prisca domus'. When Pliny named it 'princeps Etruriae', he was presumably attributing to it pre-eminence among the Etruscan cities of the Po valley. Where the impetus for its establishment came from, we simply do not know: it

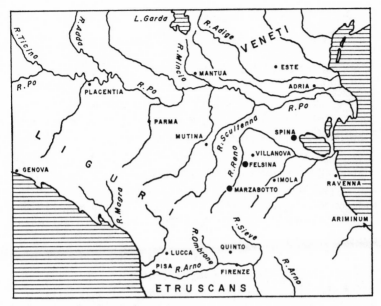

Fig. 23 Map of northern Italy

may have been from one of the cities of northern Etruria—
certainly the tomb at Quinto Fiorentino marks the northern
progress of Etruscan interests (*Pls. 84-86*)—but the late emergence of Etruscan Perusia does not make it a very likely candidate
for the role of mother-city. Nor do we know anything about the
process, or the reaction of the Villanovan settlement. Was peaceful co-existence established with the Villanovans or did the new
colony have to use force to overawe them? There is some little
evidence for a 'cultural hiatus' in the Villanovan settlement
between 550 and 520, and a consequent decline; if this could be
accepted, it would indicate that the Etruscan settlement is more
likely to have been peaceful. Again, Etruscan cultural influences
which appear to have been spreading into the area for some time,
may have prepared the ground and made the new settlement less
obnoxious. Whatever the process, the significant fact is that for
the first time a *city* had been established in an area which hitherto
had known only tribal organization. The Etruscans presumably
did not merely infiltrate into or take over a Villanovan settlement,

but sent a considerable nucleus of colonists from the south to lay out a new city, as others did at Marzabotto where more evidence survives.

The existence of Roman, medieval and modern Bologna has obliterated the plan of Felsina and its precise relation to the Villanovan settlement. The latter had consisted of several villages between the Reno and Sevena rivers; how far they were united is not known. The cemeteries lay outside the area of settlement, to the east and west, with the earliest ones naturally nearer in. The distribution of huts, as plotted on a plan, shows lines stretching north and south along the Via d'Azeglio and Via dell' Independenza, and east and west especially along roads leading west, Vie San Felice and Sant' Isaia. These naturally would suggest old routes from the Apennines to the Po and laterally along the base of the hills, but lines on a plan may be deceptive since more huts are likely to be found under relatively open streets than under the blocks of medieval buildings between them. It is thought that the acropolis of Felsina lay on the hill of the Osservanza convent west-south-west of the modern city, and that the rest of the ancient city spread northwards and eastwards from there, but only partly over the area occupied by the Villanovans. If it is legitimate to draw on the layout of Marzabotto as an analogy, then the higher ground may have contained the chief temple area and have been the religious centre, with the more populated area below it bound intimately to it; the only difference would be that at Marzabotto the sacred area was north of the settlement, but this was necessitated by the ground.

The extent of Felsina cannot be determined, since some of the Etruscan remains seem rather far apart to be included strictly in the same city. A road probably ran east and west by the line of the Via Saragozza and the Viale Gozzadini at the foot of the southern hill; apparently abandoned in Roman times, it came into use again with the Middle Ages. Some huts near the Porta Sant' Isaia suggest a way leading westwards to the cemeteries, a *via dei sepolcri*, along the earlier Villanovan route. Thus Felsina remained the centre on which old routes converged and these became even more important with the increase of trade eastwards

92 A funeral *stele* from Felsina
(Bologna) dating from the first half of
the fourth century BC, and 4 feet high.
The dead man is shown in his chariot,
as in life, but with a hint of his last
journey. Below, a she-wolf suckles a
child: probably based on a local legend
(*cf.* Romulus). See p.201.

93 Another Felsina horse-shoe *stele*,
of *c.* 400 BC. Above, a serpent and
hippocamp. In centre, the dead man
escorted to the Underworld by a
winged demon. Below, an Etruscan
cavalryman engages a Gallic warrior
on foot; this reflects the fierce struggles
when the Gauls swept over northern
Italy. See pp.202, 204 219.

94 Air view of the north-west part of Marzabotto (the top of the picture is the south), showing an area of excavation. The southern part of the city spread beyond the top edge of the picture. Below centre, beyond the modern road, is the acropolis (Misanello) with the sacred area. See Fig. 24 and p.205. 95 Podium of Etruscan altar in the sacred area. See p.206. 96 Foundations of Etruscan houses. See p.206.

to Spina and the Adriatic, northwards to the Po and over the Alps to central Europe, westwards to newer areas in Lombardy, and lastly southwards to Etruria itself. It used to be thought that the Etruscan cemeteries were kept quite distinct from the Villanovan, but what was regarded as a dividing ditch in the Arnoaldi cemetery proves to be the bed of a stream, and in 1950 a group of tombs belonging to both the fourth Villanovan period and the Etruscan occupation was found. The tombs are *a fossa* with small stones; those in the west are cremations mixed with inhumations, while in the east inhumation decisively prevails and the tombs seem richer. The sites were marked by cippi or inscribed *stelae*.

These *stelae* are a characteristic feature of the art and industry of Felsina (*Pl. 92*). Over two hundred are known, dating mainly from *c.* 500 to 350 BC. They have a rounded or disc-like top with a long rectangular stone body; the shape may represent a schematic human body or, less probably, a solar disc. Gradually they became horse-shoe shaped, and were divided into three carved zones, with the figures originally coloured. The tradition of the *stelae* goes back to Villanovan times before the full Etruscan period. One which has been found recently in connection with a tomb of Villanovan III (*cf.* p. 24) has been worked over twice: the first scene dating to the first half of the seventh century shows lotus palmettes, symbolizing the tree of life, while the second, dating to the second half of the century, depicts a chariot drawn by a horse, symbolizing the journey to the underworld. This became a common theme, and the *stele* may be linked with a stone from a Villanovan grave, the *pietra Zannoni*, which shows a man in a chariot led by a demon or deity to the underworld; this is clearly under Etruscan influence and belongs to about 500. The two other *stelae* show similar oriental motives. One, of the early sixth century, shows goats on either side of the tree of life on the disc, with below a man and animal on each side. The other, somewhat later, has a sphinx in the disc, and goats and the tree below. A *stele* of the beginning of the fifth century depicts on its disc two warriors facing each other and on its rectangular body two horses and riders. An increasingly frequent theme on the horse-shoe type is a warrior, that is, the dead man is represented in one of his lifetime activities, with perhaps a suggestion of heroization. At any rate battle scenes become more common and the reason was that the Etruscans of Felsina began to face the menace of attack by Gallic tribes who were pressing southwards and who ultimately overwhelmed the Etruscanized Po valley, which then became Cisalpine Gaul (*Pl. 93*). But while from *c.* 400 BC Etruscans fighting Gauls became a frequent subject, others more reminiscent of the southern Etruscans were popular: scenes of hunting, banquets, dancing, games, musicians, horse-racing, sphinxes, hippocamps and other monsters. Occasionally the man's name was inscribed. Thus we have the tomb of Vele Kaiknas. This seven-foot stone shows Caecina passing to the underworld in a chariot drawn by winged horses and led by demons, one of whom is blowing a trumpet; below is a boxing scene in honour of the dead, and in the bottom panel are a standard-bearer and three trumpeters. Caecina probably came from Volaterrae (see p. 169), a city where 'Fiesole' *stelae* are found (see p. 149).

It is in the context of these northern *stelae* that those of Felsina should be set. They present an interesting contrast with southern Etruscan practice in that, although they show scenes of feasting, etc., similar to the wall-paintings at Tarquinii, the latter were hidden underground for only the dead to 'see', while at Felsina the living are, as it were, invited to look at the man and his activities in life and death: in other words, these *stelae* offer a more personal and monumental record. In inspiration also they show a real artistic individuality. Although they are influenced by Villanovan, Etruscan and Greek artistic ideas, their creators have not merely copied but have selected and adapted what they wished from these traditions. With bronze work it is always more difficult to distinguish local work from imported wares, but with the *stelae* we have clearly a local school and tradition.

These local sculptors have left little beside the *stelae*. One head in the round, made from the local stone, survives from the first half of the sixth century: it is probably a sphinx and under Ionian influence. Either this start was not continued, or all other products of these artists have perished. In continuation of

Villanovan times, there was a great volume of production of bronze objects for everyday use, and some of these *oenochoae* and *stamnoi* were exported, but few bronzes are outstanding artistically; from *c.* 400 BC they become more homogeneous, which suggests greater standardization, if not mass production. Figures of athletes and bronze candelabra were popular. Two famous bronzes were found in a votive deposit at Monteguragazza, some twenty miles south of Bologna and nearer to Marzabotto than to Bologna; thus they can scarcely be classed as typical of the best work of Felsina. They are statuettes of a *kouros* and a *kore*, of *c.* 480 BC (*Pls. 98, 99*). The youth is in the tradition of Greek *kouroi*, but is not naked like a Greek athlete; his garment has slipped round his waist and he is holding out a libation-dish in an attitude of reverence. The girl holds out a flower and a pomegranate. Thus the type has been adapted to a religious purpose, while they have been compared with the Ajax from Populonia (*Pl. 63*) and the terracotta statues from Veii.

Another famous object is the Certosa *situla*, found in the cemetery on the site of the convent of the Certosa, outside the Porta Sant' Isaia of Bologna (the whole Etruscan period at Felsina has sometimes been called the Certosan). It had been used as an ossuary, and associated objects date it to the early fifth century (*Pl. 8*). Around it run four bands on which are little reliefs which illustrate aspects of local life. The top row shows a procession of soldiers, two horsemen and seventeen infantrymen, with varying equipment, *e.g.* oval, round and rectangular shields. Below comes a religious procession, presumably the funeral cortège, priests, women carrying vessels on their heads, others with faggots, two pairs of men carrying large urns, and animals for sacrifice. The next row is a cameo of country life: a ploughman has just unyoked his oxen and is carrying a light plough over his shoulder; a labourer drags along the body of a pig on which a bird has rested; two men bear on a pole the stag they have caught in the chase, while underneath runs a dog; and a hunter is driving a hare into a net. In the bottom row is a series of animals and monsters, reminiscent of oriental and Ionian art. This *situla* resembles others that have been found as far away as the Tyrol and Austria, and especially one from Este (ancient Ateste) which was the centre of an Iron Age culture in Venetia, but it may well be the prototype of the others and can be regarded as a local work, produced under strong Etruscan influence; it is a fine social document for conditions of life in Etruscan Felsina.

Another feature of the life of the upper classes was the extraordinary number of Attic vases that were imported, both black- and red-figure, including the work of some of the best painters. They range from the latter part of the sixth century to the beginning of the fourth, but the greater number belong to the first part of the fifth; after 450 BC the number begins to diminish. They were of course the possessions of the wealthy, whose taste they reflect; the everyday pottery was produced locally, with some imitations of the Attic ware. Another luxury import is seen in gold and ivory work, including a miniature chryselephantine warrior, reminiscent of the great statues of this mixed material in Periclean Athens.

Felsina thus gives the impression of a prosperous city of merchants and industrialists; farmers there must have been, but not necessarily a landed aristocracy. Indeed the tombs suggest that wealth may have been spread reasonably evenly in the community. A middle class appears to be attested by the hoplite soldiers, though no doubt these citizen-soldiers, captained perhaps by some of the men who are figured on the funeral *stelae*, only became prominent when the Gallic raids began (*Pl. 93*). A further interesting feature on Caecna's *stele* is a ship with some marines on board. This is a reminder that Felsina had interests in the Adriatic, the route by which Attic vases reached Spina, whence they came overland to the city. Nor were the upper class so devoted to industry and commerce that they had no time for culture. This passion for the best painted vases that Athens was producing, combined with the efforts of their own local artists, suggests at least a cultured minority. The Etruscans also brought with them a language and the means to write it, together with the whole conception of city life. They also had their legends and traditions, a fascinating suggestion of which survives: on a *stele* is a wolf suckling a child, an Etruscan Romulus without his brother? (*Pl. 92*). Or perhaps it is a fragment of a family rather than a city tradition.[138]

MARZABOTTO

In the valley of the Reno, some seventeen miles south of Bologna, is the site of an Etruscan city, whose ancient name is uncertain, but may have been Misa or Misna; it is near the modern village of Marzabotto. The exceptional importance of the site is that we have a new Etruscan foundation, which can be dated to *c.* 500 BC and has not been built over in later times. In contrast with Felsina, which had to take some notice of an established Villanovan settlement, Marzabotto was laid out on virtually virgin ground. There is evidence for late Chalcolithic men, and very recently some traces of the late Villanovan period (IV) have been found, but the planners are not likely to have been obstructed by existing buildings. We can now see how the Etruscans laid out a city at a given time, though it is dangerous to assume that earlier cities were based on the same principles (*cf.* pp. 77f).

The city (*Pl. 94*) consisted of two parts: a large level terrace (Pian di Misano) and a height to the north-west; the former was the site of the inhabited part, the latter a religious centre with temples and altars. But the whole was essentially a unit, planned and executed as such. The buildings in the temple area, which was originally some sixty feet above the other part, are aligned with the buildings below. The latter were regarded as an extension of the sacred citadel which had determined the ritual lay-out of the whole settlement, orientated in accordance with astronomical and priestly rules. It was a sizeable city, with a circuit of some $2\frac{1}{2}$ miles. The south-west corner, below which the Reno flows, has partly crumbled away in land-slides. The main street runs north and south, corresponding probably to an old route from Etruria to the northern plain of Italy; it is very wide—some fifty feet—and it is crossed by three streets at right angles, themselves some seventeen feet broad. The whole area, therefore, consists of blocks of rectangular *insulae*, which are much longer in the north–south direction than they are wide. They are separated by boundary channels, and within them the houses are divided into rectangular rooms, similarly orientated, although the actual arrangement of the rooms was varied (*Pl. 95*). Many of the houses are approached by a long corridor with a covered channel beneath it which drained into the channels along the streets. The corridor led to a central inner courtyard, around which the houses and rooms were arranged. In the courtyards were wells. Several of the houses on the main north–south street were dwellings, factories and shops combined. Within some were found quantities of iron-slag and tools, showing that this was an industrial area, while the manufactured goods could be exposed for sale on the wide pavements outside. Only the foundations of the buildings survive, consisting of river boulders bedded in mud, with occasional blocks of travertine. The houses were probably fairly low, not much over ten or twelve feet high; their walls were made of partly-fired bricks, roofed over with wooden beams covered with tiles. Many large tiles, some three feet wide, have been found, and the quality of the clay is good. The grid system, with its parallels at Selinus and elsewhere (see p. 76) reveals a town-planning that appears to be Greek, but there are differences; for instance in Greek cities the industrial area was banished to the outskirts, whereas here it was central. In 1964 a potters' quarter was found in the north-west part of the city (Regio II, insula 1), with furnaces for the production of bricks and tiles (Fig. 24).

The sacred area was separated from the 'town' below it not only by a terraced wall but also by the most northerly of the east–west streets that ran at its foot. Of the temples the oldest, which has also been considered to be an altar, has a travertine podium (*Pl. 96*). The large Temple C has three *cellae*, but not enough remains to afford a basis for reconstruction; part of its foundations rests on ground that has been artificially levelled, and a votive deposit has been found. On the slopes of the hill is an elaborate water system, with a central cistern and distributing channels; in fact the drainage system of the whole town is remarkable. Farther north lay a cemetery, while a second was situated east of the town. Cremation was the normal burial rite.

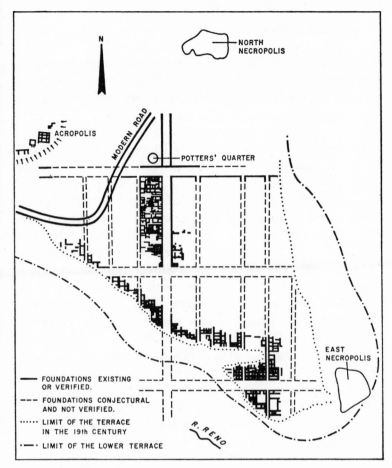

Fig. 24 *Plan of Marzabotto*

Excavation has confirmed an approximate date of 500 BC for its foundation, but why was it founded? It was a useful halting place between Etruria and the north on one of the main routes over the Apennines. As well as being protected in part by the natural heights and the river in the west, it was also probably walled: it would thus give cover against any wilder people in the Apennines, such as the Ligures Friniates. But its wide streets and large extent do not suggest a garrison town or a primarily military purpose. Rather it was established as an economic centre for trade and industry, especially for iron work. Its inhabitants doubtless practised some agriculture, raised stock, and exploited the well-wooded neighbourhood: timber was in great demand for house-building. But the bare wood was often covered with tiles, and the production of these and pottery for home use was on a considerable scale. Some temple terracottas survive: antefixes with coloured palmettes, and two heads of men in terracotta. Some pottery discs, probably jar covers, were inscribed apparently with a personal name in the genitive, for instance 'I belong to Laris Krikal'. Local bronze work is represented by brooches and bracelets, ex-voto statuettes from a temple deposit, and also an interesting bronze figure of a man wearing a *tebenna* (first half of fifth century). In contrast with Felsina, only one sculptured *stele* is known, showing the dead woman as a votary. The tombs were like boxes, made of slabs of travertine, on which were cippi or little columns: some of these cippi were bulbous like onions, one even being of marble and decorated with horsemen and soldiers. These find their nearest parallels south of the Apennines in the district of Fiesole and Chiusi. So also a *bucchero*-type impasto head of a man is linked with the art of Chiusi. Imports included a considerable number of Attic vases, which came by way of the Adriatic, Spina and Felsina. A unique find is a marble head of a *kouros*, Greek work of *c.* 500 BC. From southern Etruria came gold jewellery, both filigree and granulated, and some bronzes. The latter include a famous piece, originally the top of a candelabrum: on it are two standing figures which represent not Mars and Venus, but a soldier and his wife who is offering a libation for her departing warrior; it is dated to the early fourth century (*Pl. 97*).

Marzabotto commanded the Reno valley, but it was not alone. Where the valley debouches into the plain just south-west of Bologna there was a settlement at Casalecchio where Etruscan occupation follows immediately upon Villanovan. Finds indicate many other small settlements, together with a votive deposit of *c.* 400 BC at Monte Capra, as well as the sanctuary at Monteguragazza. The northern cities needed a secure passage to their homeland.[139]

97 Bronze statuette of
departing warrior and his
wife, of early fourth century
BC, from Marzabotto. See
p.208. 98, 99 Bronze
statuettes of a young woman
and man (*kore* and *kouros*)
depicted as worshippers, of
c. 480 BC from Monteguragazza near Marzabotto. See
p.203.

100 Painted plaque from Caere, showing a king (or ruler), before the statue of a goddess. See p.222.

101 Air view of Spina. Under the white lines of modern drainage are an ancient canal (top right), dark lines of ancient canal-ways, and light *insulae* of dwellings. See p.209.

SPINA

At the head of the Adriatic, between Venice and Ravenna, lay Spina, the third of the main Etruscan cities beyond the Apennines (*Pl. 101*). But unlike Marzabotto it was not a purely Etruscan foundation, nor was it, like Felsina, an Etruscan city superimposed on or around a Villanovan settlement. Rather it was a Greek settlement in which the Etruscans got a strong foothold; in the fifth century it became the chief port in the Adriatic and the centre through which Greek goods, especially Athenian vases, reached the markets of northern Italy.

Despite references in the Classical writers the site long remained unknown, largely because of changing conditions in the Po delta. The river Po (the ancient Padus; Virgil's 'fluviorum rex') in the course of over four hundred miles brought down great quantities of silt and splayed out into an area of lagoons and sandbars, so that Polybius could describe it as having two chief mouths, while Pliny some two hundred years later enumerated seven. During drainage and land reclamation work in Valle Trebba, some four miles west of Comacchio, a necropolis was found in 1922, containing 1213 tombs, and since 1954 another cemetery in Valle Pega has yielded no less than 2398 more. From these water-logged and muddy graves the excavators have brought to light not only skeletons clutching the money with which to pay Charon their ferry tolls, but also gold earrings, amber necklaces, alabaster perfume-bottles, children's dolls and game-counters, and above all, hundreds upon hundreds of Greek vases, which are now the pride of the Ferrara museum. Then in 1956 with the help of aerial photography the site of the city itself was discovered. The houses were built on wooden platforms and piles, on a rectangular chessboard pattern intersected by canals, at once recalling Venice or Strabo's description of Ravenna in the time of Augustus: 'the largest city in the marshes, built of (or on) wood and intersected by water; bridges and ferries provide the thoroughfares'. The area of habitation was over 740 acres. A harbour was formed by a canal, extended to some sixty feet wide, which joined the sea. This is reminiscent of the main thoroughfare at Marzabotto, as are the other details of the layout.

It is not easy to distinguish the Greek and Etruscan contributions to the settlement, since Greek writers not unnaturally asserted a purely Greek origin. Hellanicus attributed it to the Pelasgians, whom he equated with the Tyrrhenians: driven from Greece, they landed by the river Spines, left their ships there, and then pressed on inland. Dionysius elaborates the story: those left behind later built a city called Spina. Strabo reflects the same tradition, but stresses the native Umbrian background of Spina and her neighbour, Ravenna, which he says was founded by Thessalians: 'but since they could not endure the outrages of the Tyrrhenians, they voluntarily took in some Ombrici, who still now hold the city, whereas they themselves returned home'. This tradition is generally rejected (Strabo may have meant Pelasgians when he referred to Thessalians), though an abortive Thessalian colonization in the sixth century has been accepted by at least one scholar (R. L. Beaumont). On the other hand Pliny attributed the foundation of Spina to the Greek hero Diomede, while in the geographical work of Pseudo-Scylax the Etruscan background is stressed. These legends, combined with the unlikelihood of the mouth of Italy's greatest river remaining long uninhabited, have suggested the possibility of some early settlement, but there is no archaeological evidence to support this view, although there is such evidence for a foundation in the late sixth century. If a Greek foundation is accepted, no one mother-city can be named; it could have been a joint enterprise in which Athens probably played a part, since the later Greek imports were predominantly Attic. If the population was mixed, the possibility of some Etruscan co-operation from the beginning cannot be excluded. At any rate Etruscans soon moved in, since Etruscan as well as Greek *graffiti* are found on the vases, and other Etruscan elements appear in Spinate culture.

Two main facts recorded about Spina's later history can be accepted with less hesitation: her naval influence in the Adriatic and her Treasury at Delphi. The only fully Etruscan city that kept such a Treasury was Caere-Agylla. Spina's commercial interest clearly lay in maintaining good relations with the Greeks, and she could display her goodwill by joining the many cities that kept these national monuments at the great religious centre of Greece. Although Greeks and Etruscans came to blows in the west in the early fifth century, reciprocal interests kept them friendly in the Adriatic, where not only had piracy to be checked but the Greek states in the southern part, Corcyra and Epidamnus, had to be persuaded not to interfere with the passage of goods. Thus the foundation of Spina must be regarded as a Greek attempt to open up new markets in northern Italy with the active co-operation of the Etruscans who themselves had not long turned to this area.

Of the cultural level of Spina the greatest witness is the quantity of Greek vases that the inhabitants purchased for themselves and buried with their dead. The citizens were not mere middlemen, although the general similarity of the vases found there and at Felsina shows that the latter city imported her supply from Spina. The finds are virtually an epitome of Attic pottery from the end of the sixth century, and provide examples of the work of many of the master painters. In fact the appeal of the vases to the Etruscan Spinates may have been in part because they reproduced scenes from the full-scale paintings of the Greek world, which of course are now all lost to us, and Etruscans liked paintings; further, large *craters* were particularly popular, and these would show up more decoratively the scenes of the classical myths and heroes that were thus disseminated in a new area of the ancient world. Beside Attic vases Spina traded in those from other parts of Italy, though not on the same scale, and her own potters produced copies of the Greek ware. Among terracotta works are many *askoi* in the form of animals, increasing numbers of which were made from the end of the fifth century onwards. Many of these came from Athens, but others probably from Clusium. Much gold-work was imported, diadems, *bullae*, and especially earrings. Though the technique of the granulation of the diadems resembles that of Vulci, many of the earrings are curved tubes ending with the protome of an animal and these resemble work from Tarentum. Much of the goldwork therefore probably came from Magna Graecia where it was the product of a flourishing industry in the fifth and fourth centuries.

The bronze work in general seems to be of Etruscan origin, some of the best coming from Vulci and other pieces from northern Etruria, while a *situla* points to a Venetic origin. Thus Spina drew on Greece, Etruria and to some extent on its hinterland for its artistic life.[140]

ETRURIA PADANA

Etruscan power and influence north of the Apennines thus rested on these three cities. Felsina was the heart from which the arteries of trade radiated. Its productive and distributive activity was supplemented by Marzabotto, while Etruscan influence at Spina ensured a steady flow of Greek goods into the northern plain of Italy, paralleling the wares that continued to come from Etruria itself in the south. Thus this area of the earlier Villanovan culture became increasingly subjected to Etruscan and Greek influences, and a new cultural *facies*, as archaeologists like to designate it, came into being. How far this extended and, still more, over what area one can speak of the spread of Etruscan power are extremely difficult questions.

The view of Livy that the Etruscans spread over the northern plain as far as the Alps is not supported by archaeology and cannot be accepted. The area was not empty territory, and any people expanding into it would run up against other tribes—Ligurians in the west, Gauls in the north, Veneti in the east, and Umbrians coming up from the south. Livy, together with Diodorus and Servius, also speaks of a league of twelve Etruscan cities, a dodecapolis, north of the Po, and suggests that these twelve cities were sent out by the twelve cities of Etruria itself. This scheme, however, like that of the similar Etruscan dodecapolis in Campania, looks like an artificial literary creation. It is premature to speak at this time of twelve cities in the Po valley (although Plutarch does say that the Gauls destroyed no less than eighteen): urbanization can scarcely have advanced so quickly. It would not be easy to provide a certain list of the twelve: they could be Felsina, Misa (? Marzabotto), Spina, Adria, Melpum, Mantua, Parma, Mutina, Placentia, Ariminum and Ravenna. But it is unreasonable to regard such cities as linked together in any federation, when it is far from certain whether the majority should even be considered to be Etruscan in any basic sense.

One method of approaching the problem is by means of any place-names which could be related to Etruscan personal names. But any attempt to distinguish various layers of pre-Indo-European names (linguistic stratigraphy) is beset with difficulties. What then is the archaeological evidence? West of Felsina Etruscan influence clearly thins out at Mutina and Parma and decreases rapidly farther west. The natural line of expansion was along the foothills of the Apennines and the route of the later Via Aemilia. Finds at Galassina di Castelvetro in the area of Modena (Mutina) include Etruscan bronzes and Attic vases; general similarity with the material from Felsina suggests expansion from this centre. Farther west in the district of Reggio finds at Servirola San Polo on the Enza suggest at most what has been called an Etruscoid rather than Etruscan *facies*: the basic culture is local, and imported bronzes and vases are associated with others which are local interpretations of 'foreign' forms. Other isolated finds in this area likewise are not typically Felsinine. In the district of Parma only one tomb is known, at Fraore, but this was a rich example, containing some gold work. Velia, some seventeen miles south of Piacenza, has yielded a little material which suggests only commercial contacts. The dominating position of Piacenza (Placentia) itself, commanding the crossing of the Po, would attract the interest of the Etruscans if they wished to trade with, or defend themselves against, the Gauls to the north of the river. There is, however, no evidence for Etruscan occupation apart from the famous bronze liver used for hepatoscopy; this is an isolated object and is probably intrusive. Thus the picture of the district south of the Po and west of Bologna so far presented by archaeology is that small groups of Etruscans may have settled in the district of Modena and possibly Parma, but hardly as far as Velia.

In the Romagna east of Bologna there are no traces of true Etruscan settlement. There are only some 'Etruscoid' elements west of Imola, while objects at Malatesta (Imola) belong to what seems to have been essentially a Villanovan settlement. At

Persolina di Faenza some local pottery with fragments of Attic red-figure vases belongs to a sacred deposit rather than to an Etruscanized area. Greek pottery found in the territory of Rimini (Ariminum) is more likely to have come direct by sea from the Adriatic rather than from Etruria Padana, while some Etruscan bronzes found there probably came direct over the Apennines from north-east Etruria. In the hinterland of Rimini there was a flourishing Villanovan settlement at Verucchio (San Marino), but there are no traces of the Etruscans. Some Etruscan bronzes in the territory of Ravenna may have arrived by sea. As to Ravenna itself, the name could be Etruscan, since it is pre-Indo-European, while Strabo's account of its foundation (see p. 209) suggests that although there was some Etruscan pressure, Umbrians from the south remained the permanent residents.

To the north of Ravenna was Spina, with its mixed population óf Greeks and Etruscans, but Spina's relations with Adria which lay in the marshland between the Po and the Adige are uncertain, nor do we know who were the original inhabitants of Adria. It is called a Greek city by Justin, with Diomede as its founder according to Stephanus; Strabo may imply a Venetic origin, while Livy calls it 'Tuscorum colonia'. It may well be a Greek or Venetic settlement (priority can hardly be established) in which the Etruscans gained an interest. Much Greek pottery, commencing as early as c. 530, shows that it was a centre of Greek culture, where Etruscan bronzes and gold work also occur. It abounded in the late Adriatic black-glazed pottery, and Etruscan and Venetic inscriptions have been found. The latter were written in the alphabet which the Veneti took over from the Etruscans and adapted to the writing of their own language; they added the letter o, which comes at the end of their abcedaria because it was not in the alphabet of the Etruscans; this addition may be due to Greek influence. In the development of an elaborate canal system we may perhaps detect Etruscan hydraulic engineering skill. The proximity of Adria to Spina could have led to trade rivalry, but this may have been avoided by a concentration on different markets. Spina supplied Felsina and the west, while Adria may have had more contacts with the north and the Veneti. Thus in general it would seem that Etruscan expansion eastwards from Felsina was very limited, apart from Spina and perhaps Adria.

Adria and the Veneti were north of the Po. What Etruscan penetration or influence can be detected in the wide tracts of Transpadane country from the Adriatic westward to beyond Milan and northwards to the Alps? First, the Etruscans clearly did not occupy any of the land of the Veneti: even Livy, who exaggerates Etruscan expansion, records that the Veneti maintained their independence. They were an Iron Age group of Indo-European speaking people, who may have originated from Illyria, separate from but not entirely dissimilar to the Villanovans. Their centre at Ateste (Este) was famous for its metal-work, like Villanovan Bologna; this reached its peak in the first half of the fifth century. But although the Atestines resisted Etruscan domination, they absorbed considerable Etruscan influence. Their adoption of the Etruscan alphabet has already been mentioned, but even their metal-work was affected. The famous Benvenuti *situla* is closely linked to the Certosa *situla* (see p. 203), of which it is perhaps a modified copy: it shows similar warriors and country scenes but omits the zone depicting the ceremonial funeral procession.

Farther west Virgil's native city of Mantua was said to have an Etruscan origin, while Pliny could describe it even in his day as 'the only remaining city of the Etruscans beyond the Po'. Its foundation was attributed to Tarchon himself in the Etruscan histories of Verrius Flaccus and Caecina, according to one of the oldest scholiasts on Virgil. Virgil assigned the foundation to Ocnus, the son of the nymph Manto, while alternatively Mantus may be an Etruscan deity, a god of the underworld. Yet Virgil does not seem to have thought of Mantua as purely Etruscan: 'rich in ancestry, yet not all of one stock; three races (*gentes*) are there, and under each race four peoples (*populi*)':

> Mantua, dives avis, sed non genus omnibus unum:
> gens illi triplex, populi sub gente quaterni,
> ipsa caput populis, Tusco de sanguine vires. (*Aen.* 10, 201).

This passage has given rise to much discussion: the three tribes have been compared with the triple tribal division of the Dorians, and the resultant figure of twelve has been thought to come from some connection with the supposed dodecapolis. If Virgil is describing some purely internal constitutional arrangement, it seems unnecessarily complicated, but the scheme may go back to some local antiquarian tradition designed to glorify the city of which Virgil himself was so proud. Another puzzle is the possibility that Virgil came of Etruscan stock. His mother's name, Magia, may well be Etruscan, while his own *nomen* Vergilius is more common in Etruria than elsewhere and his *cognomen* Maro may be linked with the Etruscan title *maru*. Whether a Mantuan inscription, now lost, that records a 'P. Vergilius P.f. pontifex maximus' should suggest that one of the poet's ancestors was 'zilath maruchva' at Mantua is another question. However, some Etruscan connections would help to explain the very prominent (and anachronistic) role played by the Etruscans in the *Aeneid*. In view of the name Mantua and these various traditions it would be unwise to reject all Etruscan connections, but archaeology so far has given little support. A tomb containing Etruscan bronzes was found at Castiglione delle Stiviere, but that is about twenty-two miles away in the direction of Brescia.

Pliny refers to Melpum as an extraordinarily wealthy town which was destroyed by the Celts at the beginning of the fourth century. This may have been the predecessor of Milan, and the site has been sought at Melzo, a suburb of Treviglio some twenty miles or more east of Milan. Mediolanum (Milan) itself has yielded one Etruscan *graffito* (*TLE*, 720); but this is hardly enough to turn it into an Etruscan settlement, but may indicate the line of Etruscan trade interests. Similarly, a fragment of a Greek vase with an Etruscan inscription from Golasecca, the centre of an Iron Age Indo-European people south of Lake Maggiore, does not indicate an Etruscan settlement, any more than a few Etruscan inscriptions found at the Venetic city of Padua should suggest Etruscan occupation of this area where Indo-European Raetic was spoken, although this dialect may have been influenced by Etruscan at a comparatively late date. Thus there is very little to suggest any substantial Etruscan settlement north of the Po, although the scatter of Etruscan finds shows that the merchants of Felsina and Marzabotto were finding new customers both here and even north of the Alps among the Celts.[141]

ETRUSCANS AND CELTS

During the Bronze Age much of central Europe was occupied by the peoples of the Urnfield cultures, from the upper Danube to the Rhine, the Rhone, the Seine and the Low Countries. But about 650 BC there appeared in Bohemia and Bavaria groups whose chieftains were buried in wooden chambers under great tumuli, lying on a waggon with its wheels beside it, and accompanied by iron spears and swords. Their origin is not clear: in some ways they continued the culture of the Urnfield peoples whom they dominated, but iron, inhumation and waggon-burial all were new features. They may have been newcomers from the east, or perhaps their culture grew merely from contacts with other peoples, perhaps Etruscans or peoples of the Steppe. At any rate they developed into the people whom we call the Celts. From c. 550 they began to import Greek pottery and bronze jugs which came from Massalia and along the Rhone and Saone; and we begin to find Attic pottery, both black- and red-figure, in the Juras. They may even have imported Greek masons, since at Heuneburg near Württemberg their native timber and earth rampart of about 500 BC was strengthened by a great mud-brick wall which suggests builders from the Mediterranean world. Of about the same date was the stronghold near Châtillon-sur-Seine with the famous tomb of the princess at Vix. Her body lay on a waggon, her ornaments were Greek, and around her was a great mass of bronze vessels, including an Etruscan beaked flagon and above all the famous *crater*. This great vessel, apparently of Tarentine or Laconian origin, is five and a half feet high, with a figured frieze showing a procession of warriors alternately on foot and in four-horsed chariots. The Celtic chiefs liked big vessels, whether in bronze or pottery. These Greek wares at first came from Massalia and the Rhone valley, but during the fifth century this trade began to weaken, perhaps because of the changing

political conditions that resulted from the replacement of the
earlier Hallstatt by the La Tène culture. However, with the
dwindling of Massalian trade, Etruscans and Cisalpine Gauls
clearly stepped in and kept up the supply of Greek wares to the
Celts. This trade grew with the establishment of Etruscan commercial bases at Felsina and Marzabotto, which through Spina
could trade direct with Greece. The Etruscans must have been all
the more eager to develop trade with the Greeks in the Adriatic
after their defeat of Cumae in 474 BC by the western Greeks,
when they found their commercial prospects limited to areas
nearer home. These new influences on Celtic society led to the
flowering of the La Tène period. Thus, for instance, in chariot
graves from *c.* 450 in Champagne and the Middle Rhine, the
four-wheel chariot is replaced by the two-wheel, perhaps under
Etruscan influence, and Etruscan beakers are found in the tombs.
However, native Celtic artists soon began to imitate these, and
the new distinctive art of the period emerged.

The Celts were gradually tempted to move over the Alps and
occupy the northern plain of Italy from which they ultimately
drove the Etruscans. When and how this process took place are
controversial questions. Livy preserved a tradition that the
invasion of Italy occurred in the reign of Tarquinius Priscus at
Rome, *i.e. c.* 600 BC, but this date has been almost universally
rejected as being some two hundred years too early. Melpum is
said to have fallen to them in 396 BC, while the *stelae* at Felsina
show that this city held out until about the middle of the fourth
century. But it may be that the date of *c.* 400 for their arrival
needs modifying. The fact that Felsina was still Etruscan in the
early fourth century does not mean that there were no Celts in
the Po valley before that. The first waves, perhaps the Senones,
may have come much earlier during the fifth century and their
attitude need not have been hostile. Recent finds at Casola Val di
Senio near Faenza have revealed some Celtic burials which contain not only Celtic arms but also Attic black-figure pottery
which cannot be later than the first decades of the fifth century.
This would suggest that Celts and Etruscans were first penetrating
into this area about the same time, and considerably earlier than

the conventional dating for the Celts. A common interest in developing trade possibly at first promoted co-operation rather than hostility. However that may be, later waves of Celts were resisted. Livy records (5, 34) that the Etruscans were routed by the Gauls near the Ticinus; this episode cannot be dated, but some Etruscans apparently had moved up to the foothills of the Alps in order to try to check an invasion—it need not have been the first—and failed. Operations in this district strengthen the possibility of some Etruscan control of Milan, which would form a base for action farther north.

When the final attacks fell upon Marzabotto and Felsina, the heart of Etruria Padana, we have evidence in the *stelae* for the stiff resistance of Felsina until *c.* 350 BC (*Pl. 93*). On these we see the horsemen of Felsina matched against naked Gauls: that the Etruscan is depicted as the victor, although the stone commemorates his death, need occasion no surprise. At Marzabotto we see only the aftermath: a Gallic cemetery has been found, containing iron swords and other grave-goods typical of the La Tène period. The Gauls, perhaps here the Boii, appear to have occupied the site for a short time but not for very long: north of the main axis of the town are small huts, containing La Tène armlets and fibulae, and the dead were buried in abandoned houses. But these Etruscan cities were not the only victims: in 390 Rome itself succumbed to a Gallic raid. However, she soon recovered, consolidated her power and then took the offensive against central Etruria. In this phase Etruscans and Gauls joined hands as allies against the rising might of Rome, an alignment that was also reflected in the cultural field. The tombs of the Gauls who settled around Bologna contain pottery, bronzes and even mirrors from central Etruria, and at the same time these Celtic warriors added defensive equipment of Etruscan manufacture, such as bronze helmets, greaves and even breast-plates, to their native weapons of offence, iron swords and spears.

By this time the northern plain of Italy was being transformed into what the Romans called Gallia Cisalpina, and the more limited part of it which could accurately be called Etruria Padana now disappeared as an independent cultural unit. But not before it had made a very considerable contribution to the history of Italy. By commercial activity it raised the whole level of life over a large area and by the wide distribution of Greek and Etruscan works of art in bronze and pottery, it created and satisfied an enlarged cultural area. And not least among its 'exports' must be counted the Etruscan alphabet which enabled many hitherto illiterate peoples as far north as the Alps to commit their thought to writing.[142]

CHAPTER VIII

THE POLITICAL AND SOCIAL STRUCTURE OF THE CITIES

POLITICAL ORGANIZATION

POLITICAL LIFE for the Etruscans, as for the Greeks, was based on the city-state, an independent and autonomous unit. First, therefore, we must examine the institutions that were created for their administration and then look at the relations of these cities one to another.

The earliest stage of their organization is simply a matter for surmise; our first glimpse of them reveals kings in control. If the Etruscans came from the east as conquering bands, presumably each leader held regal power when once his group had seized a strong position and had grown into a permanent settlement. If, however, Etruscan civilization developed out of little Villanovan settlements gradually merging into larger units, then the process by which leaders of villages, tribes or clans gained control of the 'cities' must have been more complex. But as soon as we can speak of cities, we should probably also assume the existence of monarchy.

The title of the king was *lauchme* or *lauchume* (Lucumo in Latin). As so often, our evidence derives mainly from a much later period when the word survived after the regal period as the title of the priest who inherited the king's sacred functions, as did the Archon Basileus at Athens or the Rex Sacrorum at Rome. Thus the Zagreb inscription records a word *lauchumneti*, meaning 'in the *lauchumna*' or priest's house (*cf.* the Regia in the Forum at Rome), and the function of a priest at Tarquinii in the second century BC is described by the verb *lucairce*. The root also became a family name (Lauchumni, Lauchumsnei) in the district around Perusia and Clusium, as King has become a common surname in England, and Rex a *cognomen* at ancient Rome (as Quintus Marcius Rex).[143]

We also happen to know what the Etruscans called the authority of a ruler, since the late Greek lexicographer Hesychius, probably of the fifth century, has recorded that the Etruscan equivalent to the Greek word ἀρχή was (in a Greek form) δρούνα; this will be an Etruscan word, *truna* or *thruna*, and may be connected with the pre-Greek word τύραννος, which the Greeks took from the Lydians to describe an unconstitutional ruler. It is uncertain to what extent this Etruscan conception influenced the Roman idea of *imperium*, by which was meant the executive authority of kings and magistrates. For the detailed rights and functions of the Etruscan kings we have little direct evidence, but clearly by analogy with Rome and elsewhere they must have been supreme leaders in war, in religion and in the administration of justice. It was probably to this last function that Macrobius referred when he said that 'every ninth day the Etruscans used to go to greet their king and to consult him *de propriis negotiis*' (*Sat.* 1, 15, 13).

Much more is known about the outward trappings of the kings, since many of these survived at Rome when they were taken over by the later Republican magistrates from the Tarquins. Dionysius of Halicarnassus says that these comprised 'a golden crown, an ivory throne, an ivory sceptre surmounted by an eagle, a purple tunic decorated with gold, and an embroidered purple robe like those the kings of Lydia and Persia used to wear, except that it was semicircular and not rectangular. This kind of robe is called a toga by the Romans and *tebenna* by the Greeks, but I do not know where the Greeks learned the name, since it does not appear to me to be a Greek word' (3, 61). Some of these attributes can be seen in a painting from Caere, which shows a man, perhaps a king, seated on a folding ivory seat like the later Roman *sella curulis*, used by magistrates, in front of the statue of a goddess. In his left hand he holds a sceptre (without an eagle) and he wears a white (not purple) tunic with short sleeves, and a short purple cloak, embroidered on the edges, which corresponds to the short toga of the Romans which they called a *trabea*, a garment which Dionysius elsewhere (2, 70, 2) translated as *tebenna*. He also wears typical Etruscan shoes with turned-up toes (*Pl. 100*).[144]

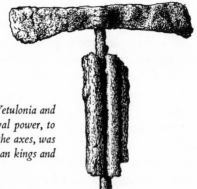

Fig. 25 Iron model of fasces *found at Vetulonia and dating to c. 600 BC. This symbol of royal power, to scourge with the rods and execute with the axes, was borrowed from the Etruscans by the Roman kings and later magistrates*

The most striking symbol of sovereignty was the axe and bundle of rods (*fasces*), which showed the king's power to execute or scourge. These also were taken over by the Romans, first by the kings and then by the consuls, but their Etruscan origin is specifically mentioned by Florus (1, 1, 5) and Silius Italicus (*Pun.* 8, 483ff). Silius, whose source is perhaps Cato's *Origines*, assigns the invention to Vetulonia, and by a remarkable coincidence it is Vetulonia that has supplied the only surviving specimen. This was found in 1898; there can be no reasonable doubt that the object does represent a *fascis* and dates from *c.* 600 BC. It is, however, a model reduced in size for votive or funerary purposes, and it differs from the later Roman *fasces* in that the axe is two-headed, not a single blade (Fig. 25). But this is not surprising because the axe would be of the same type as that used in war, and again by a lucky chance we have a representation (Fig. 1) of a warrior from Vetulonia, brandishing just such a double-bladed axe. His name was Avele Feluske (Aulus Feluscus) and he is shown with a plumed helmet and round shield on a *stele* which was erected in his memory by a fellow warrior, Hirumina Phersnachs or Herminius of Perusia. Though the double-axe is a well-known cult symbol in Minoan religion, in Etruria its significance is likely to be secular rather than sacred. According to Dionysius the king of each city was preceded by one lictor carrying a *fascis* of rods and axe, but when the twelve cities united in any military campaign the twelve axes were entrusted to one supreme

commander. Dionysius, who records that when the Etruscans sub-
mitted to Tarquinius Priscus of Rome they brought the twelve
axes to him, mentions another tradition that assigned the use of
twelve axes to Romulus. At any rate, the Tarquins probably had
twelve, which were later taken over by the supreme magistrates of
the Roman Republic.

In the course of time the authority of the kings weakened as
that of the nobles increased, and monarchy was superseded by
oligarchy during the sixth and fifth centuries BC. This was not
an isolated phenomenon but rather a process that was to be
found in many parts of the Mediterranean world, for instance
among the Phoenician cities in Syria and Africa no less than
among Greek cities such as Athens or Corinth. There is, however,
the possibility that before the king's power was undermined
completely by the nobles in some cities he may have attempted to
counter their strength by a reorganization of his city's institutions
in order to give greater influence to the military potentiality of a
middle class.[145] This raises the question of what constitutional
rights the citizens of an Etruscan city may have had, if any.
One of the most striking and perplexing features of Etruscan
society is the apparently deep gulf between the aristocracy and a
dependent population, and the apparent absence of a middle
class (p. 237). But it can hardly be supposed that a free population
other than the nobility did not exist or that it lacked all institu-
tional organization. Here we can proceed only by analogy. At
Rome the earliest division was into three tribes and thirty *curiae*;
the latter had religious functions and also formed voting units in
a political assembly (Comitia Curiata). *Curiae* existed in other
Latin cities (*e.g.* Lanuvium) and it is not unlikely that an equivalent institution was found in Etruria.[146] But even if such groupings
existed, this is insufficient evidence to establish that they developed
into a popular assembly, though by analogy this might be
expected. At Rome this arrangement was superseded by the
Servian organization which established military units (*centuriae*)
and property classes, increased the efficiency of the army, and
gave more power to the middle class legionary 'hoplites'; the
army was also increased in size through the enfranchizement of

many men whom trade and commerce had attracted to Rome under Etruscan rule. The army was reorganized on the basis of hoplite tactics like the Greek phalanx, an organization which the Romans are expressly said to have borrowed from the Etruscans.[147] What Servius Tullius did at Rome other Etruscan kings may have attempted in their own cities, namely to bolster up their own declining powers by trying to create a counterweight to a militant and aggressive nobility. Such a device did not work for long at Rome—the dynasty of the Tarquins soon fell—and may not have worked in Etruscan cities, if it was tried (see p. 258).

How the monarchy succumbed to aristocracy in the various Etruscan cities—and the process need not have been identical everywhere—we have unfortunately little precise knowledge. One example is quoted: at Veii after the defeat of the king Lars Tolumnius by the Romans, the monarchy was abolished in 432. Twenty years later, however, it was temporarily restored: 'the Veientines, weary of the annual canvassing [unfortunately the nature of the magistracy is not indicated] which sometimes caused dissension, chose a king' (Livy 5, 1, 3). Livy goes on to say that this offended the feelings of the other Etruscan peoples who hated the king personally no less than the institution of monarchy and so they refused to help Veii in its struggle against Rome. The passage, if taken literally, shows that the majority of the Etruscan cities had abandoned monarchy by the end of the fifth century, and also that they hated it (though here Livy's motivation may reflect the hatred of the Romans of the Republic). In fact the restored monarchy at Veii did not last long because the city was destroyed in 396. It is only at Rome that we get a detailed picture of the end of an Etruscan monarchy, the expulsion of Tarquinius in 510, but even there the process is not certain, since many modern scholars refuse to accept the later Roman tradition of what happened and believe that the monarchy was ended not by revolution but by evolution, with the powers of the king gradually devolving upon other leaders. This latter view may not be acceptable (see below pp. 262ff), but it belongs to a pattern of unsettled conditions that many interpret as an intermediate stage between monarchy and settled oligarchy. As Lars

Porsenna was said to have captured Rome after the expulsion of Tarquinius, many other Etruscan warriors may have been on the warpath, such as Caelius and Aulus Vibenna of Vulci (see p. 256) or indeed Avele Feluske of Vetulonia (p. 223). But even if military adventurers did succeed for brief periods in establishing personal power, they were soon reduced to the level of their fellow nobles, and the cities were administered thereafter by local aristocracies.

These leading oligarchs in each city were called *principes* by Roman writers; the equivalent Etruscan term is not known, but since Livy (10, 13, 3) mentions them alongside Samnite magistrates he presumably equated the *principes* with magistrates. Further, there was an *ordo* of *principes*, which was presided over by a *princeps civitatis*.[148] This will have formed the governing class and met in an assembly corresponding to the Roman Senate.[149] But although this Order was exclusive it seems to have contained grades within itself, perhaps like the *maiores* and *minores gentes* at Rome, since Livy, writing about the senate at Arretium in 208, seems to contrast seven *principes senatus* with 'the other senators' (27, 24, 4). But fortunately we can bring more life to these rather shadowy *principes* of the literary sources by means of two other forms of evidence: inscriptions that record their titles, and sculptured monuments that show their insignia and appearance.

The inscriptions are epitaphs from monuments, some of which depict a magistrate exercising his office.[150] Forty-three such inscriptions survive, ranging from the fourth to the first century BC. Thus they represent Etruria at a late stage of its development, but since the earliest of them antedate the Roman conquest, their evidence may—with caution—be applied retrospectively. Another limitation is their distribution: they come from ten centres, mostly from southern Etruria and especially from Tarquinii and the surrounding district. The reason might be that this area received better treatment from Rome and that therefore its earlier local institutions survived more easily than at Perusia, Cortona or Arretium.[151] The three main magistrates that they attest are the *zilath*, the *maru* and the *purthne*. These have been regarded as a hierarchy, corresponding with the praetor, aedile and quaestor in the Roman *cursus honorum*, for instance by A. Rosenberg;[152] but the evidence is too complicated to allow so neat a solution. The words themselves, which appear in a variety of forms, verbal as well as substantival, do not help very much. The etymology of *zilath* is not known, though it clearly means 'magistrate'. *Maru* has some connections with *maron*, the name of a magistrate found among the neighbouring Umbrians, but *maron* probably was derived from the Etruscan usuage.[153] The word is best known in its survival as a *cognomen*, which the poet Virgil (P. Vergilius Maro) received from the Etruscan background of his native Mantua (*cf.* p. 216). *Purthne* has been linked with the Greek πρύτανις, which was the name for a magistracy at many places, including Corinth, whence Demaratus migrated to Etruria. But although the Etruscans could have borrowed the term from the Greeks of the eastern Mediterranean or from those in south Italy, more probably both Greeks and Etruscans derived their words from a pre-Greek root *prut*, meaning 'first'.

Many questions arise: how were these three magistracies related to each other? were they, some or all, collegiate? were all men with the same title performing the same functions? were the duties of any sacral as well as secular? what is the meaning of *zilath* when it is found with no less than eight different qualifying words? were the magistracies the same in all the major cities? Even more questions arise when it is asked what was the relation of the titles of these magistrates of the major cities to those held by officials either in the smaller towns or in the wider context of the League of the Etruscan cities. Here only a general picture can be suggested, such as might commend itself to the majority of scholars, conjectural in many details and subject at any time to modification through the discovery of new inscriptions.

Zilath is generally regarded as the chief magistracy. This may well have comprised a college, with zilaths exercising different functions: an analogy has often been drawn with the nine archons at Athens who consisted of the three chief magistrates (the archon Eponymous, the Basileus and the Polemarch) together with the six Thesmothetae. Any differentiation of function or rank is difficult to establish: the *zilath parchis* may have dealt with the nobles, the *zilath eterav* with clients and *zilch cechaneri* with cult (*sacris faciundis?*), but the interpretations are uncertain. That one zilath was probably eponymous is suggested by an inscription from Tarquinii which seems to be dated by such a magistracy: 'zilci velus(i) hulch(u)niesi', which almost certainly means 'when Hulchnie (a member of the gens Holconia) was zilath'.[154] The college of zilaths must have had a president who was sometimes designated simply by the word zilath (possibly being the eponymous zilath), but he may also have been given the title *purth*.[155] Lastly the title *maru* belonged to priests: thus we hear of a *maru* of Bacchus (*maru pachathuras*: *TLE*, 190). But they were also magistrates, and like the zilaths they perhaps formed a separate college with some specialization of function, but in any case they appear to have had a lower rank than the zilaths. They have been compared with the Roman aediles.

All the magistrates were normally annual, but numbers affixed to an office in inscriptions show that it could be held more than once. A man apparently could become zilath at a fairly early age: one of twenty-five years old is attested at Vulci, and even if this was exceptional, thirty may have been a normal age. Even though we cannot determine the magisterial *cursus honorum* with any accuracy, nevertheless inscriptions, like Roman *elogia* as well as sepulchral monuments, proudly proclaimed the offices men had held. Thus one from Vulci (*TLE*, 324) records Larth Tute, the son of Arruns and of Ravnthu Hathli, who had been seven times zilath and once *purth* and who died aged seventy-two. The zilath who died aged twenty-five, Sethre Tute, son of Larth and Vela Pumpli, was probably the son of the septuagenarian.

A number of monuments, which have recently been gathered together and discussed by R. Lambrechts,[156] vividly depict some of these supreme magistrates at the height of their glory in a procession, which is both triumphal and funerary. They are a group of sarcophagi, mainly from Tarquinii and southern Etruria, and a number of alabaster urns from Volaterrae (*Pl. 102*). Seven of the sarcophagi have inscriptions which refer to the magistrate, whose figure is modelled reclining on the lid of the sarcophagus. On the front of the sarcophagi and urns a procession is depicted, which with great variety of detail always shows a similar theme. Thus even where inscriptions are now missing, the type of monument can be identified. Since some forty of these monuments are known, it may be wondered whether all of them really contained the ashes of a zilath. Although the visitor to the Volterra museum who is surrounded by such a vast number of urns might not doubt the possibility, yet the theme appears to have become conventional and gained a general religious significance. These monuments, however, all date from the Etrusco-Roman period; they thus represent the end of a long development, but there can be no doubt that earlier examples, and all the inscribed ones, actually belong to a magistrate and reflect the splendour of his office.

The magistrate is generally shown in a chariot, with four or two horses, but sometimes he is on foot. He wears a tunic, a toga-like mantle and a gilded crown on which, in a few cases, traces of colour survive: the *elogium* of a magistrate of Tarquinii specifically mentions his '(corona) aurea' (*cf.* p. 91). The triumphal procession consists of a number of men, from two to ten, but it would be hazardous to make constitutional deductions from the number of the attendants, because this is likely to have been determined less by the magistrate's rank than by artistic considerations such as space. They consist of lictors, who carry *fasces* without axes, a group of musicians with a variety of instruments (*cornicines, citharistae, tibicines* and *tubicines*) and sometimes men with a spear or staff whose duty may have been to clear the way, like the Roman *viatores*. Other servants carried a curule chair, a travelling-bag (*mantica*), writing-tablets (*pugillares*), a box for papers (*scrinium*) or a book (*volumen*). Sometimes a horseman is shown, but whether he was an outrider or a messenger from the Underworld to conduct the *zilath* to his future home is uncertain. Thus the magistrate is revealed in all his authority, but stress is naturally laid on his civil attributes in monuments that date from this late period: the lictors, for example, no longer carried an axe. This, however, may merely reflect a parallel development with Rome where axes were no longer carried within the city-bounds after the right of appeal had been granted to the people, traditionally in 509, possibly in 300 BC; the difference lay rather in the fact that Roman magistrates still exercised military *imperium* when they left the city, while Etruscan power was increasingly overshadowed by Rome.

It must, however, be remembered that this picture of the Etruscan magistracy rests largely on late evidence which comes from a relatively limited number of cities. We have no direct evidence for the magistrates at Veii, Populonia, Cortona, Perusia or Arretium, and generalization must therefore be dangerous. Further, a recent brilliant attempt to use two monuments to illustrate the earlier period has not met with general acceptance. These show two reliefs of seated figures, one of the fifth century from Clusium, the other of *c.* 500 BC from Velletri, though perhaps of Veientine manufacture and now in Palermo. The figures, which hold spears or sceptres and augurs' crooks (*litui*), have been interpreted as magistrates (*zilath* with sceptre, and *maru* with *lituus*), but the more usual view that they are an assembly of gods or even a family reunion at a funeral is more probable.[157]

Since cities governed not only the area within their walls but controlled large territories beyond, the question arises of the relation of the two. Thus the *ager Tarquiniensis* included not only Tarquinii but several large settlements or towns at Norchia, Musarna (Viterbo), Tuscania, Bieda (Blera) and Visentium (Bisenzio). Here are attested the three main magistracies: *purth* at Norchia, *maru* and *zilath* at Tuscania and all three at Musarna. Were these local magistrates, or magistrates of Tarquinii who lived elsewhere, or magistrates who represented the whole *populus Tarquiniensis* (as seems to be suggested by the occasional use of the word *spur-*, which probably refers to the *populus* or *civitas* as opposed to the whole Etruscan nation)? It happens that at Musarna seven members of the Alethna family held office, but one of these is said to have 'been *zilath* at Tarquinii'; this addition seems to imply that the others were local officials. This may well have been so in the late period of the inscriptions; under Roman control these smaller places may have been independent of Tarquinii and have retained for their local officials the titles of earlier days. But it is hazardous to apply this evidence to an earlier period, and better to confess ignorance of the precise way in which Tarquinii administered its territory in the seventh and sixth centuries.[158]

THE ETRUSCAN 'LEAGUE'

Etruscan cities were autonomous individual states, but they were linked by a common language, culture and possibly racial origin. They would naturally therefore tend to form some wider association, as did other peoples in Italy: many Latin cities, for instance, united in one or more leagues. Was there then an Etruscan League? To this a variety of answers has been given, since the evidence for some association cannot be dismissed but is ambiguous and scanty. Some believe in a full federal League of twelve cities, other water this down to a loose religious bond and emphasize the political disunity of the cities[159] (Fig. 26).

The ancient sources frequently refer to twelve cities or peoples (*duodecim populi*) or to 'all Etruria' (*omnis Etruria*) in contexts that imply some unity of action. Further, some form of association lasted nearly a thousand years, since it is found as late as the reign of Constantine (though after a revival in the early Empire when the number of peoples was increased to fifteen) and inscriptions from the second to fourth centuries AD attest the existence of *praetores Etruriae XV populorum* (see p. 283). What then was the nature of the bond that linked the cities together: was it religious or political or both? And it is well to recall that the great religious festivals of the Greek world at Delphi and Olympia, which attracted competitors and visitors from all Greece, did not lead to direct political association; they were a unifying influence, but not in the strictly political sphere.

The Etruscans clearly had a federal sanctuary at the Fanum Voltumnae, where every year games (*sollemnia ludorum*) were held and a fair grew up which attracted merchants and itinerant traders. The site of this shrine, which has not been discovered, probably lay near Volsinii, since the games were still being celebrated in the fourth century AD *apud Volsinios* in accordance with ancient custom.[160] Voltumna, according to Varro, was the chief Etruscan god (*deus Etruriae princeps*); the Romans called him Vertumnus. Since *fanum* means a place dedicated to a deity, the early form of building is not known, but a fine temple is likely soon to have been built. The title of the president of the games in imperial times was *sacerdos*. At this Fanum Voltumnae a council met, which Livy calls *concilium Etruscorum* or *concilium Etruriae*. This consisted of the twelve *lucomones* in early days, representing their cities, and later the chief magistrates of the cities. Although no doubt it remained an aristocratic body, its membership is likely to have been wider than this and to have included other representatives from the cities. Thus Livy refers once to a numerously attended meeting in 404 BC (*frequenter*: Livy, 4, 61, 2) and in reference to another occasion he writes 'in all their councils the *principes* of the Etruscans were openly criticized' (10, 13, 3); whoever the critics were, whether other nobles or even less privileged people, a wider body than the twelve chiefs is implied. One of the twelve was elected as leader by the twelve cities.[161] Livy refers to such an election when the people of Veii decided to revert to monarchy, as mentioned above (p. 225): the new king was hated by the rest of the Etruscans 'because he had violently broken up the solemn festival in his anger at not being elected and since by the votes of the twelve peoples another man had been preferred to him as *sacerdos*, he had suddenly taken away the actors, most of whom were his slaves, in the middle of the games'. Thus under the earlier kings the head of the League was a *lucumo* or *rex*, and by the end of the fifth century he was in Roman terms the *sacerdos*. His Etruscan title was probably *zilath mechl rasnal* or 'the magistrate of the nation (*mechl* is opposed to *spur* or city) of the Etruscans (the Rasenna)'. To look for other League officials who might be parallel to city magistrates and to see the League as a city writ large is hazardous.

Further problems arise. When was the league formed, when did it meet, what were its functions and which were the twelve peoples that formed it? The problem of the origin of the League is not likely to be regarded in the same light by those who believe in an eastern origin of the Etruscans as by those who support an autochthonous origin. The former may see some truth behind

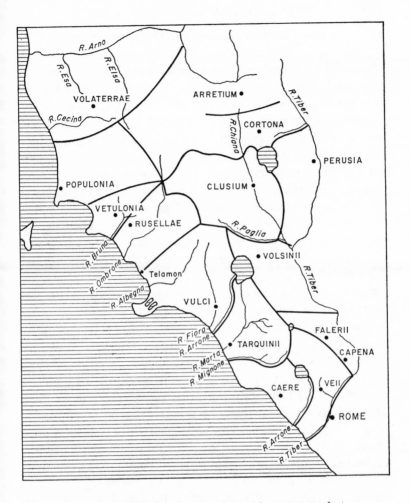

Fig. 26 *The territories of the Etruscan cities, showing the approximate limits*

the tradition of early unity recorded by the geographer Strabo and may find a development analogous to that of the Greek settlement of Ionia and the formation of an Ionian League. The latter will see a gradual movement to greater unity among Villanovan settlements, now culturally 'Etruscanized', and they will interpret the Ionian analogy, if they consider it relevant at all, as a pattern consciously imitated by the Etruscans in the sixth century. According to Strabo when Tyrsenos arrived in Italy from Lydia he founded twelve cities, but this unity under a strong ruler later collapsed, and the Tyrrhenoi were divided up into separate cities. The legend cannot be accepted in this form: if invasion came from the east, it probably came in several small groups, though an initial group, *e.g.* at Tarquinii, might have become more powerful than others; yet if the Etruscans were foreign invaders in an alien land they would have been more conscious of their unity than if a widespread population began to absorb new cultural influences. Thus a feeling of unity may have existed from quite early days, and even have found expression in a common cult-meeting which in course of time developed some political aspects. An analogy might then fairly be drawn with the Greek settlements in Ionia where they established the Panionion, a federal sanctuary of the Ionian League, whose site, unlike that of Fanum Voltumnae, appears to have been discovered.[162] This League, which in its fully developed form comprised twelve independent and autonomous city-states, first consisted of a smaller number of settlements, the chief of which appears to have been Ephesus under a monarchy. Its king became the 'champion of the early Ionian settlers who met at the Panionion. This primitive league was not a league of city-states. Kings ruled its member-towns with the King of Ephesus as their chief. . . . When the towns of the primitive league developed into city-states in the eighth century, their kingships, too, became religious offices and the old quasi-feudal ties with the chief king lapsed. The religious celebration of the Panionic festival remained to reinforce the feeling of being a separate people.'[163] A similar process could have occurred in Etruria, with perhaps Tarquinii playing the role of Ephesus, if once the Etruscan migration is admitted. Further, Etruscan leaders might well know something about the political development that was taking place in Ionia, just to the west of Lydia. An alternative explanation is to assume that there was little unity until the cities became politically mature and that at some point, possibly in the sixth century, twelve cities deliberately created a league; this might, as many believe, or might not have been done under the conscious influence of the Panionion.[164]

How often did the council of the League meet? If any authentic information can have survived in Livy's sources, the normal time appears to have been once a year: this is specifically stated if a passage (4, 25) is given its natural interpretation: he says that in 432 BC at a meeting at the Fanum Voltumnae a matter (a declaration of war) was postponed for a year ('prolatae in annum res') and it was decreed that no council should be held before then. This implies that the next regular meeting would be in a year, but that special meetings could be summoned. Such emergency sessions could be called by individual cities (Livy 4, 23) or by foreign allies such as the Samnites (10, 15). More important, and more obscure, is the question of the functions of the council. In one passage Dionysius refers to joint military action: whenever the twelve cities decided on a common expedition, the kings of the cities customarily handed over the twelve axes to the one who received full powers, that is to the president of the council (3, 61). Dionysius also records the joint declaration of war against Rome, together with the decision that any city that refused to take part in the expedition should be excluded from the League; also to conclude a separate peace with the enemy was regarded as a breach of federal obligation; and on another occasion the League was unwilling to declare war but allowed volunteers from the cities to serve with Veii against Rome (3, 57; 8, 18; 9, 1). Whether or not much reliance should be put in Dionysius, common action was apparently not often taken: more often we hear of city engaged against city, while Veii's appeal for help against Rome met with no joint response from the other Etruscans (pp. 225, 268). But if united activities were rare (see p. 273), that does not mean that they never occurred, but rather that if loyalty to the League clashed with the interests of a city, the city's interests would take first place.

The general impression conveyed by all these factors taken together is therefore that representatives of the Etruscan cities met regularly for religious purposes, that they had some feeling of national unity which might occasionally find expression in joint action, but common political action was not frequent enough to turn their meetings into a strong federal League whose obligations could often overrule city interests. This failure to establish real unity of purpose was ultimately to prove fatal to the cities when they came into conflict with Rome.

Which were the twelve cities? No ancient source names them: hence much modern speculation. To some extent the question may be misplaced, since it presupposes a more static condition than historical growth suggests. At some point the number was established at twelve, and *duodecim populi* may have remained a conventional title until reorganization in the Roman Empire raised the number to fifteen. As already seen (p. 140), some cities, like Vetulonia, declined early, while others gained independence later; and whatever be thought of the statement of Servius (*ad Aen.* 10, 172) that Populonia was founded after the establishment of the twelve peoples, it at least implies a tradition that this city was not among the founding members of the League, perhaps because it was overshadowed by Volaterrae. Again, as the cities came under Roman control—*e.g.* Veii after its destruction in 396—they will have made no independent contribution to the League, even if they remained titular members of the Twelve. Alternatively, the list may have been revised in the light of the fluctuating fortunes of the various cities. If a list is to be attempted, it would include Veii, Caere, Tarquinii, Vulci, Rusellae, Vetulonia, Volsinii, Volaterrae, Clusium, to which may be added Cortona, Perugia and Arretium. But perhaps the number of active members varied, since at any rate in the late period smaller groupings seem to have been allowed within the larger body: this is suggested by an issue of bronze coins in the third century BC, bearing the names of Populonia, Vetulonia and either Camars (Clusium) or Caere (p. 145).

THE SOCIAL STRUCTURE

Political power in each city was held by a limited number of men. Since the evidence is insufficient to establish the existence of a popular assembly, the rule of the Few may have been unfettered by the criticism, constitutionally expressed, of the people.

Indeed the general picture given by our sources is one of an opulent and powerful aristocracy on the one hand and an immense body of clients, serfs and slaves on the other.

The governing class, and as far as is known the whole free citizen body, rested on the basis of families or clans, a gentilician structure. This comes out most clearly in the Etruscan system of personal names. Whereas Greeks and Jews used a personal name and a patronymic, to which the Athenians later added that of a man's deme or parish, the Etruscans followed the method used by other peoples in Italy, namely a personal name combined with that of the *gens*. This no doubt was also the normal practice of the early Romans, who gradually added a third name (*cognomen*) to distinguish the families within the same *gens*. In Roman usage a patronymic did not form part of a man's name, but was often added by nobles who were proud of their ancestry. The Etruscans too added the name of the father and often (unlike the Romans) that of the mother; those of the grandparents were even included on occasion. Thus we find 'Lars, son of Arruns Pleco and of Ramtha Apatronia' (Larth Arnthal Plecus clan Ramthasc Apatrual: *TLE*, 136), who was twice *zilath* at Tarquinii, while a fellow citizen recorded his own ancestry as 'Laris Pulenas, son of Larce, nephew of Larth, grandson of Velthur, greatgrandson of Laris Pule Creice' (lris pulenas larces clan larthal papacs velthurus nefts prumts pules larisal creices: *TLE*, 131). Such pedigrees suggest a strong feeling for family. To what extent the families developed a hierarchy of prestige, or even if they fell into two separate groups as the Roman patrician and plebeian *gentes*, we do not know, but the families that frequently secured magistracies and priesthoods for their members are likely to have formed a distinct, if not a closed, circle and to have strengthened their interdependence by marriage ties.

One puzzling feature is the apparent absence of a middle class. It may be that the gulf between the aristocracy and the servile or semi-servile class was always very deep. This would be especially likely if the Etruscans were a conquering minority who reduced the Villanovan population to serfdom, though perhaps less easy to account for on the evolutionary theory. But even so, it must be remembered that so much of the evidence is late and that this wide separation might partly be a development of later times. There must surely have been in earlier times a considerable body of middle-class farmers throughout the countryside, while the use of hoplite tactics presupposes such a class. Whenever Etruscan soldiers abandoned the older more 'heroic' methods of fighting, in which individual prowess was demanded, and turned to the battle-line (phalanx) of heavy-armed infantry this would by analogy seem to presuppose the existence of a large enough body of men who could afford to provide their own hoplite armour. It has now been shown that the introduction of hoplite armour and of the hoplite phalanx need not have occurred at the same time.[165] It appears that in Greece hoplite armour was adopted by the aristocracy piece by piece without making any sudden and radical change in tactics: it was only when the phalanx formation was adopted, that social and political changes in the structure of the warrior class necessarily followed. In other words the older idea that the appearance of hoplite armour implied the rise of an independent middle class must be modified. Now the Etruscans had adopted the equipment of the Greek hoplite before 600 BC and probably were using the hoplite phalanx during the sixth century. Thus the new armour and arms were adopted when kings or aristocrats were in control of the cities. These changes imply, if not the emergence of a middle class with political influence, at least the existence of a considerable body of middle-class farmers who could afford to equip themselves in the newer fashion, unless of course the nobles were sufficiently rich and sufficiently confident in the loyalty of their retainers to have provided the arms themselves. But perhaps the farmers, many of whom probably lived in the cities (see p. 63), were bound more closely to the ruling class by ties of clientage than elsewhere. At any rate where Etruscan society is seen most clearly, it is sharply divided into *domini* and *servi*.

The *domini* of course comprised the ruling aristocracy, the men who held office and swayed policy, but perhaps the group should not be defined too narrowly; the term might cover a larger section of society. The number of Etruscan *gentes* known from inscriptions is very considerable: many who did not fall into the category of *servi* may have regarded themselves as in some way *domini* (after all, every Roman was *dominus* to his *servi*). Thus many farmers of substance may technically have been clients of the nobles whose land they worked as *possessores*, but at the same time when they regarded the large servile or semi-servile population they might consider themselves as *domini*. In other words we should perhaps not think of a complete social chasm between the classes, but of many families who were technically clients, helping to bridge the gap; the more fortunate of them might think of themselves as belonging to the *domini*, the less fortunate as being a privileged section of the lower class.

Clients are probably to be identified with a class known as the *etera*. These were not completely free, since their names are always accompanied by a second name in the genitive case, implying some kind of dependence; on the other hand, they generally have a 'gentile' name and were often buried in family tombs. Thus in the tomb of the family of the Venete (Venetii) at Perusia we find: Se. Venete La. Lethial clan' and 'La. Venete La. Lethial etera', where no distinction is made in the formula between the son (*clan*) Sethre and the *etera* Larth.[166] Various interpretations of *etera* have been offered (*e.g.* 'slave' or 'foreigner', *servus* or *peregrinus*), but that of 'client' seems the most probable, whether or not a connection exists with the Greek ἑταῖρος ('companion' or *sodalis*). The client-patron relationship played a basic role in Roman life, and though a strict equation of *etera* with *cliens* need not be pressed, a similar institution probably existed in Etruria. Further, at Tarquinii there was a magistrate called *zilatheterau*, who presumably looked after the interests of the *etera*; he can scarcely be compared with the *tribunus plebis* at Rome, since he was an aristocrat and not a plebeian himself. There was also a class known as *lautneteri*; these must have been either *etera* who sank to the status of freedmen (*lautni*) or more probably freedmen who were treated as clients. Many of the *etera* were no doubt closely attached to their patrons' houses, helping them in politics or commerce and finding their last resting place in the family tomb. But the majority of the tombs of *etera* known to us are separate, and this suggests that the term *etera* may also include land-workers, the *agrestes*, who cultivated the land of their patrons as *possessores*.[167]

Our knowledge of the servile and semi-servile classes in Etruria, as of so many aspects of Etruscan life, is very limited in time and space. We see slaves painted on the walls of tombs, but these are virtually confined to Tarquinii; we have epigraphic material, but none of this is earlier than the third century and mostly comes from Clusium and Perusia; the literary sources provide Latin equivalents to Etruscan terms (thus *lautni* is equated with *libertus*), but we cannot be sure that the legal status of the freedman is the same among both peoples; we know something of the conditions which precipitated a slave revolt at Volsinii in the third century, but even here we depend on later authors whose source was the fuller account given by Livy in one of his lost books (*cf.* p. 275).

The word *lautni* is derived from *lautn* meaning 'family' or *gens*. In Latin *familia* originally meant the slaves and servants in a house, and only gradually came to include the whole family in the English sense under the control of the *paterfamilias*. In Etruscan the *lautni* may originally have been slaves, but late bilingual inscriptions show that the Romans translated the word by *liberti*, freedmen, so that this must have been their status, at any rate by the third century. Once again the comparison must be only general, since we cannot tell whether a slave gained his freedom under similar legal processes in Etruria as in Rome; even the terminology varies, for some Latin writers such as Orosius, use the word *libertinus* rather than *libertus*. Further, although a Roman freedman had certain obligations to his former master, those of the *lautni* may have been greater. As examples we find 'Avle Alfnis lautni' (Aulus, freedman of Alfius), 'Velia Tutnal lautnitha' (Velia, freedwoman of Tutia), or 'Larth Scarpe lautuni' who appears in Latin as 'L. Scarpus Scarpiae l. popa' (Lucius Scarpus, freedman of Scarpia, priest's assistant); in this last case the Etruscan has taken a Roman *praenomen* and had adopted the gentile name of his former mistress; or 'Leucle Phisis lautni' whose Latin memorial records 'L(ucius) Phisius l(ibertus) Laucl(es). Thus the

102 Alabaster urn from Volaterrae. Procession of dead magistrate to the
Underworld. His four-horse chariot is preceded by two horn-blowers and two
lictors with *fasces*; two servants (one with *pugillares*) follow, and an outrider
salutes him. (The cover belongs to another urn). Late (first century BC?).
See p.228.

103 The temple site of Sant' Omobono in Rome. Of the two Etruscan temples (those of Fortuna and Mater Matuta?) one lies beneath the Church of Sant' Omobono. In front of the temples are altars on the axial lines of the *cellae*. The site has yielded much early material, including a head of Minerva. (*Pl.110*). See p.251. 104 Air view of the Regia in the Roman Forum. See p.249.

lautni had at least two names, and their burials were not much poorer than those of freedmen. They must normally have married within their class, but on occasion not only did freedmen marry freedwomen but freedwomen are even found as wives of freedmen although this was regarded as scandalous: thus 'H. Ecnatei Atiuce lautnic' records 'Hastia Egnatia and the freedman Antiochus'.[168] Many of the freedmen or slaves known to us from around Clusium and Perusia had Greek names (such as Apollonius, Apluni; Evander, Evantra; Nicephorus, Nicipur), but as Roman usage suggests, this does not always imply Greek nationality. However, many Greeks were no doubt captured by Etruscan warriors and pirates in early times, while in the later days, to which the inscriptions belong, the Roman conquests in the Greek world as elsewhere were beginning to flood the slave-markets and consequently to increase the servile population in Etruria, especially on the ranches (*latifundia*).

The vast number of slaves below these more privileged dependents remain for us an anonymous mass: they did not receive a tomb to record their names. Some, however, appear to have been called Lethe (Lethi or Lethia in the feminine). This perhaps designated slave-status and came to be applied to individual slaves as a kind of *praenomen* which might be passed to the next generation: thus we find a Larthe Venete who had married a Lethni (their son's epitaph ran, 'Se. Venete La. Lethial clan' or 'Sethre Venete, son of Larth Venete and of Lethi'). Lethe is attested both early and late, since it appears, as *lethaies*, at Veii in the seventh century and as *lethae* near Orvieto about 500 BC, while it is found around Clusium, Perusia and Arretium later.[169] A great number of slaves was employed in the houses of the rich; they are depicted on the paintings at Tarquinii. No doubt families vied with one another in the size and splendour of their *familia urbana* and Diodorus records (5, 40, 1) that the Etruscans invented the *atrium* in order to separate masters from the confusion caused by the crowd of slaves. Others, whose lot was no doubt much harder, worked on the land, or in industry or in the mines, often in appalling conditions.

This sketch of the political and social structure of the cities represents only some aspects of their public life: its economic basis in agriculture, industry and commerce has been sketched in the third chapter and in considering the development of the individual cities. It is impossible within the scope of this work to refer to the rich culture and private life of the Etruscans, to their costume and jewellery, their food and banquets, their music and musical instruments, their dances, races, athletics and sports, their art and architecture, their literature, language and religion. Some glimpses of these may have been revealed, but there is no shortage of good books which deal more systematically with the Etruscans' private lives and antiquities; among these J. Heurgon's *La Vie quotidienne chez les Étrusques* deserves special mention.

CHAPTER IX

ETRUSCAN ROME

THE EVIDENCE

OUR KNOWLEDGE of early Rome, including the period of Etruscan rule, rests upon a variety of evidence: literary, archaeological, linguistic and religious. The surviving literary tradition inevitably suffers from the fact that the Romans unfortunately did not start to write their history until half a millennium after the accepted date of the city's foundation. When Fabius Pictor and other annalists attempted the task near the end of the third century BC, fact and legend were not always easy to differentiate although the historians had some reliable information to draw upon, such as the Annales Pontificum, official lists of magistrates (Fasti), some documents such as laws, treaties, calendars, and the traditions, oral and written, of many leading families, though probably no 'lays of Ancient Rome'. Even the work of these early annalists and their successors is lost, so that our main sources are writers of some 200 years later, especially Livy and Dionysius of Halicarnassus, who used the annalistic tradition. Further, the survival of some early religious ceremonies into later times enables us to draw some deductions about the process by which the earlier villages coalesced to form the city of Rome, while the religious calendar of the Republic still reflects some customs of the sixth century or earlier. Finally archaeology provides much information about the huts and burials of the early settlements and about some of the buildings of the Etruscan period; this material is now being published in the great work by E. Gjerstad, *Early Rome*, projected in six volumes, three of which have now appeared.

The varied and uncertain nature of the evidence has naturally led to very diverse interpretations: some scholars accept the main outline of the literary tradition while others reject it; some believe that the archaeological evidence supports tradition, others that it necessitates some modification. These points must be stressed here because the early history of Rome has evoked keen interest and controversy in recent years, and any brief statement is bound to give an unduly oversimplified account of extremely complicated issues. For a judicious and masterly survey reference should be made to 'An interim report on the origins of Rome' by A. Momigliano.[170]

Evidence for pre-Iron Age settlements at the site of Rome has recently come to light. Flint and copper implements of the Chalcolithic period, long known, are now believed to come from the Esquiline hill, while Apennine pottery of the Bronze Age in the Forum Boarium near the Tiber has been found by E. Gjerstad in a filling of earth which was probably moved there in rebuilding a temple in 212 BC; the settlement from which it came was probably on one of the neighbouring hills, the Aventine, Capitoline or Palatine. But although this gives dramatic evidence for settlement on the site before and after c. 1500 BC, and thus adds nearly a millennium to the history of pre-urban Rome, so far there is no certain evidence of continuity of habitation with later times.[171]

The Iron Age settlements seem to mark a fresh start. Small villages of shepherds and farmers with wattle-and-daub huts spread over the Palatine, Esquiline, Quirinal and probably also the Caelian hills. The slopes and valleys between were used for burials until, probably in the early seventh century, overcrowding in the villages led some of the inhabitants to move down the slopes; before the end of the century, perhaps by 625, the site of the future Forum Romanum had been partially drained and dwelling huts are found there too. The tombs on the Esquiline are almost exclusively *fossa* inhumations; on the Quirinal the earliest are *pozzo* cremations, which are followed by *fossa* inhumations; an early tomb found in 1954 under the House of Livia on the Palatine was a cremation. In the Forum there were both cremation and inhumation burials (*Pl. 105*), but with cremation dominant in the earliest tombs; it is generally believed that these cremations represent the burials from the Palatine settlement, and the inhumations those from the other hills, while many think that the inhumations should be associated with the Sabines whom the later Romans believed to have formed a substantial element in the early population. However that may be, the inhabitants of all these villages were fundamentally similar to those of other Iron Age settlements in Latium. Those on the Palatine (*Pls. 1, 3*) resembled those on the Alban Hills, while material from the Esquiline is paralleled at Tivoli and southern Latium. Further, although the villages showed some individual characteristics in their pottery, they all shared essentially the same culture.[172]

The dating of this growth is more controversial. H. Müller-Karpe, who believes that the earliest settlement was subject to Aegean and Mycenaean influences, places the beginning in the tenth century, while the eighth saw the supersession of the cemetery in the Forum by a market centre. But this view has not won general support.[173] Gjerstad on the other hand places the days of the separate hill-dwellers from *c.* 800 to 700 (his Periods I and II); in Period III (700–625) the inhabitants began to move down the slopes and huts are found built over earlier tombs. Then comes the drainage of the Forum valley which in Period IV (625–575) enabled the area of settlement to spread (*cf.* the huts near the equus Domitiani). All these dates are of course approximate, with a margin of 25 years. During these last two periods the isolation of the villages was breaking down, their products were becoming more standardized, partly through the emergence of more professional craftsmen, some men were apparently becoming richer (a *fossa* tomb of *c.* 650 on the Esquiline contains the remains of a man's armour and chariot), and above all external influences increased, more particularly in Period IV when Etruscan *bucchero* and metal work from Veii and Caere appears, together with Etruscan imitations of Greek Protocorinthian and Corinthian pottery. Though the inhabitants lived in huts, their cultural demands were increasing.[174]

Thus far archaeology. But how does this square with the literary and religious evidence? Romulus is said to have established Roma Quadrata on the Palatine (see p. 75), and there is a slight balance in the archaeological evidence to suggest that the Iron Age settlement on the Palatine was marginally older than the others. Concerning the date, the later Romans had uncertain ideas, but the majority were in favour of a date around 750 BC, until Varro's estimate of 753 was officially accepted. Although these dates resulted from artificial calculations, it is a remarkable coincidence that they correspond with the archaeological date for the Iron Age huts on the Palatine; further, if the date of the first settlement should prove to be slightly earlier, there is always Timaeus' date of 813 to remember. Thus while few believe in a historical Romulus, the general tradition about his date makes good archaeological sense.

Religious cults which survived into historical times throw light on the process of amalgamation. The dancing warrior priests, the Salii, were divided into two groups, the Salii Palatini and Salii Collini (*i.e.* of the Quirinal). Further, the Luperci, who at the festival of the Lupercalia used to run around the Palatine in a ceremony of purification, were also divided into two groups, the Quirinales and the Fabiani, while it is known that the Fabian *gens* had a private cult on the Quirinal. All this points to the union of two originally separate villages. The festival of the Septimontium, however, seems to have been celebrated by the original elements of three groups: the Palatine (= Cermalus, Palatinus and Velia), the Esquiline (= Oppius, Cispius and Fagutal) and the Caelius. Finally, a procession which included the Pontifices and Vestals, used to visit twenty-four shrines of the Argei, six in each of four regions, namely Palatine, Velia, Caelius, Esquiline and Quirinal. Here is a union of four areas, and since the procession went round each separately, the rite may possibly go back to a period when there were four separate villages. From all this evidence the picture that emerges is first of separate villages such as Romulus' Palatine, followed by the Septimontium groupings of Palatine, Esquiline and Caelius. These were probably linked by common interests and religious cult, and not necessarily by a physical union within a single defensive rampart; in fact nothing is certain about any village or common walls for these early times, the likelihood being that the villages relied for defence on the steep hill-sides, though there *might* have been some earthwalls across the Oppius, Cispius, and Quirinal. Tradition also records the story of the Rape of the Sabine women which resulted in the joint rule of Romulus and the Sabine Titus Tatius until the latter's death. Though this dual monarchy may be an attempt to explain the origin of the later collegiate magistracy of the consulate, the resultant 'urbs geminata', to which Livy (1, 13) refers, may reflect the union of Palatine and Quirinal. When this was organized as Rome of the Four Regions, which still excluded the Capitoline and Aventine, we are passing from the pre-Etruscan to the Etruscan city.

The transition is heralded by the importation of Etruscan and other pottery, as we have seen (p. 245), which increased in volume in Gjerstad's Period IV. It has recently been argued by G. Colonna that this period should be subdivided, IV A being applied to the last Forum burials and IV B to the orientalizing elements.[175] In the latter period not only Etruscan pottery but Etruscan ideas were reaching Rome, and huts were giving place to houses with tiled roofs, and changes in burial pits occurred. Thus Rome is entering into the cultural circle of Etruria, and the beginning of this period IV B should be placed in the last quarter of the seventh century, at the very time when according to Roman tradition the first Etruscan king, Tarquinius Priscus, gained his throne (616 BC). Henceforth, Rome can be considered an Etruscan city in the sense that it became an *urbs* rather than *pagi*, that it was brought within the general ambit of Etruscan civilization, and that for much of the sixth century it was ruled by Etruscan kings until Tarquinius Superbus was finally expelled, traditionally in 510 BC.

THE BUILDINGS OF THE CITY

One outstanding aspect of the growth of the city under the Etruscans is its amazing speed: within a century a collection of huts had developed into a city with a civic centre, public buildings and temples of which the greatest could vie with any in Etruria and indeed in the contemporary Greek world. This was the result of Etruscan influence on Villanovan Latins, and it strengthens the view that an external foreign Etruscan influence had promoted the similar rapid growth of Villanovan villages into cities in Etruria itself a century or more before this time. Behind the physical growth of the city lay the driving power of a unified source of authority, the will of the scattered villages to strengthen their individual positions by co-operating as a single body, and the technical skill in architecture and engineering that produced the new buildings (Fig. 27).

The focal point of the new city was the Forum, which became usable only with adequate drainage to draw off the water that came down from the valleys between the Esquiline, Viminal and Quirinal and from the other hills. The earliest hut-settlement of *c.* 660 had suffered from flooding (*c.* 625) but drainage works were undertaken, possibly by Tarquinius Priscus and the area of possible habitation was extended. The main drain, the Cloaca Maxima, was attributed by tradition to the second Tarquin; like its predecessors it was still probably an open ditch, since the surviving *capellacio* work seems to belong to the years after 390 BC. At any rate by the early sixth century the older graves were covered and the huts destroyed and on top of them a pebble floor was laid for the new centre. The huts were replaced by houses with walls of sun-dried brick covered with painted stucco and having tiled roofs. Some regular streets were no doubt planned, the most famous being the Sacra Via, which came down over the Velia following the course of a stream; in the Forum it led between the Regia and the Temple of Vesta, and ultimately went on to the Capitolium, while the Vicus Tuscus continued on from the Forum to the Cattle Market (Forum Boarium) near the Tiber. This Vicus was a quarter inhabited by Etruscans, perhaps largely craftsmen and traders, and here stood a statue of the Etruscan god Vortumnus, of which the later base was found in 1549. The date of the earliest road-bed of the Sacra Via was either during Period IV of the pre-urban epoch, or in the initial period of the unified city, *i.e. c.* 575, accord-

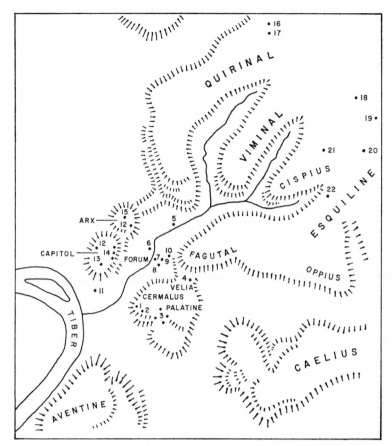

Fig. 27 Plan of early Rome. 1 Walls on the Palatine. 2 Huts. 3 Huts, tombs, cisterns, etc. 4 Huts on Velia, 5 Tombs under Forum Augusti. 6 Huts at Equus Domitiani. 7 Huts and tombs near Temple of Caesar. 8 Finds near Temple of Vesta. 9 Regia. 10 Tombs and huts at Sacra Via. 11 Forum Boarium, with temples. 12 Walls on Capitol. 13 Temple of Jupiter Capitolinus. 14 Finds on the Capitol. 15 Antefix from the Arx. 16 Tombs on the Quirinal. 17 Agger on the Quirinal. 18 Agger on Esquiline (at Stazione di Termini). 19 Tombs on the Esquiline. 20 Agger on Esquiline. 21 Huts on the Cispius. 22 Tombs on Esquiline

ing to Gjerstad's assessment of his stratigraphic excavations.[176]

In the Forum stood the Regia which Rome's second king, Numa, according to tradition, had given to the Pontifex Maximus (*Pl. 104*). It was on the north side of the Sacra Via whose east-west orientation was determined here by the direction of the southern wall of the Regia. The date of the earliest building can scarcely be later than *c.* 575 since the *latest* finds in the lowest stratum are of the sixth century, while some of the pottery belongs to Gjerstad's Period IV or even III. Near by have been found fragments of terracotta revetments, which have reliefs of panthers, lionesses and minotaurs in procession (*Pl. 109*); their style suggests the first half of the sixth century, and they probably formed part of the decoration of the Archaic Regia. Of the earliest round temple of Vesta on the other side of the Sacra Via nothing has been found, but within the temple area a votive deposit provides material, including Greek pottery, which runs from 575/550 down to much later times. Further, a pit just south-east of the temple, excavated in 1930, contained exclusively archaic material which was probably the crockery and domestic utensils used in the adjacent House of the Vestal Virgins; the date appears to be *c.* 575–550, if some of the finer pottery, which may be a little older than this, was not in use until this period.

The Comitium, the later assembly-place of the Roman people, lay in the Forum near the Capitoline hill. Its use as a political centre may be coeval with its first pavement, but below this is a gravel surface, probably contemporary with the pebbling of the Forum *c.* 575 (*Pl. 106*). Below the so-called Lapis Niger a votive deposit contains objects from *c.* 570 to the first century, demonstrating an early cult. Among them are fragments of terracotta revetments which probably adorned the cult-building; they include a horseman, part of a feline, and a gorgon antefix. Others have been found near by, depicting a chariot scene, paralleled on terracottas from Veii and Velitrae, a pair of galloping horsemen like that from Velitrae and another feline (*Pl. 107*). Lastly, mention should be made of the Volcanal which was an assembly place before the Comitium was so used; it formed a platform from which the king could address the people. Since sanctuaries of Vulcan had to be built outside the city, this Volcanal at the foot of the Capitol must precede the time when the Forum was part of the city, and belong to the period of village settlement, when there was perhaps an open-air altar which *may* be represented by some early tufa foundations just behind the Arch of Severus.

The early development of the Forum Boarium, now revealed by the excavations around the Church of Sant' Omobono, resembles that of the Forum Romanum: by c. 575 BC earlier huts were destroyed and a floor was laid out (Pl. 103). As early as this an open-air sanctuary had been established, to be followed by two temples built symmetrically on a platform with altars in front of each on the axial line of their cellae: one temple is now under the Church.[176a] The first temple belongs to the beginning of the fifth century; and since the temples of Fortuna and Mater Matuta, which were said to have been founded by Servius Tullius, were in this area, the identification is usually accepted. They were reconstructed by Camillus in 395. The excavations produced considerable quantities of imported Greek pottery, dating from c. |570 until c. 450 (Pl. 119) terracottas, fragments of plaques showing horses, chariots and charioteers, and two terracotta sculptures, a head of Minerva, and a torso of Hercules (Pl. 110).[177]

The early inhabitants of Rome had curiously neglected the Capitoline hill: no certain archaeological evidence exists for its occupation before the sixth century, despite the legend that Titus Tatius lived on the Arx, its northern height, and despite its obvious advantages as a natural stronghold.[178] However, the Tarquins made up for that and, by including it within the city and by establishing a great temple to Jupiter Optimus Maximus on its southern side, they made it the religious centre of the city. In the north-west corner of the Arx was an open space (templum), where public auspices were taken; the thatched hut of the observer was preserved at least until the time of Augustus. In view of the significance attached to auspices by the Etruscans, this area is likely to have been important in the sixth century. Other buildings include an unidentified temple with a votive deposit, which was traced in 1925–7 west of the Via del Campidoglio and dates to c. 500. Soundings at the temple of Veiovis suggest that the cult began c. 500. A cistern under the Palazzo dei Conservatori may go back to the regal period. Several architectural terracottas have been found, including the famous antefix of the slightly smiling woman's head from the Arx (Pl. 111). Lastly, a votive deposit in a pozzo at the Clivus Capitolinus has pottery starting from the late sixth century and including a *bucchero* bowl inscribed with one of the three Etruscan inscriptions found in Rome: 'ni araziia laraniia' (*Pl. 118*).[179] And, whatever its precise date, one of the finest sculptures of early Rome should be mentioned here: the Capitoline wolf (*Pl. 120*).

The Capitoline temple was the crowning architectural glory of Etruscan Rome. Only parts of the stone substructure and fragments of terracotta antefixes and tiles survive. It was vowed, according to tradition, by Tarquinius Priscus, nearly completed by Tarquinius Superbus, and dedicated on September 13th of the first year of the Republic to Jupiter, with his companion deities Juno and Minerva. Jupiter occupied the middle of the three *cellae*, and his cult statue was made in terracotta by Vulca, a Veientine master sculptor (*cf*. pp. 108f); it was clothed with a tunic adorned with palm-branches, and a gold-embroidered purple toga, the costume that Roman generals later wore when celebrating a triumph. The superstructure of the temple was of wood covered with painted terracotta, and on the central acroterium above the pediment was placed a quadriga, in which stood Jupiter holding sceptre and thunderbolt, also the work of Vulca. Three rows of six columns formed a *pronaos* in front of the *cellae*, while a row of three columns made a portico on each side of the temple. Its width was possibly some 180 (Roman) feet, its height some 65, and its columns 8 feet in diameter (*Pls. 113-5*). Figured friezes probably ran along both architrave and raking cornice: they may well have depicted a solemn procession of chariots and a chariot race, such as those shown in other surviving revetments. One of the antefixes that has been found shows the head of a Silenus (*Pl. 112*).[180]

In addition to its architectural splendour, the religious significance of the temple was profound. Under the Etruscans the Romans first learned to envisage their vaguer deities in anthropomorphic shape and to build temples, in place of simple altars, for them. Further, Jupiter Optimus Maximus became the official state-god of the community, while Vulca's representation of him revealed to Rome the Etrusco-Greek art which flourished at Veii. With this new cult was linked the Etruscan ceremony

of holding a triumph which the Romans borrowed from them. After the solemn procession to the temple the triumphator, the king in regal times, sacrificed to the god whom he had represented in the procession, and then went down to the Circus Maximus in the valley between the Palatine and Aventine, where the Roman Games were celebrated in the god's honour. The first Games held were ascribed to Romulus, but in view of the Etruscans' love of horseracing they were no doubt elaborated by the Tarquins, who are said to have built the first wooden stands for the spectators, though apparently there was no permanent construction before 329 BC.

One other famous sixth century shrine must be mentioned, although its precise site has not been established, that of Diana on the Aventine. This hill had not been included in the Rome of the Four Regions, and indeed did not come within the sacred *pomerium* until the time of the emperor Claudius, but the site was chosen by Servius Tullius for a federal Latin temple; here he persuaded the neighbouring Latin towns to build a common sanctuary of the League. As in the case of the Sant' Omobono open-air sacred area, the earliest form was more probably an altar perhaps in a grove (*cf.* 'lex arae Dianae in Aventino': *ILS* 112), rather than the temple that tradition assigns to Servius. Despite attempts to prove that this temple was later than 500, a mere imitation of the federal Latin sanctuary at Aricia, the original date should stand.[181] Rome was clearly trying to win the political leadership of Latium from Aricia, while Servius, a Latin, may have had an eye on the interests of a Latin league in case of trouble from Etruria.

Finally, there is the vexed question whether sixth-century Rome was encircled by a stone wall. Tradition ascribed such a defence to Servius Tullius (578–535). Some archaeologists assign to him some parts of the surviving 'Servian' wall which in the main belongs to the fourth century, but others believe, perhaps rightly, that the allegedly early small blocks of grey tufa (*cappellaccio*) are later than the sixth century (*Pl. 113*). More probably an earthwork (*agger*), constructed across the Viminal and designed to block the heads of the valleys that lead into Rome from the

east, may be ascribed to Servius. The work is dated by Gjerstad to c. 475, but this is on the strength of a single piece of Attic pottery found in it, which may well be intrusive; regal Rome, like contemporary Ardea may have been protected only by its natural position and by an *agger* and fosse.[182]

Thus under Etruscan rule Rome became a centralized city with a unified government, with public buildings worthy to be set alongside those of Etruria itself. Most have perished, but something of the spirit of public life is reflected in the gaily coloured decorations of the temples and in the scenes shown on the friezes: banqueting scenes, horsemen, chariots and men walking in procession, chariot races, strange feline beasts and minotaurs, together with the quantities of Greek imported pottery, suggest a background congenial to the new rulers and remote from the lives of the men who had lived in the huts on the site less than a century before.

THE RULE OF THE TARQUINS

No detailed discussion of sixth-century Rome can be attempted here, but some aspects may be mentioned. From the point of view of Etruscan history it is tantalizing that the one city about whose internal government we know something from literary sources was far from being a representative Etruscan city. In fact Rome, though it probably gained its very name from the Etruscans, remained essentially a Latin community and its organization should not be used as evidence for that of the cities of Etruria, although its general development may mirror something of what occurred in them. We must remember that we are dealing with a Latin people who had some Etruscan rulers and were swept out of their earlier parochialism into the wider world of Etruscan social, economic and cultural life.

The three pre-Etruscan kings in the seventh century may well be historical figures, though little of the tradition about them can be accepted with confidence, since both earlier and later institutions tended to be attributed to them.[183] Numa, the priest king, was traditionally the creator of many of Rome's religious priesthoods and practices. He may have established a new

calendar, perhaps a twelve-month one in place of a ten-month, though if Aprilis derives from Etruscan *apru*, this change may rather belong to the Tarquins. Then the warrior Tullus Hostilius may be credited with the destruction of Alba Longa, as tradition asserts: Aricia seems then to have taken over the lead from Alba. Ancus Marcius, wise in peace and strong in war, probably built the wooden Sublician bridge over the Tiber at Rome which would allow men, unhampered by the rivalry of Veii in the north, to make their way to the salt-pans at Ostia: the salt-trade was becoming important and Ancus probably established settlers, though not a colony, near Ostia. Thus towards the end of the seventh century the communities at Rome had coalesced sufficiently to unite under common leadership in establishing some order at home and in advancing their joint authority both towards the coast and in the Alban Hills. In one sense Rome can justly be called a city at this time, but many aspects of city-life were to be developed only under Etruscan guidance. To call, with Gjerstad, this period 'Pre-urban', as opposed to the urbanized Rome of the Etruscans, may be a useful label so long as it is not applied too narrowly, does not provoke arid discussion of what is meant by a 'city', and does not lead to his date of *c.* 575 being given canonical authority for the foundation of the city.

Then followed the Etruscan L. Tarquinius Priscus (traditionally 616–579), the Latin Servius Tullius (578–535) and the Etruscan Tarquinius Superbus (534–510). It is clear that, however much later Roman tradition tried to play down the fact, the Tarquins were Etruscan rulers: their name alone denotes this (the Lucius may arise from confusion with the title Lucumo). In some ways they are shadowy figures and since many similar actions are attributed to both of them, some critics regard them as a single person. But much of the confusion may have arisen from the survival of a body of rather generalized tradition about the two men, which later Roman historians tried to sort out, not all attributing the same deeds to the same Tarquin. The date given to Priscus fits well with the archaeological evidence of the beginning of Etruscan influence at Rome, and even Gjerstad's date of *c.* 575 for the unification of the city is not too far out, unless it is given a rigid interpretation which excludes a fairly wide margin of error (Gjerstad himself will not abandon Priscus and therefore lowers Priscus' initial date to 575. It would surely be better to abandon his traditional initial date, assign him a shorter reign, and retain the date of his death.)

Traditionally Tarquinius Priscus came to Rome, peacefully, from Tarquinii: this alleged origin may be due to the similarity of name, since the family of Tarcna, latinized as Tarquitius, had a family tomb at Caere which has inscriptions from the fifth to the third century. He was said to be the son of the immigrant Corinthian Demaratus (see p. 85), but even if this were doubted, the historicity of Demaratus need not be involved. He had married a noblewoman, the Etruscan Tanaquil, whose dominant influence is dramatically described by Livy, so that it has been said that 'the events of her life are un-Roman and literary':[184] they may not, however, be un-Etruscan. Of Tarquin's alleged activities his establishment of Games (cf. p. 253) and a system of drainage, two typically Etruscan interests, may be accepted. He is said to have added a hundred members to the Senate, who were known as *minores gentes*. He will clearly have encouraged a number of Etruscan families to come to settle in Rome, a process which presumably continued under Superbus. Several Etruscan names are preserved in those of the tribes set up by Servius, such as Lemonia, Menenia, Papiria, Voltinia. Thus the Tarquins strengthened their position by an Etruscan *clientela*. Finally, if he should be identified with the Cn. Tarquinius Romanus depicted in the François tomb at Vulci (see pp. 122f) who was killed by M. Camitlnas, when the latter, with Mastarna and A. Vibenna, was trying to rescue C. Vibenna from Tarquin, then his end was violent in Etruscan tradition as well as in Roman, though the story varied. According to Livy, he was killed by agents of the two sons of Ancus, though Tanaquil's skill secured the succession for her son-in-law Servius.

Servius Tullius was, according to Roman tradition, a Latin of humble birth who had been brought up by Priscus, whose daughter he had then married; he owed his throne to Tanaquil's boldness in concealing Priscus' death until Servius was secure in

105   Air view of the Iron Age cemetery (Sepulcretum) in the Roman Forum
at the end of the excavations of 1902, before it was filled in again. It contains
cremations (round *pozzi*) and inhumations (trench-like *fosse*). See p.244f.

106 Section which shows the stratification of Boni's excavations in the Comitium in the Roman Forum. This work, undertaken in 1900, has been supplemented by E. Gjerstad's excavations, especially that near the Equus Domitiani in the Forum which revealed 29 strata from the time of the Roman Empire down past the Republican, Regal, and pre-urban hut levels to virgin soil. These superimposed strata in the resultant earth-wall thus reflect the history of the centuries.

107–109 Terracotta moulded reliefs from Early Rome. See p.250. 107 Warriors, charioteers and winged horses, from the Cispius. 108 Warrior riding on horse, from the votive deposit under the Lapis Niger in the Forum. 109 A Minotaur flanked by two felines (right, a lioness, left a panther) from near the temple of Caesar in the Forum.

110 Head of a statue of Minerva, found near Sant' Omobono in the Forum Boarium, Rome, *c.* threequarters life size. Perhaps originally the acroterium of a temple. In an Ionian style, late sixth century. See p.251.

111 Terracotta antefix in the shape of an oval female head crowned by a
semicircular diadem and with an archaic smile. Found in the garden of the
Aracoeli, it decorated a temple of the Arx Capitolina. See p.251.   112 Antefix
in the shape of the head of a Silenus, from the Cispius. See p.252.

113 Stretch of the 'Servian' Wall on the Aventine in Rome showing cross-section. Though attributed to Servius Tullius, it may date from after 387 BC. See p.253. 114 Substructure wall of the podium of the temple of Jupiter Optimus Maximus on the Capitol. It now forms part of the Museo Nuovo Capitolino. See p.252.

power. His name, which is Latin, helps to guarantee his historicity, since it was later used only by plebeians, while a fictitious king would probably have been given a patrician name. However an Etruscan tradition, which apparently was unknown to or rejected by Roman historians until it was given currency by the emperor Claudius, equated Servius with the Etruscan Mastarna who according to the François tomb-painting had helped A. Vibenna to rescue his brother Caelius in the mêlée in which Cn. Tarquinius was killed (*Pl. 46*). According to the Etruscan version of events, as given by Claudius, Mastarna had been a close friend of Caelius Vibenna in all his adventures and then, driven out by a change of fortune, he had left Etruria with the remains of Caelius' army, occupied a hill in Rome, which he named the Caelius after his former leader; he changed his name to Servius Tullius and obtained the kingship at Rome. Here there is a contradiction. The earlier painted version suggests that the violent death of Tarquin left a vacant throne, but the Roman tradition suggests no violent seizure of power by Servius. In fact the Roman writers believed that Caelius, with his Etruscan companions, had been invited to Rome by Tarquinius to help him (so Tacitus; Varro gives Romulus) and was given the hill of the Oak (Querquetulanus) which later received Caelius' name. Claudius, or rather his source, must therefore have used a romanized version of the Etruscan story, one which had dropped the whole episode of the violent struggle with Tarquinius.[185] Further complications, *e.g.* that Mastarna should be identified with Porsenna, need not be discussed here, except to note the embarassing fact that Mastarna seems to be a Latin and not an Etruscan word: Macstr-na = mag(i)st(e)r-na, and *magister populi* was probably the original name of the Roman dictator. However, the Etruscan version cannot be dismissed out of hand: the painting is a historical document of great value and a certain Aulus Vibenna (Avele Vipiiennus) dedicated a *bucchero* vase at Veii in the mid-sixth century (*cf.* p. 109) which goes some way to establish the historicity of the two Vibenna brothers. If then we have to choose between an Etruscan or Latin origin for Servius Tullius, the latter will seem more probable in the light of the great veneration accorded to him by later generations, though it must be recognized that both the Roman and Etruscan traditions had a strong motive in claiming him. But if a Latin king held the throne between two Etruscan rulers, it does not necessarily mean that all Etruscan influences ceased during the middle of the century.

Three achievements are usually attributed to Servius: the creation of the centuriate organization, the building of the walls of the Rome, and the establishment of the cult of Diana on the Aventine. If modern archaeologists want to rob him of the wall, at least he is credited by many with care for the defence of the city, which he strengthened with earth ramparts and ditches at weak spots. His establishment of the cult of Diana (see p. 253) was a bold attempt to assert Roman political leadership in Latium. The cult was that of Diana of Ephesus, the source no doubt also of the goddess' cult at Aricia, which Servius was trying to outdo. Since Strabo states that the statue was set up in the same way as that of Diana at Massalia, while the Massaliote one copied the Ephesian, Servius may have got some technical advice from the Massaliotes or refugees from Ionia.[186] The Aventine was later a plebeian quarter of the city and doubtless was inhabited by many resident aliens as well as poor citizens and the new cult would appeal to this class, to whom Servius by his reforms was hoping to extend citizenship. These reforms, which in their essential features are assumed here to belong to the period of Servius, though more relevant for the future history of Rome than for the contemporary history of Etruria, may have some significance for the latter. As we have already seen (p. 225), by a timocratic reorganization of the state Servius may have tried to strengthen the power of the monarchy against increasing pressure from the nobility, by appealing to the middle-class which could supply legionary hoplites; at the same time he was enabled to enfranchise many of the men whom trade and industry had attracted to Rome under Etruscan rule. With this increase in population he could raise the size of the army from the old force of 3000, based on the *curiae*, to a new legion of 6000, based on his new structure of *classes* and *centuriae*. One result must have been to slow down the process by which the nobles were claiming more religious, social and political privileges for themselves, and thus beginning to form a separate class, the patriciate. Finally, the growing influence of Greece is noteworthy; not only was the worship of Diana a Greek cult and much Greek pottery was reaching Rome, but Servius' reforms were made only a few decades after Solon had introduced a timocratic reform in the Athenian state: one would like to know the extent to which Greek ideas had been reaching Rome since the days of the elder Tarquin, whose father was a Greek.[187]

Servius was murdered by the younger Tarquin, the son or more probably grandson of Priscus, who was driven on to the deed by the ambitions of his wife, Tullia, Servius' own daughter. Though depicted by the literary sources as a kind of Greek tyrant decked out in Roman regalia, his historical existence can hardly be questioned. At home he is credited with building the Capitoline temple and the Cloaca Maxima. His external achievements include a treaty with Gabii, some twelve miles east of Rome; the treaty was written on the ox-hide covering of a shield and was preserved in a temple on the Quirinal until the time of Augustus; it is not likely to have been a forgery. Thus during the regal period Rome's power in Latium had greatly increased; she controlled some 350 square miles of territory. In fact her importance was such that Carthage had probably negotiated a treaty with her (see p. 176). In it Rome speaks for the cities of the Latin coast who were 'subject' to her, that is probably allies (*socii*) who, like Gabii, recognized Rome's military leadership in individual treaties: these cities were Ardea, Antium, Circeii, Terracina and probably Lavinium. Rome's further claim to speak for those Latins 'such as were not subject' suggests that she was acting as spokesman for a league of which she was a prominent member. Thus under Etruscan rule Rome had become a city which interested even distant Carthage.

This interest was doubtless due both to the traditional friendship of Carthage with the Etruscan cities, and to the fact that Rome was now a commercial centre. In industry and trade Rome owed much to Etruria: the technical skill of the Etruscans in metal and clay had set an example for Roman craftsmen to follow, and the eight labour guilds which are attributed to the regal period are quite credible: these were bronze-smiths, potters, gold-smiths, carpenters, dyers, leather-workers, tanners and flute-players. Even if Rome did not produce more than required by the home market, which included a luxurious court, her geographical position enabled her to share in the commerce which passed between Etruria and Campania, and between the salt-flats at Ostia and the hill-tribes to the east.

Rome's debt was not confined to the economic sphere. The building of temples, besides providing work for skilled and unskilled, promoted a new conception of deity, while it was from the Etruscans that Rome learnt to elaborate the practice of augury, which played a fundamental part in public life. From the same source she borrowed the trappings and insignia of her later magistrates (see p. 222), as well as hoplite tactics in the phalanx and some military equipment. Etruria was also the main channel through which early Rome became acquainted with many aspects of Greek life. No doubt Rome learnt much too in less visible ways—powers of organization which made possible a united city life. But the debt must not be exaggerated. Basically industry was less significant than agriculture, and while no doubt part of the population became bilingual, it is remarkable how few Etruscan words survived in Latin. The Romans remained what they had been before, a Latin people.

The importance of Etruscan Rome, which is summed up in G. Pasquali's famous phrase, 'La grande Roma dei Tarquinii', has recently been questioned by A. Alföldi who writes: 'the prosperity of Etruscan Rome—a boom which was not lacking elsewhere in Latium—does not mean the sovereignty of Rome over the Latin nation' (*Early Rome and the Latins*, p. 319). Briefly, Alföldi has argued that the picture of early Rome which we find in Livy and writers of his day was invented by Fabius Pictor. In Alföldi's view Rome was one of the lesser Latin cities which endured Etruscan rule for some 150 years until *c.* 505; the rulers were not only the Tarquins but included kings from Caere, Vulci, Veii, and Clusium: it was only a considerable time after the Etruscan period that Rome became the leading Latin city. Fabius, aware of this, deliberately antedated Rome's rise to power and attributed to her in the sixth century that strength and predominance over other Latin cities that she gained only in the later fifth. Patriotism led him to wholesale falsification, which was accepted by later Roman writers. This attempt to scale down the importance of Etruscan Rome, though argued with great learning, is scarcely likely to win many supporters: it involves so many difficulties that it is easier to believe that what the Romans themselves said about their early days may well be nearer to the truth. So detailed a reconstruction demands mention but can scarcely be discussed here: its merits and weaknesses will appear in further scholarly debate.[188]

THE END OF ETRUSCAN ROME

The fall of Tarquinius Superbus at Rome, the collapse of Etruscan power in Latium, the history of Lars Porsenna, the establishment of a Republican constitution at Rome, all form parts of a complicated pattern. First, a brief glance at the relatively simple account given by the ancient historians; then the much more complex interpretations put upon the ancient evidence, both literary and archaeological, by modern scholars.

Superbus had three sons. While Sextus was in Rome, his two brothers with their cousin L. Junius Brutus consulted the oracle at Delphi about a portent; in view of the connection of Caere with Delphi (see p. 184) and of the Tarquins with Caere, the historical background of this story is perfectly reasonable, whatever may be thought about its actual historicity. Thereafter the rape of Lucretia, wife of Tarquinius Collatinus, by Sextus provoked an uprising against the Tarquins which was led by Brutus: Sextus fled to Gabii where he was killed, while his father and two brothers took refuge in Caere. At Rome the monarchy was abolished and replaced by two annually elected consuls, of whom one was Brutus; meanwhile Tarquinius Superbus gained help from Tarquinii and Veii whose forces met the Romans in an indecisive battle at Silva Arsia. Next Tarquinius secured aid from Lars Porsenna of Clusium who marched to Rome but failed to capture it on arrival, thanks to Horatius' defence of the bridge (and it is noteworthy that in the legend Horatius' companions, Larcius and Herminius, both had Etruscan names). After a siege the bravery of the Romans, revealed by the exploits of Mucius Scaevola and Cloelia, led to Porsenna's withdrawal. So says Livy, but later Romans such as Tacitus and the elder Pliny knew and exposed the bitter truth—that in fact Porsenna had captured Rome. Indeed, the purpose of Porsenna's attack may not have been to restore Tarquinius at Rome: at any rate, though successful, Porsenna did not restore him. Then followed the defeat of Porsenna's forces by the Latins and Aristodemus of Cumae at Aricia (c. 506), whether the action had been precipitated by an abortive southward push by Porsenna or by a Latin counter-attack (cf. p. 194).[189] Tarquinius next took refuge with his son-in-law Mamilius Octavius of Tusculum who persuaded the Latins, according to Roman accounts, to take up the exiled king's cause and fought the Romans at the battle of Lake Regillus. In fact Tarquinius probably had nothing to do with promoting the action: rather, the Latins, who had co-operated successfully at Aricia, were organized in a league from which Rome was excluded, and the two opponents clashed. Soon afterwards in 496 Tarquinius died at Cumae where he had found a final refuge with Aristodemus.

The linchpin of the traditional account of the establishment of the Republic is its connection with the expulsion of the Tarquins: it was due to revolution. Some modern scholars, however, impressed with supposedly analogous developments elsewhere, have attributed its establishment rather to evolution and rejected the traditional account: thus at Athens the authority of the king declined and was gradually transferred piecemeal to three magistrates. Others, although ready to accept that the end of the monarchy was abrupt, are not willing to believe that the dual consulship was devised suddenly in 509 as an anti-revolutionary safeguard: it must have resulted from earlier prototypes by an evolutionary process, e.g. two auxiliaries of the king, or praetors. Other historians have postulated an interval of time between the monarchy and two magistrates of equal authority during which one magistrate (or a college of magistrates in which one predominated) exercised control, *e.g.* a *praetor maximus*, while others again have tried to show that dictators or *magistri populi* existed under the monarchy. Since we are less concerned with Republican Rome, we need not pursue these questions further, but they have been mentioned in order to indicate the kind of difficulties and reconstructions that are encountered if once the traditional account is abandoned.[190]

The rock to which the traditionalist must cling is not of course the mass of detailed legend, but rather the Fasti, the list of Rome's early magistrates which starts with the first consuls of the Republic. It is generally agreed that the early lists are not free from errors and falsifications, but that is no reason to reject them as valueless, nor indeed to take refuge in the theory that the officials listed were not consuls. One objection to their reliability has been the fact that they contain the names of some plebeians such as Cassius, whereas all the early consuls have been regarded as patricians. But patricians and plebeians in early times sometimes had the same names while original patrician names sometimes passed over into plebeian families: that is, not all names in the Fasti which were later plebeian need be plebeian inventions. Further, since many now place the emergence of the two Orders after the end of the monarchy or else hold that such a division had not become clearly defined before its end, it would be difficult to believe that none of the consuls with later plebeian names in the early Fasti could have held the office. Another line of attack has been to point to a considerable number of Etruscan names among the holders of the office: this must mean, it is argued, that the Etruscan king had not been expelled, or in other words this part of the Fasti must apply to the regal rather than to the Republican period and therefore, if the dates of the Fasti are accepted, the date of the establishment of the Republic must be lowered until after the appearance of these Etruscanized consuls. Nothing of the sort! The Roman tradition associates the beginning of the Republic with the expulsion of the family of one Etruscan, not with a wholesale expulsion of all the Etruscans who had settled in Rome. As Professor Momigliano says, the expulsion of the tyrant Hippias from Athens in 510 BC, did not lead to the ejection of all his followers; and no modern historian would try to eliminate the Peisistratid element which existed in Athens for the next two or three decades. Momigliano has further underlined the important fact that the chronology of the annal- istic account of the fall of the monarchy is roughly confirmed by an independent Greek tradition. This is the account given by Dionysius of Halicarnassus about the activities of Aristodemus and in particular the help that he gave to the Latins in 505 against Porsenna: whether or not Dionysius derived his account from a local history of Cumae, it clearly came from a source other than the Roman annalists.[191]

It has been necessary to emphasize the essential reasonableness of accepting the outlines of the Roman account, because we must now examine another attempt to explain the Fasti in a different way; and this is necessary not because the theory has won wide acceptance but because it has been adopted by Gjerstad, who uses it as a framework for the interpretation of the archaeological evidence. In 1945 K. Hanell advanced the view that 509 BC was the first year of the new cult of Jupiter Capitolinus but not the first year of the Republic, and that the surviving list of consuls of the first half of the fifth century represented not consuls but merely eponymous magistrates of the new cult of Jupiter: in fact at first there was only one each year, the *praetor maximus*; thus one name of each consular year has to be eliminated, unless with Gjerstad both are accepted. At the same time the pre-Julian calendar was introduced in connection with the foundation of the temple. The monarchy continued until the mid-fifth century. This view has been adopted by Gjerstad, who accepts the length of reigns assigned by the annalistic tradition to the kings; he therefore brings down the period of Etruscan rule in Rome from *c.* 616–510 BC to *c.* 530–450. This theory, if adopted, would result in having to put the struggle of the Orders, the treaty of Cassius and many other events into the regal period. Such telescoping produces dislocation on a scale that can hardly be contemplated.[192]

How then does Gjerstad think that this reconstructed dating of the Etruscan regal period gains support from the archaeological evidence? Briefly, because one of the temples of the Forum Boarium and the *agger* (representing the Wall) belong to the early fifth century and are traditionally assigned to Servius Tullius; thus Servius must be brought down to this century. But the late dating of the *agger* depends on a single Attic sherd, while the temple could have been falsely assigned to him by tradition: he could in fact have been responsible for an earlier altar on the site.[193] Beside these specific points, Gjerstad wishes to prolong the regal period 'because Etruscan art continued to flourish in Rome until about 450 BC. At that time, contact with the high Etruscan culture is suddenly broken' (*Legends*, etc., p. 61): he also points to the Etruscan names among the magistrates. But others might interpret these facts in an opposite sense: as has been said, the expulsion of Tarquinius would involve a slow decline of Etruscan influences at Rome, rather than an abrupt ending; Rome was not suddenly whisked off the map to another world, but continued to live in the same cultural area, and the contacts of over a century would not be snapped instantly. This is clear from the fact that Greek pottery continued to be imported, though perhaps on a declining scale until the mid-fifth century; terracottas from temples are found, while there was a positive spate of temple-building, that of Saturn in the Forum in 496, of Mercury in 495, of Ceres, Liber and Libera on the Aventine in 493, of the Dioscuri in the Forum in 484 and of Dius Fidius in 466; further, that of Ceres is expressly said to have been decorated by Greek artists.

The slowing down of cultural life after *c.* 475 has led R. Bloch to argue that the end of Etruscan rule at Rome should be dated to this time.[194] With the expulsion of the Tarquins not all Etruscan leaders left, but some continued to support the plebeians against the landed Latin nobility. In other words, the fall of Tarquinius was followed by a decade or two which could be called sub-Etruscan, marked by the activities of men like Porsenna, a transitionary period which should be set against the background of the weakening of Etruscan power in Latium and Campania at a time when the control of many Etruscan cities also was passing from kings to oligarchies. In these disturbed times ambitious nobles, with their bands of clients, followers and mercenaries, could strive for power. If, in earlier times, Servius had tried to curb them by introducing hoplite tactics, more lawless days allowed men to fight in more personal order, as when the clan of the Fabii and their clients fought against the Veientes on the Cremera in *c.* 475, and perished almost to a man. Conflicting feelings towards Etruria may also have influenced internal history. Magistrates with Etruscan names are found until 487—*e.g.* Aquillius Tuscus—two years before Spurius Cassius, who favoured friendship with the Etruscans, and aimed at personal power, only to be overthrown and followed by the powerful Roman aristocratic clan of the Fabii and their war against Veii. The temporary reappearance of some Etruscan names in the Fasti in 461–448 coincides roughly with the interruption of war with Veii and internal plebeian pressure in Rome. However that may be, if in general we should perhaps not seek a definite date for the end of Etruscan Rome, but rather think in terms of a receding tide, that need not involve the rejection of the traditional date of the expulsion of the Tarquins.

CHAPTER X

ROME AND THE ETRUSCANS

ROME AND THE SOUTHERN CITIES[195]

UNDER ETRUSCAN RULE Rome had been a spearhead thrust into the side of the Latins, but after the expulsion of the Tarquins and Rome's subsequent alliance with the Latins the spearhead was turned to the north and menaced Etruria. The city which might be expected first to clash with Rome was her neighbour Veii, since two areas of potential rivalry existed: the salt-pans at the mouth of the Tiber, and Fidenae which lay east of the Tiber and commanded the entrance to the Cremera valley on the opposite bank. This valley led to Veii, and the river was probably crossed by ferry; if Rome gained Fidenae, Veii's influence in the Tiber valley and her link with the tribes of central Italy would be threatened or cut.

Border raids may have occurred, but the first real clash is recorded in 483–474. The Romans are credited with a victory in 480 against Veii which probably received no help from other Etruscan cities, despite Livy's contrary view. The Romans, or traditionally the Fabian *gens*, established a block-house near the Cremera, which would cut Veii's communications with Fidenae and put an end to her control over traffic in the Tiber valley, especially any moving southwards. Disaster followed: with great variety of detail the story is told that the whole Fabian *gens* except one youth was annihilated on the Cremera. Veii's hold on the west side of the Tiber down to the salt-flats was strengthened, and the Veientes are even credited with occupying the Janiculum hill across the river from Rome itself. Thereafter an uneasy peace reigned for some forty years: Rome, with the Latins, was busy campaigning against the Aequi and Volsci, while the Etruscan naval defeat at Cumae (474) weakened the foreign trade of the cities and restricted their ambitions.

Rome's next step was to win permanent possession of Fidenae, but details of the tradition are confused. With Veii's help Fidenae revolted, though Veii in turn got no help as the result of an appeal to the Etruscan League which met at the Fanum Voltumnae. Four Roman ambassadors were murdered; Cornelius Cossus won the *spolia opima* by killing in battle Tolumnius, prince of Veii; and Q. Servilius Fidenas captured Fidenae by driving a tunnel underneath it in 435. Nine years later Fidenae revolted again, and was again reduced. Though there may in fact have been only one war, two memorials of the contest survived; statues of the envoys stood on the Rostra at Rome until Sulla's day, while the breastplate of Lars Tolumnius, which Cossus had dedicated to Jupiter, was seen by Augustus who read the inscription: unless the emperor was guilty of misrepresentation, the historicity of the second war is attested, while a sixth-century inscription at Veii names an Etruscan Tolumnius (Velthur Tulumnes: *TLE*, 38); the tunnelling episode however is doubtless borrowed from the later siege of Veii. Whether the struggle had originated in an attempt by Veii to recover control over the left bank of the Tiber or whether Rome, encouraged by a recent victory over the Aequi, had taken the initiative, the result was that Veii might now have to face the prospect of a Roman attack; it was about this time that she decided to strengthen her position by building walls (see pp. 107f).

At the end of the century came the final struggle, and after a long siege Veii fell (*c.* 396), having received little help from other Etruscan cities. A federal Etruscan council is said to have met, but made excuses not to help because of the increasing threat from the Gauls in the north and because of their dislike of the revival of monarchy at Veii. The essential reason, however, was probably lack of national sentiment: the northern cities had little direct interest in supporting Veii, and if they wanted to have access down the Tiber valley to send their goods southward they may have judged that Rome held the key position and that it was more politic to abandon Veii to its fate. Even Veii's neighbour, Caere, maintained a benevolent neutrality towards Rome. Veii, however, received some support from Capena and Falerii farther up the Tiber valley. These cities were unwilling to see their market at Veii disappear and probably feared that if it was destroyed they would be the next objective in a northern advance by Rome.

The story of the ten years' siege of Veii is recounted in a splendid narrative by Livy which, although embroidered with many a dubious episode, contains a hard core of historic fact. The length of the siege is copied from that of the Trojan war; statuettes of Aeneas and Anchises found at Veii show that the Trojan legend was already known there (cf. p. 82). Livy may have included the account of the draining of the Alban Lake (see p. 69) because of the story that Veii fell when the Romans successfully drove a tunnel under the city. The tradition of this mining operation might have arisen from the mere fact of the numerous *cuniculi* in the neighbourhood (cf. p. 108), but two factors suggest, though they do not prove, a historical basis. The tunnel between Fosso Formello and Fosso Piordo runs under the most probable site of the Roman camp near the north-west, which is on the only relatively level ground by which the city could be approached. Secondly, at this point the walls, which had been constructed at this time in anticipation of a Roman attack, were built over a number of *cuniculi* which had been filled in with earth and stones. Could the Romans have entered the city by clearing one of these tunnels?[196] At any rate Veii fell to Camillus' siege; the tutelary goddess, Juno in Roman eyes (Uni Turan?), was persuaded to accept a new home in Rome through a religious process of *evocatio*, a ritual that may well have been Etruscan; and a golden bowl was probably sent as a thank-offering to be placed in the Treasury of the Massaliotes at Delphi, as tradition records.

Rome quickly came with terms with Veii's allies, Capena, and Falerii, who had apparently helped only by raiding Roman territory. They were brought to heel, whether or not Livy is right in believing that Falerii, despite the natural strength of its position, was actually captured (cf. p. 112). This move brought the Romans far up the Tiber valley, and to Sutrium and Nepet, which Livy described as the gateway ('velut claustra inde portaque') to Etruria (cf. p. 115). Here, although the precise dating escapes us, Rome settled two Latin colonies; it may have been in 390 and 383, or 383 and 373. Thus she shared her conquest with her allies, but she kept the *ager Veiens* for her own use, since it marched with the *ager Romanus*; it was annexed and distributed to Roman settlers who formed four new tribes. This had great importance for Rome's internal history and military strength; externally these new moves meant that her northern horizon now reached the Ciminian Forest and Etruria lay open to attack. Indeed Rome may already have had a brush with Volsinii in 392, if Livy be believed.

Thus Veii, 'urbs opulentissima Etrusci nominis', was the first of the great Etruscan cities to be humbled by the future mistress of Italy. But Rome herself was on the eve of disaster. Even before the settlement just mentioned was completed, a horde of Gauls had swept down from the north and sacked the whole city except the Capitol (390 traditionally; better 387). Now Rome and the Etruscans were faced with the same danger, and Clusium, which came first in the path of the advancing storm, had, it is said, appealed to Rome for help. If the two cities had made any contact at all in earlier days, it is likely that Clusium and other inland cities in the north would have wished to preserve good relations with Rome, who could control the lower Tiber valley along which any of their goods would pass to Latium or farther south. Such a land route would become more significant after the Etruscan defeat at sea in 474, but its importance must have diminished when Campania began to slip out of Etruscan control from the later fifth century. Further, if Lars Porsenna was in fact ruler of Clusium, his occupation of Rome (cf. p. 262) may have brought the cities temporarily closer together and then left a legacy of bitterness. However that may be, Clusium's appeal in 390 must be regarded with some doubt: the story could have arisen from the version of events given by Diodorus, namely that the Romans heard of the Gallic invasion and sent a force to Clusium to reconnoitre. Whatever damage Clusium suffered from the raiding Gauls, it was not to be compared with the sufferings which Felsina, Marzabotto and other Etruscan cities in Cisalpine Gaul were enduring at this time (see p. 219). Rome's fate was sharp but relatively short. When the Gauls withdrew, not only had the city to be rebuilt, now within the protection of a new 'Servian' wall, but her authority in central Italy had been shaken, and she had to repeat the work of the fifth century in the first half of the fourth.

In the time of their peril the Romans had found a friend in Caere, which had not helped Veii in her struggle with Rome, and had even provided a refuge for the sacred cult objects and priests of Rome when the Gauls were attacking the city. After the Gallic withdrawal Rome rewarded Caere with a contract of hospitality (*hospitium*). Rome was also free now to settle the district around Sutrium and Nepet, which may have been raided by other Etruscans (389); despite a possible slight clash with Tarquinii, in the main the two peoples were at peace for the next thirty years. A recent attempt has been made to connect this lull with the emergence of a philo-Etruscan element in the Roman governing class and an understanding with Caere by which the two cities co-operated in their efforts to defeat further Gallic raiders and the threat by sea from Dionysius of Syracuse who sacked Caere's harbour at Pyrgi in 384/3.[197] At any rate mutual tolerance would benefit both Rome and Caere, even if not formally expressed.

Rome's increasing domination of Latium may have alarmed the Etruscans. At any rate in 359 Tarquinii took up arms and was joined by Falerii two years later. In 353 even Caere joined Tarquinii, but was quickly defeated and granted a hundred years' truce. Two years later Tarquinii and Falerii succumbed and received a forty years' truce, which Falerii in 343 exchanged for a permanent alliance (*foedus*) with Rome. The result of these campaigns was that the coastal route to northern Etruria was now safer, and Rome was free from danger on her northern front for forty years. Caere's precise status is, however, doubtful. At some time she was given the private privileges and obligations of Roman citizenship (*civitas sine suffragio*). The date is uncertain but it was probably not until *c.* 274 BC; if it was in 353 it may have been a device by which Rome could control Caere without subjecting it to the fate of Veii.

At this time of Etruria's waning and Rome's waxing strength, the main centre of civilized life lay not in the west but in the east where Alexander the Great was changing the course of history. It is noteworthy that 'Etruscans' as well as Bruttians and Lucanians are said to have been among the peoples that sent congratulatory embassies to him as he was returning to Babylon in 323 BC. Since this statement by Arrian (7, 15, 4) derives *via* Ptolemy from the official Journal of Alexander's expedition, it is generally accepted as genuine, but one would like to know much more about it. Who were the 'Etruscans': some individual cities or representatives of the 'League'? What were their motives: concern about their trade in western waters, or the desire to find a counterweight to the growing strength of Rome? The later story that the Romans sent a similar embassy is usually rejected as less well attested, but could the view be right according to which the Etruscan embassy included some Romans? At any rate the embassy went at a time of comparative quiet between the Etruscan cities and Rome.

ROME AND THE NORTHERN CITIES

The Romans were lucky in that during the earlier part of their long struggle against the Samnites in the central Apennines Etruria remained quiet. The Etruscans may have recalled how their own control of Campania had been overthrown by the Samnites and they did not wish them to replace the more civilized Romans as their southern neighbours; further, some cities such as Caere, Tarquinii and Falerii, were on friendly terms with Rome and perhaps would hesitate to break their sworn agreements. However, when they saw Rome's power increasing they may have been more willing to intervene to restore the balance, especially as Tarquinii's forty years' truce was expiring. In 310 the forces of Tarquinii and perhaps of Volsinii advanced against Sutrium. But Q. Fabius Rullianus boldly forced his way through the dread Ciminian Forest into central Etruria where he is credited with a victory. Livy's narrative reveals many interesting details. The consul's brother had been sent ahead to reconnoitre, dressed as a peasant, because he had been educated at Caere, was learned

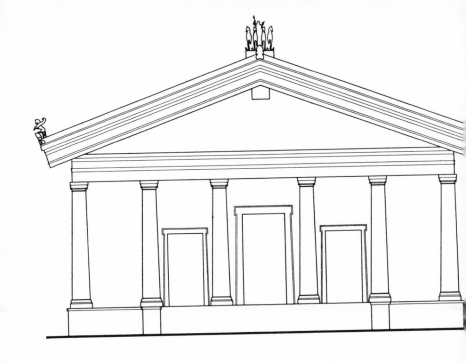

115 Reconstruction of the facade of the Temple of Jupiter on the Capitol after E. Gjerstad. 116 gives details of the reconstruction. The proportions of fragment of a terracotta frieze showing a procession (*Pl.107*) correspond to the interaxial measurements of the Temple of Jupiter. See p.252.

117 Terracotta statuette of
Aeneas and Anchises from Veii,
of the early fifth century BC.
Other similar evidence shows
that the legend of Aeneas was
known in Etruria during the
sixth century. Thus Etruria and
Rome had at least one hero in
common. See pp.82, 269.

118 Small *bucchero* bowl with an Etruscan inscription (*ni araziia laraniia*) from the Clivus Capitolinus; it dates to *c.* 525 BC. 119 Fragment of Black-figure crater with Hephaistos on a donkey, from a deposit in the Comitium in the Forum; it dates to 570–560 BC. See p.251.

120 The Capitoline wolf. The finest archaic work from Rome and a product of Etrusco-Italic art. Both its school (Veientine?) and date (*c.* 500 BC?) are uncertain. Figures of the twins Romulus and Remus were added to it in the Renaissance. They symbolize the fact that Rome drew much cultural nourishment from Etruria, but the Romans were not Etruscans: the wolf was only a foster-mother. See p.252.

in Etruscan literature and knew the language well. Livy adds that it was the custom at this time for Roman boys to be regularly schooled in Etruscan literature, no doubt to gain knowledge of their religious *disciplina*. Further, a definite geographical stage is marked by the Romans' advance through the forest: when they reached the crest, they looked over the rich ploughlands of Etruria (*opulenta Etruriae arva*), the more open rolling fertile north. Finally, as the troops scattered to plunder they were attacked by improvised companies of Etruscan peasants who had been hastily raised by the leaders (*principes*) of the district: here, for a moment, we get a glimpse into the feudal structure of Etruscan society. Livy also mentions that some historians recorded that the battle was fought on the eastern side of the Ciminian Forest near Perugia; if so, Fabius perhaps chose a more practical if less heroic route.

The Etruscans had had enough, and a thirty-years' truce was arranged with Cortona, Perusia and Arretium: Volsinii was reduced and in 308 the alliance with Tarquinii was renewed for another forty years. Livy says that all the Etruscans (*nomen omne Etruscum*) asked for a treaty, but on payment of an indemnity were granted an annual truce. Livy may have been thinking of the Etruscan League, and while it is possible that a general council met to consider policy, it is improbable that Rome had any direct dealings with it: rather, Rome always made individual arrangements with the separate cities.

In 302 Rome was again involved, this time on behalf of the powerful family of the Cilnii (of whom Maecenas was a later descendant) of Arretium, who had been expelled by the people. It was in line with Roman policy to support the ruling class in the cities and so they restored the Cilnii either as the result of large scale war or (an alternative and perhaps more reliable version given by some writers, as Livy records) by diplomacy (see p. 167). By this time Rome had also won the great Samnite War, but a Gallic invasion in 299 tempted both Samnites and Etruscans to try conclusions with her once more. But the Etruscans' participation was somewhat half hearted: if they had any share in the final battle at Sentinum (295) where the Gauls and Samnites were decisively defeated, it was a very small one. During the next two years Etruria was reduced and pacified, suffering defeats, according to Livy, near Volsinii and Rusellae; Volsinii, Perusia and Arretium received truces for forty years. Falerii, which had been loyal to Rome since 343, suddenly revolted but was reduced (292); at first granted an annual truce, she may have had her *foedus* renewed before long. A few years later more Gauls crossed the Apennines and besieged Arretium which remained loyal to Rome, who lost a consul in trying to relieve the city (284). But not all the Etruscans were so faithful. Amongst others Vulci and Volsinii revolted and held out even after the Roman victories over the Gauls until 280. They may even have been in communication with Tarentum and with Pyrrhus who had invaded southern Italy, but they were defeated in time (280) to allow Rome to concentrate on the Pyrrhic War.

A general settlement with Etruria seems to have been reached in 280 and to have included not only Volsinii and Vulci, but also Tarquinii, Rusellae, Vetulonia, Populonia and Volaterrae. The legal nature of the arrangements made at this time and earlier is debatable. The usual view is that in Etruria Rome did not pursue her normal policy of wide grants of Roman citizenship or alternatively of alliance by treaty; since the Etruscans were more alien, at any rate in language, than the majority of people that Rome encountered elsewhere in Italy, and since the nature of the country made campaigning difficult, Rome made less attempt to assimilate them into the Italian confederacy but was content to keep them at bay by means of truces (*indutiae*) of varied duration instead of establishing permanent treaties (*foedera*). The one exception to this was Falerii which received a *foedus*, but it has recently been argued that this status may well have been granted to other leading cities when Rome was ready to reach a more lasting arrangement.[198] This may well be the case, though the evidence hardly allows any confident conclusion. Rome's only departure from her policy of withholding all forms of citizenship was in the case of Caere, whose history is ambiguous (*cf.* p. 271). In *c.* 273 BC Caere must have been suspected of some act of disloyalty, because it obtained peace from Rome only at the price of ceding half its territory; this may well be the occasion of her receiving *civitas sine suffragio*.

The fate of two other cities requires mention: Volsinii and Falerii. Unlike Arretium, which maintained its industrial position by producing pottery instead of metal work, Volsinii was suffering a decline in the productivity of her mines and in her commerce. This promoted internal social unrest, which our sources depict as an uprising of the slaves (perhaps rather serfs) against their degenerate and luxurious masters who had allowed them to intermarry with the upper classes and to manage the city. When the slaves rose, the masters appealed to Rome, which favoured the ruling class and intervened on its behalf. In 264 a Roman army destroyed the city and removed the masters and any loyal serfs to a less defensible site by Lake Bolsena. Rome next had to face her first war with Carthage, during which the Etruscans remained loyal, but in its final year (241) Falerii revolted. If her treaty had in fact not been renewed, she might have had an annually renewed truce for fifty years from 292 which would now just have expired. Rome reacted sharply and sent a double consular army against the city which was quickly stormed; half its territory was annexed as Roman *ager publicus*, its arms, horses, slaves and household goods were taken, and the inhabitants were forced to abandon their strong hill-site (Civita Castellana) and to build Falerii Novi in the plain where the ruined church of Santa Maria di Falleri within the circuit of the Roman walls still preserves the name.

Roman predominance in Etruria was symbolized in the religious field by the removal of Etruscan deities to Rome. Juno had been summoned to Rome from conquered Veii, and now Fulvius Flaccus, the victor of Volsinii, dedicated on the Aventine a temple to Vortumnus who was worshipped especially at Volsinii (*cf.* p. 130), while one of Falerii's chief deities was given a shrine on the Caelian hill with the title of Minerva Capta. In the material field Rome made use of some of the land she took from Etruscan cities for the settlement of colonies or centres of influence. A *colonia maritima* of Roman citizens was probably established *c.* 289 BC at Castrum Novum on territory that had belonged to Caere. In 273 a Latin colony was sent to Cosa in the territory of Vulci: its fine walls, temples, and other buildings make it for us the very paradigm of a Latin colony. For the Etruscans it was a symbol of Roman power which cut their coastline in half. Maritime colonies were also sent to three places that had belonged to Caere, namely Pyrgi (see p. 102) probably before 241 and perhaps in 289, Alsium in 247, and Fregenae *c.* 245. Some of these were designed to guard the coast against the Carthaginians, but they will also have acted as watchdogs over south-western Etruria.[199] For the rest of the land, the colonies which had been established in central and northern Italy against Gaul, Samnite and Umbrian sufficed to prevent any Etruscan forces from straying too far from their homeland. Then in addition the Romans soon began to develop the road system by driving the Via Ameria and then the Flaminia northwards, together with the Cassia and the Clodia (see p. 117). Thus with colonies and roads the Roman network was imposed on Etruria, and the days of the great independent Etruscan cities had passed.

ROMAN ETRURIA

As part of the Italian Confederacy under Rome's control, Etruria did not necessarily suffer serious economic loss: witness the contributions made by some cities in 205 to Scipio (p. 64). True, she had to provide troops to the joint army, as did all allies when the need arose, but her levy does not seem to have been heavy. In 225 BC to meet a renewed Gallic attack the Romans and Campanians put 273,000 men into the field, while the joint contribution of the Etruscans and Sabines was only some 54,000. This time the Etruscans were no longer allied with the invading Gauls but fought loyally alongside the Romans to defeat the invaders at Telamon in Etruria itself and thus to drive them from Italy. During Hannibal's subsequent invasion the Etruscan cities closed their gates to him: though his route took him past hill-towns such as Cortona and Perusia, he could not delay to attack them and despite his overwhelming victory at Lake Trasimene, Etruria stood by Rome. Later as the strain of war increased there was some restlessness at Arretium in 209 but

Rome quickly checked it, and four years later many of the cities sent their aid to Scipio for his proposed invasion of Africa.[199a]

Etruria suffered much less than many other parts of Italy from Hannibal's devastations, and little is heard of it during the early second century. A slave revolt was crushed there in 196: this may foreshadow the development of the large ranches run by foreign slave labour which Tiberius Gracchus later saw near the Etruscan coast and deplored. But even if *latifundia* was increasing, its incidence in Etruria may have been uneven. However, it was perhaps with an eye to possible unrest in Etruria as well as to relieve her own population problem that Rome established a few more colonies there. In 183 a Latin colony was placed in central Etruria at Saturnia, where a *praefectura* had already existed, and another followed on the coast at Graviscae two years later. Heba too was founded either about this time or, if it is thought that Livy cannot have omitted to mention its foundation, after 168. Finally in 177 a colony of Roman citizens was sent to Luna (Spezia) to strengthen the area in connection with the wars against the Ligurian tribes; this would help to shelter Etruria from their incursions.

Evidence for the effect of the Gracchan land legislation on Etruria is lacking. We hear of some Etruscans going to Rome in 91 BC to agitate against Drusus' land legislation for fear it might affect them adversely; they may well have been magnates who were afraid of losing some Roman *ager publicus* which they were holding. In the Social War that followed, Etruria remained essentially loyal to Rome. If, as threatened for a moment in 89, the rebel Italians had been able to break through into Etruria, they might have caused some embarrassment, since there may have been some fighting in Etruria late in 90, but as it was Etruria gave Rome little trouble. Like the rest of Italy, it welcomed the offer of Roman citizenship made under the lex Julia, and thus, together with the rest of Italy, was united in a single state.

In the civil war between Marius and Sulla the sympathies of Etruria were with Marius. When he landed at Telamon from his exile in 87 he was able to raise a force of some 6,000 men, but

Etruria was more seriously involved in the struggle of his successors with Sulla in the civil war of 82 when the Marian leader Carbo raised large forces in Etruria, and Clusium and Arretium became the centre of one of the war zones. When Sulla was victorious he exacted a terrible price from the Italian cities which had opposed him, inflicting fines and confiscating land wholesale. Needing land on which to settle his veterans he therefore ejected owners, both private and communal, on a large scale in order to make room for his soldiers, many of whom probably had little desire to settle down as farmers. In Etruria colonies were established at Arretium, Clusium, Faesulae and Volaterrae but probably not at Florentia.[200] Volaterrae was one of the chief victims: here the Marians had made a last stand, and their stronghold had withstood siege by Sulla until 80. Meantime Sulla had passed a law depriving the inhabitants and those of Arretium of their Roman citizenship, in addition to the subsequent loss of territory which they suffered. Sulla's measure about their citizenship was illegal and was soon recognized as invalid, but his action led to frequent disputes in the future; Cicero, for instance, was involved in several cases on behalf of the rights of Volaterrans and Arretines such as when he defended Aulus Caecina, who came of an old Volaterran family, against a charge of incapacity to inherit. Even as late as 45 BC he was protecting the interests of his friends at Volaterrae whose land was threatened.

The long term effects of these Sullan colonies on Etrurian economy are hard to gauge. In some cases where land was confiscated it was not redistributed, thus leaving the original owners in *de facto* occupation. In most of the colonies the new colonists seem to have been settled in separate communities from the old: thus we know that at Faesulae they were distributed in *castella* and did not come within the walls of the old city. They seem to have remained two distinct communities; this obviously left the older inhabitants greater independence than they would have enjoyed if the veterans had been mixed up with them; there was less opportunity for brutal or overbearing dominance by the colonists. In fact in the course of time it seems that in some cases at least, as happened at Faesulae and Clusium, the colonists were ultimately absorbed by the older community. The effects of this colonization on the prosperity of Etruria have been interpreted very differently: to some this change has appeared to herald increasing prosperity, to others deterioration. It is certain that much immediate misery followed: the plight of the dispossessed was hard, while many of the ex-soldier settlers had little taste for the routine of life on the land and began to drift off in search of fresh campaigns and booty. Thus a nucleus of discontented men was formed and Etruria became the centre whence Catiline drew much support, with his headquarters at Faesulae. In so far as many settlers left their holdings, these would tend to revert to larger estates, and the check to *latifundia* which the Sullan settlement had secured was diminished. Indeed, the ultimate state of Etruria may not have been very different in this respect from its earlier one. But there was one significant change: the influx of so many veterans, with their Latin language and customs, must have accelerated the gradual submergence of the Etruscan tongue and habits. Italy was steadily becoming more unified but at the cost of the gradual disappearance of much local culture.

Further troubles lay ahead. Among the many crimes with which Cicero charged Clodius was that of plundering Etruria (*vastarat Etruriam*), while at the outbreak of the civil war in 49 BC Pompey wrote to Domitius Ahenobarbus: 'Curio is massing the garrisons in Umbria and Etruria and marching to join Caesar'.[201] Worse followed in the subsequent struggle between Octavian and Antony, when the latter's brother, Lucius Antonius, opposed Octavian and was driven into Perusia where he endured a cruel siege: hunger, which became proverbial as *Perusina fames*, at last compelled capitulation in 40 BC. The city was sacked and burnt, the town councillors and Octavian's Roman political opponents were put to death, although the scandalous story that they were sacrified on the anniversary of the murder of Julius Caesar, his adoptive father, on an altar dedicated to his memory, should be dismissed as deriving from anti-Octavian propaganda. This same year, Menas, the lieutenant of Sextus Pompeius, ravaged the Etruscan coast.

Thus from the time of Sulla until that of Augustus Etruria suffered from wars and devastation. In 46 BC some of the land of Veii and Capena was used for the settlement of veterans (Cic. *ad Fam.* 9, 17, 2), and it may well be that Lucus Feroniae in the Ager Capenas now received the status of colony from Caesar rather than later from Augustus; and, incidentally, the later occurrence of a non-collegiate praetor at Capena may reflect a survival from Etruscan days. The building programme for the new colony, however, apparently had to wait until the time of Augustus since the number of the original settlers was probably reduced by the wars. The process at Veii, which Augustus made a *municipium* before AD 1, was perhaps similar. At any rate the large number of dedications there to the Julio-Claudian emperors suggests a period of moderate prosperity in the first century AD. A colony was established at Sutrium, perhaps by the triumvirs after the death of Julius Caesar, although Falerii Novi did not gain this status until the third century AD (Pliny's reference to an Augustan colony probably should be to Falerio in Picenum). Augustus restored Perusia with the title of Augusta, while Rusellae is said to have been an Augustan colony. Aqueducts of the Julio-Claudian period have been found at Vulci, Vicus Matrini and Forum Novum, as well as an Augustan one at Lucus Feroniae.[202] Though unhealthy conditions, including perhaps malaria, may have been hastening the decline of some of the coastal cities, many of even smaller towns of the interior may well have enjoyed reasonable prosperity during the early Empire, and the later literary pictures of decay may be premature. Some of the inland cities fared very well: if not all could vie with the prosperity created by the pottery industry of Arretium. Strabo at the time of Augustus could classify even Sutrium with Arretium, Perusia, and Volsinii among the larger inland towns.

The disappearance of the Etruscan language was naturally a protracted process. Its decline can be seen in the many brief bilingual inscriptions, especially those from around Clusium and Perusia, which give the name of the deceased in both Etruscan and Latin; these continued until at least the end of the Republic. In the family tomb of the Volumnii near Perusia (*cf.* pp. 161f) six urns of travertine, with recumbent figures and Etruscan inscriptions, are followed by one of marble of the first century BC, with the name of 'P. Volumnius A.f. Violens Cafatia natus' in Latin, while on the roof is added in Etruscan 'pup. velimna au cahatial' (*TLE*, 605); this member of the family obviously did not want to be too far out of step with his ancestors. At Rome the link with old Etruria was kept alive in the late Republic by the number of men with Etruscan names (endings in -a, -as, -anus denote Etruscan origin, however remote). Licinius is an Etruscan name (Lecne) hidden by a Latin termination, while other men such as Perpenna, C. Carrinas and C. Norbanus, some of whom had a stormy history, may be mentioned.

At Rome there were also men interested in Etruscan literature and lore. A certain Volnius (Velna) wrote tragedies in Etruscan, probably at the time of the Gracchi or later. He is mentioned by Varro who knew of some works on Etruscan history from his friends Caecina and Tarquitius. These *Tuscae Historiae*, written in Etruscan, after the eighth Etruscan *saeculum*, show that Etruscan history was being written between 206 and 88 BC. Thus in addition to whatever Etruscan traditions Cato had used in his *Origines* or Fabius Pictor in his Annals (the Fabii had close connections with Etruria: *cf.* p. 272), more information was being made available at Rome in the late Republic. A fragment of a work written in Latin by Caecina survives: it describes Tarchon's founding of Mantua and other Cisalpine cities. The Caecinas were one of the great families of Volaterrae: when one of them went to Rome where he had a racing chariot, he took with him swallows dyed in the colours of the victorious team, which he released to convey the result of a race to his friends in Etruria (Pliny, *NH* 10, 71). Cicero defended A. Caecina in 69 in a case of inheritance (see p. 278) and was a friend of the same man's son, with whom he corresponded in 46. This Caecina, taught by his father, was an expert in divination and the Etruscan discipline and wrote on these matters; his works were later used by Pliny (bk. 2) and Seneca (*Quaest. Nat.* 2, 3, 9). Another man who helped to keep Etruscan lore alive in Rome was the *haruspex* Tarquitius Priscus, mentioned in one of the *elogia* of Tarquinii (*cf.* p. 91), another friend of Varro: he produced a poetic version of the prophecies attributed to Vegoia (*cf.* p. 73) and his other works included the *Ostentaria Tusca*, a translation of an Etruscan work on prognostication.[203] Thus in a period of increasing interest in astrology and eastern cults, men turned also to the lore of Etruria, the more so since this might be considered more respectable: anomalously, Etruscan customs now appeared to have been regarded as romanized and part of the Italic tradition, in contrast to the wilder beliefs that were reaching Rome from the East.

Maecenas, whose descent from the ruling class of Etruscan Arretium was proclaimed by the poets Horace and Propertius as well as by the genealogical trees (*stemmata*) which adorned his home, was always at hand as Augustus' friend and counsellor, to remind the emperor of the glorious past of Etruria (*cf.* p. 167). It was, however, the emperor Claudius who did most to keep alive Etruscan traditions, since his personal interest in Etruscan matters led him to write a history of the Etruscans in twenty books, composed in Greek. He may not have read Etruscan himself, but he used Etruscan sources, and his work received publicity when in his speech to the Senate about admitting Gallic nobles to the Senate he showed his knowledge of Tarquinius Priscus, Servius Tullius, Mastarna, Caelius and other aspects of early Etruscan history. When he extended the Museum at Alexandria, it was arranged that his Etruscan History should be read aloud as a public recitation every year. It was significant for the Principate that the emperor was a scholar endowed with a sense of Rome's past, and equally so for the preservation of the dying Etruscan traditions that he should have particularly interested himself in them.[204]

Religion was at the heart of Etruscan culture, and Claudius therefore dealt with central matters when he revived both the diviners (*haruspices*) and the Etruscan League. The *haruspices* had been members of the aristocracy in the various cities, the guardians and interpreters of the *Etrusca disciplina*, an art which had been handed down from father to son. When in their later days these priesthoods were on the decline the Roman Senate had already tried to stem the decay: a measure was passed, probably in the second century BC, requiring that either six or ten sons of the Etruscan *principes* in each city should be trained in the *disciplina*. These were the men who probably formed the *ordo LX haruspicum* mentioned in an inscription probably of the late Republic.[205] A *summus haruspex*, possibly the head of the College, had warned Caesar not to cross to Africa before the winter solstice, while a *haruspex* with the Etruscan name of Spurinna, possibly the same man, warned him of the Ides of March. These official diviners should be distinguished from the crowd of soothsayers and fortune-tellers who brought the *disciplina* into disrepute: it was probably of these latter that the elder Cato was thinking when he recorded his surprise that one *haruspex* did not laugh when he saw another. In AD 47 Claudius urged the Senate to take action, that 'the oldest discipline of Italy might not become extinct'; in view of its decline through public indifference, combined with the progress of foreign superstitions (*externae, e.g.* oriental or Egyptian cults, as opposed to the now 'internal' Etruscan beliefs), Claudius proposed the restoration of the Order. Details are not known: no doubt it had a centre at Rome, but it had a treasury at Tarquinii, which may well have been its official centre in view of the city's ancient claim to Tages, Tarchon and the revelation of the *disciplina* (see p. 84). Etruscan lore was now part of the Roman inheritance.[206]

Claudius is also the most likely author of the revived Etruscan League, which now comprised fifteen cities. The celebrations at the Fanum Voltumnae took in a new lease of life and continued at least until the time of Constantine: though they lacked any political meaning, they provided games and other festivities. We hear both of a *sacerdos* and of a *praetor* and an *aedilis Etruria XV populorum*. The praetorship might be held by Roman senators, and even the emperor Hadrian did not disdain the office. At Caere remains of a monument were found (see p. 140) with reliefs of figures personifying Vetulonia, Vulci and Tarquinii. This was probably a monument of the revived League, with the other figures missing, and may well have been a local reproduction of an original set-up in Rome by the grateful League. With it was found a large seated statue of Claudius (now in the Lateran Museum), around whose throne the figures were presumably set.

Claudius seated amidst the cities of Etruria may personify Roman Etruria and provide a suitable image with which to close this book, but one other significant picture may be recalled. Some three and a half centuries later, long after Christianity had been officially recognized and divination had been officially banned, in AD 410 when Alaric the Visigoth was advancing on Rome in one of her darkest hours, some Tuscans turned to their ancestral ritual and by summoning thunder and lightning from the heavens hurled the invader back from their city: Divus Claudius would have approved, and understood.[207]

NOTES

CHAPTER I

1 The oldest form of the name in Greek is Τυρσηνοί (Hesiod, *Theog.* 1010); this and Τυρρηνοί are the Ionic forms which correspond with the Doric Τυρσανοί and Τυρρανοί. The latter appears in the dedication of an Etruscan helmet to Olympian Zeus by Hieron of Syracuse after the battle of Cumae in 474, namely τυραν' (*cf.* note 135); this gave rise to a false etymology, *e.g.* the Augustan grammarian Verrius Flaccus said that the Etruscans were called tyrants (*tyranni*) because of their cruelty. The root of the early Τυρσηνοί—Τυρσανοί, *i.e. turs-*, appears in Latin as Tusci, and after metathesis as Etrusci. It is found in place names: Tyrra in Lycia and Tyrsus in Sardinia. According to Dionysius (1, 26) those who believed the Τυρρηνοί to be indigenous in Italy derived the name from τύρσις (a tower; *cf.* Latin *turris*), but whether with any justification cannot be determined. The Etruscans themselves used the root Ras- as their name; how the two forms became current cannot be said, though such duplication is not unparalleled, *e.g.* the use of Hellenes and Graeci

2 Etruscan origins. See especially M. Pallottino, *L'origine degli Etruschi* (1947), *Etr.*, ch. 2, and *St. Etr.* 1962, 3ff: J. B. Ward-Perkins, *Harvard Studies in Classical Philology* 1959, 1ff. *Cf.* also note 41

3 For the French analogy see Pallottino, *Etr.* 112; for the Norman, Ward-Perkins, *op. cit.* 15 and *CIBA*, 49

4 On prehistoric Italy see T. E. Peet, *The Stone and Bronze Ages in Italy and Sicily* (1909); D. Randall-MacIver, *Italy before the Romans* (1927); J. Whatmough, *The Foundations of Roman Italy* (1937); F. von Duhn and F. Messerschmidt, *Italische Gräbekunde*, I, II (1923, 1939); Pauly-Wissowa, *RE*, Supplementband ix (1962), s.v. Italien (Urgeschichte), 105–371; G. Patroni, *La preistoria*² (1951); A. D. Radmilli, *Piccola guida della preistoria Italiana* (1962), *La preistoria d'Italia* (1963); S. Puglisi, *La civiltà appenninica* (1959); C. H. Trump, 'The Apennine Culture', *Proc. Prehistoric Soc.* 1958, 165ff, *Central and Southern Italy before Rome* (1966); G. Säflund, *Le Terremare* (1939); C. F. C. Hawkes, 'The origins of the archaic cultures in Etruria', *St. Etr.* 1959, 363ff; M. Pallottino, *Etr.* ch. 2

5 *Cf.* C. H. Trump, *Central and Southern Italy before Rome* (1966), 142

6 On the Iron Age and Villanovans, see note 4 and D. Randall-MacIver, *The Iron Age in Italy* (1927), *Villanovans and Early Etruscans* (1924); *Civiltà del Ferro* (Bologna, 1960); M. Pallottino, *St. Etr.* 1939, 85ff

7 On the northern Villanovans, see note 6 and R. Scarani, *L'Emilia prima dei Romani* (1961); *Mostra dell' Etruria Padana*, 2 vols. (2nd ed. 1961), with full bibliographies in vol. 2; P. Ducati, *Guida del Museo Civico di Bologna* (1923); R. Chevallier, *Latomus* 1962, 99ff; G. A. Mansuelli, *St. Etr.* 1965

8 On Iron Age Latium, see P. Gierow, *The Iron Age Culture of Latium* II, i, *The Alban Hills* (Lund, 1964) and now I (1966) with emphasis on Latian influences in south Etruria

9 On the recently found Villanovan sites near Salerno see P. C. Sestieri, *St. Etr.* xxviii (1960), 73ff; *Riv. Sc. Preist.* xv, 1960; *Fasti Archaeologici* 1959; E. Lepore, *Parola del Passato* 1964, 144ff. *Catalogo*: Mostra della Preistoria nel Salernitano (Salerno, 1962); B. D. 'Agostino, *St. Etr.* 1965, 671ff; M. Napoli, *St. Etr.* 1965, 661ff. Pontecagnano almost certainly is the Picentia of Strabo (5, 4, 13) and probably its earlier name was Aminaea (Hesychius s.v. 'Aμυναὶα): *cf.* Napoli, *op. cit.* For Capua, W. Johannowski, *Klearchos* 1963, 62ff and *cf.* above pp. 191f

10 On the urn-fields, see H. Müller-Karpe, *Beiträge zur Chronologie der Urnenfelderzeit, nordlich und südlich der Alpen* (1959); H. Hencken, *CIBA* 29ff

11 See E. Richardson, *The Etruscans* (1964), 5 and 30ff

12 Pallottino, *Etr.*, 116

13 On linguistic problems, see E. Pulgram, *The Tongues of Italy* (1958); L. R. Palmer, *The Latin Language* (1954). For Pallottino's theory see *Etr.* especially 50ff, 63ff. For Pulgram's criticism see *op. cit.* 223ff. See also Patroni, *La preistoria* (1951), 989f

CHAPTER II

14 This important passage would require further treatment here, if only reasonably firm conclusions could be drawn from it, but unfortunately there are many uncertain elements. The main points are: (*a*) the date of Hesiod, (*b*) what parts of the *Theogony* should be ascribed to Hesiod (*i.e.* to the author of *Works and Days*), and (*c*) what is the probable date of those parts which are considered to be later additions to the Hesiodic nucleus of the *Theogony*. Briefly, (*a*) Hesiod is placed variously between *c.* 800 and the early seventh century, (*b*) the parts describing goddesses with mortal lovers (which includes 1101ff) is generally regarded as an addition, and (*c*) the expansion and interpolations to the *Theogony* may perhaps be placed 'during the period of rhapsodic transmission, down to the time when the written texts of the poem were produced in some numbers between the late seventh or early sixth and the fifth century B.C. (G. S. Kirk, *Hésiode et son Influence*, Fondation Hardt, *Entretiens sur l'antiquité classique*, VII (1960), p. 63). The source of the material may be other Hesiodic poetry (*cf.* Kirk, p. 75). Thus clearly the value and interpretation of the passage about the Etruscans in Italy will differ according as it is placed in the eighth, seventh or sixth century

Alcinus, a writer of the mid-fourth century BC, recorded (see Festus, 326L; Jacoby, *F. Gr. H*, no. 560 F. 4) that Aeneas married a Tyrrhenia, whose son was Romulus. Again, any implication for the relations of Etruscans and Latins that may lie behind this passage cannot be pursued here. *Cf. F. Gr. H.* III b Kommentar, p. 520, and W. Hoffmann, *Rom und die Griechische Welt im 4 Jahrhundert* (1934), 113ff

15 On Xanthus, see L. Pearson, *Early Ionian Historians* (1938), ch. iii; on the value of his testimony on this point, see also H. H. Scullard's remarks in *Ancient Society and Institutions* (ed. E. Badian, 1966), 225, where certain inaccuracies on the part of Dionysius in recording Herodotus' story are noted

16 The reading of Herodotus' reference to Krestonietai has been questioned because Dionysius (i, 29), in quoting Herodotus, speaks of Krotonietai. These latter must be the people of Cortona in Etruria, since Croton in S. Italy cannot come into the picture. For arguments about the reading of *Creston*, see How and Wells, *Commentary on Herodotus* I, 79ff. If *Creston* is rejected, Herodotus cannot be quoted as evidence for Pelasgians in this area, but Thucydides still can be (and in view of Thucydides, it might be better to accept the reading of Creston)

17 On the difficulty that the Pelasgians were credited with the foundation of some specific cities in Etruria (Cortona, Caere, Pisa, Saturnia, Alsium) and not of others (as Tarquinii or Veii), see M. Pallottino, *L'origine degli Etruschi*, 41ff. M. B. Sakellariou (*La Migration grecque en Ionie* (1958), 418ff), argues that the passages in the sources which link (a) the Pelasgians and Tyrrhenians, and (b) the Pelasgians and Etruria have no historical value

18 Dionysius I, 89. On his purpose see H. Hill, *JRS* 1961, 86ff

19 Herodotus' story that the followers of Tyrrhenos adopted the name of Tyrrhenoi only when they arrived in Italy has been taken literally by some (cf. Pallottino, *L'origine*, 39) to suggest that we should not look for a people *called* the Etruscans in Asia Minor. But this is surely too narrow an interpretation: the name of Tyrrhenos himself is said to come from Lydia, while Pallottino admits Τυρσηνοί as the inhabitants of a small Lydian city, Τύρρα or Τύρσα)

20 Lemnos inscription. For recent discussion see W. Brandenstein, *PW*, s.v. Tyrrhener, cols. 1917–1937, with bibliography. Compare, for instance, the Lemnian terminations *-z, -eiz, -ai, -aith, -ale, -ial* with Etruscan *-s, -eis, -ai, -aith, -ale*, the Lemnian words *aviz, zivai, arai* with Etruscan *avils, zivas, aras,* and the phrase *aviz sialchviz* with Etruscan *avils sealchls*

21 Thus Pallottino finds in the similarity between 'Lemnian' and Etruscan, which he attributed to the basic substratum of pre-Indo-European, an argument in support of the autochthony of the Etruscans, and he would take Herodotus I, 57 as representing a different tradition on Etruscan origins from that in I, 94 (the Lydian story): see 'Erodoto Autoctonista?', *St. Etr.* xx (1948–9), 11ff

22 See for recent discussion G. A. Wainright, 'The Teresh, the Etruscans and Asia Minor', *Anatolian Studies* 1959, 197ff and cf. *Journ. Egyptian Archaeology* 1960, 24ff. Other identifications of the *Trs.w* include linking them with the land of Taruisa or the city of Tarsa (both mentioned in Hittite documents; the latter is identified with Tarsus), the *Tjwr* of Syria (men-

tioned on a stele of Seti I), not to mention Trojans, Thracians, the inhabitants of the Tauric Chersonese, Tyrus on the Euxine or even Tiras, son of Japheth (*Genesis*, 10, 2). M. B. Sakellariou (*La Migration grecque en Ionie* (1958), 464ff) doubts the identification with the Tyrrhenians, thinks that Lydia was never inhabited by a people with the ethnic name of Tyrrhenians, and believes that the town of Tyrrha lay not, as generally thought, between Smyrna and Phocaea, nor on the coast of Mysia to the north, but in the interior of Lydia

23 See G. A. Wainwright, *Anat. St.* 1959, 201ff

24 The *Saecula* were recorded in Etruscan Histories (*Tuscae Historiae*) which were translated into Latin by an Etruscan on behalf of the Roman scholar Varro. There were ten *saecula*; the eighth ended in 88 BC according to Plutarch, *Sulla* 7. Censorinus, *De die nat.* 17, 6, attributed 100 years (round figures) to the first four *saecula*, 123 years to the fifth, and 119 to the sixth and seventh. Allowing 120 years for the eighth, we get 969 BC as a starting date. But if Augustus was wrong in ending the ninth in 44 BC, we may have a different system of calculating, which with an average of 110 years would put the start in the mid-eleventh century

25 See Lord William Taylour, *Mycenaean Pottery in Italy* (1958); F. Biancofiore, *La civiltà micenea nell' Italia meridionale* (1963). P. Caretelli (*PP*, 1958, 207ff, 1962, 5ff) has argued for a Mycenaean origin for the 'Achaean' colonies of Metapontum, Sybaris and Croton

26 See the controversial views of H. Müller-Karpe, *Vom Anfang Roms* (1959): for criticism of them, see M. Pallottino, *St. Etr.* 1961, 11ff and *Arch. Class.* 1960, 1ff

27 On the swords see R. Maxwell-Hyslop, *Proc. Prehistoric Soc.* 1956, 126ff, whose views appear acceptable to C. F. C. Hawkes (*St. Etr.* 1959, 368ff)

28 For this view see especially C. F. C. Hawkes (*St. Etr.* 1959, 368ff), who is careful not to claim more than a hypothetical possibility for it. Pallottino (*St. Etr.* 1961, 26ff) regards these arguments as acute and thinks that Hawkes is right in seeing the process of the orientalizing of Etruria in terms of individual economic absorption by a world that was already politically established and ethnically defined; however, as one who rejects the theory of migration from the East, Pallottino naturally does not accept this aspect of Hawkes' argument. Here mention should be made of the views of J. Bérard (*Rev. des Études Anc.* 1949, 201ff and *La colonisation grecque de l'Italie méridionale* 2nd ed. 1957, 470ff, 497ff) who avoided the chronological gap by putting the arrival of the Etruscans in Italy in Trojan times and regarding the orientalizing civilization of the eighth and seventh centuries as a 'renaissance' and not a 'naissance': the modern idea of an immigration in this later period is firmly rejected. This view, which lacked archaeological evidence in Italy, could now be given some support by the evidence from Populonia as interpreted by Mrs Maxwell-Hyslop

29 For the Raetic language, see Whatmough, *FRI*, 166f. For the views mentioned, see G. De Sanctis, *Storia dei Romani*, I (1907), and L. Pareti, *Le Origini Etrusche* (1927); the latter has reiterated his theories in *Storia di Roma*, I (1952), 110ff and also *St. Etr.* 1957, 537ff. Two archaeologists, F. von Duhn and G. Korte, at first supported the northern theory, but later abandoned it in favour of the eastern. The northern view received support from two philologists, W. Corssen and E. Lattes, who believed that Etruscan was an Indo-European language, and from P. Kretschmer (*Glotta* 1943, 213ff) who argued that the language belonged to a widespread 'Raeto-Tyrrhene' or 'Raeto-Pelasgic' racial-linguistic group which spread southwards from the Danube area. But see M. Pallottino, *St. Etr.* 1961, 8ff

30 See F. Schachermeyr, *Etruskische Fruhgeschichte* (1929). For the views of J. Bérard, see above note 28

31 The inscription from Ischia is on a skyphos known as the 'Cup of Nestor', because its owner suggests in the verse which he has scratched on his cup that Nestor's cup in Homer is not to be compared with his. It thus provides not only one of the oldest (the oldest?) examples of Greek alphabetic writing but it also shows its owner's knowledge of the Homeric poems. See G. Buchner and C. F. Russo, *Rendiconti . . . Lincei*, 1955, 215ff; D. L. Page, *Cl. Rev.* 1956, 95ff. Its date may be *c.* 725-600

32 On early Greek scripts see L. H. Jeffery, *The Local Scripts of Archaic Greece* (1961). W. L. Brown, *The Etruscan Lion* (1960), 35, would date the Massiliana tablet 'hardly before 675'

33 Cremation and inhumation co-existed in Athens during the Geometric Period, but the reasons are not clear. The main evidence comes from the cemetery at Kerameikos (Potters' Quarter). In the period after the break-up of the Mycenaean empire, the earliest sub-Mycenaean graves are inhumations in rectangular pits. About 1100 BC three cremations are found, and thereafter cremation became the predominant custom until interment was resumed *c.* 800. The older view that cremation was brought into Greece by the Dorians is not easy to reconcile with present views of chronology, and the practice is not found in many Dorian areas. But the explanation eludes us. Some argue that refugees arrived at Athens, bringing their dead in this more transportable form, others think of plague as a possible cause. But in view of the uncertainties, Attica should hardly offer any analogy for Etruria

34 *Cf.* E. M. Richardson, *MAAR* 1962, 159ff and *The Etruscans* (1964), chs. ii and iii, esp. pp. 54 and 62. One of her strongest arguments derives from sculpture, whose history she traces (see *MAAR*). From before *c.* 700 BC the Villanovans developed a Wiry Geometric style (not unlike the Geometric bronzes of Greece): small cast bronze figurines for decoration, *e.g.* lively horses and riders, who have spindly bodies and large round heads, and nude women, from Tarquinia. This art was developed further

at Vetulonia during the years *c.* 675-650 when some orientalizing elements began to appear (*e.g.* a long braid of hair down the back of women, which was never worn in Greece but has a long history in the Near East). These early bronzes were exported from Etruria (*e.g.* to Picenum and north of the Apennines) as were those of the next stages which Mrs Richardson names Geometric Overlap and Orientalizing Geometric. Then came the fully orientalizing figures of the seventh century, together with the great new tumulus tombs. These figures represented a repertoire of new types which superseded the older nude figures, horsemen, and warriors brandishing spears: they are rounded and have 'full heavy forms, in tranquil poses, with hieratic gestures, the whole frozen and immobile within a closed outline' (*MAAR*, p. 162). This new style was also used successfully in terracottas, while later a backwash of native Italic Geometric re-appeared

So impressed is Mrs Richardson by this change that it is here that she would bring the Etruscans into Italy. The great objection to this is that any large-scale immigration in the mid-seventh century is unlikely to have escaped all mention in our surviving literary sources. On the other hand the transition from Italic Geometric to orientalized Etruscan is, on her own showing, somewhat protracted, and one could surely suppose a gradual flowering of oriental influences which had been planted earlier. But since this would not go back as far as the *fossa* graves of 750–700 the Autochthonists might use the evidence to support the infiltration of influence rather than the immigration of men

Another archaeologist, R. A. Higgins, who also supports an Eastern origin, sums up his view: 'The Oriental influences in Etruria are not of the same order as the contemporary Orientalizing phase in Greece. Although there are obvious resemblances, the process in Etruria was much more sudden in its inception, and far deeper-rooted in its effects' (*Greek and Roman Jewellery* (1961), 133)

Etruscan origins are discussed by H. Hencken in an article (*Antiquity* 1966, 205ff) in which he summarizes the argument of his forthcoming book, *Tarquinia, Villanovans and Etruscans.* He suggests that some cremating urn-fielders joined up with some of the raiding Peoples of the Sea in the Eastern Mediterranean, and that some of these may be the urn-field cremators who appeared on the Italian coast *c.* 1200 BC; he would call the latter pre-Villanovans rather than proto-Villanovans. Proper Villanovans should not be dated before at least the tenth century, while a second Villanovan period began from the mid-eighth century (with occasional vases of Late Geometric type in graves). The orientalizing period *c.* 700 is linked with the conquests of Assyrians and Cimmerians in Asia Minor. Finally Dr Hencken asks: did Herodotus indeed 'telescope into one story two separate settlements in Etruria, one of urn-field people coming from the Aegean and one of Lydians escaping from the Cimmerians?' (p. 211)

35 See Pallottino, *Etr.* 96–102. For the Urartu bronzes and Gordium, see Pallottino, *East and West*, ix (1958), 29ff; E. Akurgal, *Anatolia*, iv, 67ff; R. S. Young, *AJA* 1958, 139ff. Pallottino's position is both strengthened and weakened by the views of G. M. A. Hanfmann, an expert in Lydian archaeology, who wrote, 'The alleged emigration of the Etruscans from Lydia to Italy receives more support from linguistics and general historical considerations than from the archaeological material found in Lydia' (*Studies Presented to D. M. Robinson*, I (1951), 180). On the other hand Hanfmann, although not accepting an Etruscan migration from Lydia in the eighth to seventh centuries, is not unattracted by the idea of an earlier one, perhaps connected with the *Trs.w* of the Egyptian documents: *Abhandl. der Akad. Wissenschaften in Mainz*, 1960, 510ff

36 *Cf.* G. M. A. Richter, *Handbook of the Etruscan Collection, Metropolitan Museum of Art* (New York, 1940), p. xviii

37 See *CIBA*, 67

38 Sir Gavin de Beer, *Revue des Arts* v (1955), 139ff, *The Listener* 1955, 989ff

39 The population problem is discussed by D. A. Bullough, *CIBA*, 93ff. For the revised map, see A. E. Mourant, *ibid.* p. 112

40 See *Ciba Foundation Symposium on Medical Biology and Etruscan Origins* (1959), edited by G. E. W. Wolstenholme and C. M. O'Connor

41 Oriental and Autochthony theories. A detailed bibliography of this question need not be given here. For summary and discussion of the modern literature published before 1938 see P. Ducati, *Le Problème Étrusque* (1938). For the more important recent contributions, see above note 2 and works quoted in subsequent notes. For a recent assessment of the literature, see Pallottino, *St. Etr.* 1961, 3ff. It may be well to list here some of the supporters of each theory. The Orientalists, if the term be used in its widest possible connotation, include P. Ducati, *op. cit.*, G. Patroni, *La preistoria*² (1951), W. Brandenstein, *PW*, s.v. Tyrrhener (1948), R. Bloch, *The Etruscans* (1958), A. Grenier, *Les religions étrusque et romaine* (1948), P. L. Zambotti, *Il Mediterraneo . . . durante le preistoria* (1954), P. Bosch Gimpera, *El problema indoeuropeo* (1960), K. Bittel, *Grundzüge der Vorgeschichte Kleinasiens*² (1950), R. Dussaud, *Prélydiens, Hittites et Achéens* (1953), L. R. Palmer, *The Latin Language* (1954), J. Bérard, *op. cit.* note 28, G. A. Wainwright, *op. cit.* note 22, F. Altheim, *op. cit.*, note 44, H. Hencken, *op. cit.* note 34, J. B. Ward-Perkins, *op. cit.* note 2, G. Säflund, *Historia*, vi (1957), 10ff, R. Maxwell-Hyslop, *op. cit.* note 27, C. F. C. Hawkes, *op. cit.* note 27. Among the Autochthonists are numbered U. Antonielli, *St. Etr.* i (1927), 34ff, A. Trombetti, *ibid.* 213ff, F. Ribezzo, most recently in *St. Etr.* xxi (1950–1), 200ff, G. Devoto, *Gli antichi Italici*² (1951). M. Pallottino may be included among the Autochthonists only in the sense that he rejects the arrival of the Etruscans in the eighth or seventh centuries, but he would reject Antonielli's concept of an Etruscan people in Italy in prehistoric times

42 See H. Hencken, *CIBA*, 30ff

43 See M. Pallottino, *Etr.* 116, *St. Etr.* 1961, 21ff

44 Altheim's work is more interesting for its attitude to the problem than important for its detailed contribution. He had not seen Pallottino's *L'origine degli Etruschi* when he wrote, although he knew Pallottino's ideas of formation from the second edition of *Etruscologia* (1947), and, with him, he rejected any idea of Etruschicità before the formation of the Etruscan nation on Italian soil. Altheim pours into the melting-pot, from which the Etruscan nation was formed, what he calls Tyrrhenians from the East, together with Greeks, Latins and Umbrians. Few will follow him in this rather wild idea: for criticism, see Pallottino, *St. Etr.* 1961, 23ff; A. Momigliano, *Rivista Storica Italiana*, 1951, 398ff

CHAPTER III

45 See Cato, *Orig.* 2, 20; Virgil, *Aen.* 10, 184; Rutilius, *de redit. suo* 282; Pliny *Ep.* 5, 6; Strabo 5, 1, 7. *Cf.* also Sidonius Apoll. *Ep.* 1, 5 (*pestilens regio Tuscorum*) and Tibullus 3, 5, 1

46 'Wann die Malaria in Italien eingewandert ist, können wir nicht wissen': so Kind, *PW*, s.v. Malaria. Brought by the Etruscans: see N. Toscanelli, *La Malaria e la fine degli Etruschi* (1927). This view is criticized by B. Nogara, *Gli Etruschi* (1933), 116ff. For a reply see J. Heurgon, *VQE*, 126ff. Came with Hannibal: W. H. S. Jones, *Malaria, a neglected Factor in the History of Greece and Rome* (1907)

47 *Cf.* J. B. Ward-Perkins, *Landscape and History in Central Italy*, The Second J. L. Myres Memorial Lecture (Oxford, 1964), 14

48 *Cf.* G. Negri, *St. Etr.* 1927, 363ff, on the vegetation of Etruria

49 In general, see L. A. Moritz, *Grain-Mills and Flour in Classical Antiquity* (1958)

50 Fenestella, see Pliny, *NH*, 15, 1ff

51 See R. Pampanni, *St. Etr.* 1930, 293ff and A. Neppi Modona, *CIBA*, 68

52 For the tools see G. Vitale, *St. Etr.* 1928, 409ff; 1930, 321ff; 1933, 321ff

53 Columella 6, 1; Faliscan oxen, Ovid, *Amor.* 3, 13, 3. Cheese, Pliny, *NH* 11, 241. Tanaquil, Pliny, *NH* 8, 194. Polybius 12, 4, 8

54 Rutilius, *De Red. suo*, 615ff. Varro, *RR* 3, 12, 1. Pyrgi, Athenaeus, 6, 224. Tunny-towers, Strabo, 5, 2, 6. Fish in lakes, Columella, 8, 16

55 *Cf.* A. N. Modena, *CIBA*, 68

56 Cuniculi: see S. Judson and A. Kahane, *PBSR*, 1963, 74ff, J. B. Ward-Perkins, *Hommages à A. Grenier* (1962), 163ff. *Cf.* also *Pl.* 11

57 Mines and mining: see especially G. D'Archiadi, *St. Etr.* 1929, 39ff; A. Minto, *St. Etr.* 1954, 297ff

58 See Tenney Frank, *Roman Buildings of the Republic* (1924), 20, with photograph of this quarry

59 See 'Tarquitius Priscus', *Latomus*, 1953, 402ff by J. Heurgon
60 *Cf.* A. Piganiol, *Cahiers d'histoire mondiale* 1953, 344ff
61 On the dating of Vegoia's prophecy, see J. Heurgon, *JRS* 1959, 42ff
62 See S. Mazzarino, *Historia* 1957, 98ff, especially 104ff, to which the account in the text is much indebted
63 See J. Heurgon, *VQE*, 135
64 Table of Veleia, = *ILS*, 6654. *Cf.* Mazzarino, *Historia* 1957, 101ff
65 So G. Devoto, *Tabulae Iguvinae*, p. 158. But G. Pulgram, *The Bronze Tablets of Iguvium* (1959), 329 writes that *tuder* has 'no sure connections outside Italic'
66 So F. Castagnoli, 'Recenti richerche sull' urbanistica ippodamea', *Arch. Class.* 1963, 181. For the whole problem, with photographs of sites, see this article
67 See A. Boëthius, *The Golden House of Nero* (1960), 12, and *cf.* 39, and also in *Classical, Medieval and Renaissance Studies in honour of B. L. Ullman* (1964), I, 3ff
67a On temples see A. Kirsopp Lake, *MAAR* 1934, 89ff; A. Andrén, *Rendiconti della Pontificia Accademia di Archeologia*, xxxii (1959–60), 21ff. On temple decorations, see A. Andrén, 'Architectural Terracottas from Etrusco-Italian Temples', in *Acta Inst. Rom. Sueciae*, iv (1939–40); A. Minto, *St. Etr.* xxii (1952–3), 9ff. On houses, see A. Boëthius, *Clas. Med. and Renaissance Studies in Honour of B. L. Ullman* (1964), i, 3ff: J. Heurgon, *VQE*, 174ff; E. Richardson *The Etruscans* (1964), ch. viii. For references to individual sites, see relevant notes
68 See, *e.g.* A. Alföldi, *Die trojanischen Urahnen der Romer* (1959)
69 For the legends of Odysseus in Italy, see E. D. Phillips, *JHS* 1953, especially 58ff

CHAPTER IV

70 Tarquinii, see M. Pallottino, *Mon. Ant.* 1937; P. Romanelli, *Not. Scav.* 1948, 133ff (for the city-site) and *Tarquinia. La Necropoli e il Museo* ('Itinerari dei Musei e Monumenti d'Italia', 1951); C. M. Lerici, *Nuove testimonianze dell' arte e della civiltà Etrusca* (1960), M. Moretti, *Nuovi monumenti della pittura Etrusca* (1966). For Iron Age chronology, M. Pallottino, *St. Etr.* 1939, 83ff
71 For the ancient sources of these two legends, see M. Pallottino, *Mon. Ant.* 1937, 234ff: Dennis, *CCE*, i, 398ff
72 Demaratus, see A. Blakeway, *JRS* 1935, 129ff: for harsh criticism of the legend on archaeological grounds, see L. Banti, *ME*, 55
73 For the probability of the export of Villanovan objects from Tarquinii to Vetulonia, see G. Camporeale, *St. Etr.* 1964, 38
74 D. Randall-McIver, *VEE*, 55

75 See H. Hencken, *CIBA*, 41fr. On the Bocchoris vase *cf.* A. Momigliano, *JRS* 1963, 105. Beside the Bocchoris vase, another possibly nearly contemporary object provides help for dating *a fossa* burial (The Warrior's Grave) at Veii, namely a bronze lion's head (a rhyton?). In this grave all the other bronzes are Villanovan and there is a local imitation of an eighth-century Protocorinthian scyphos. The lion's head closely resembles such a vessel depicted on Assyrian reliefs at the palace of Sargon II at Khorsabad which was built 713–707; it also resembles one found in the royal tomb at Gordium. But even though it was probably imported from Assyria this does not provide so neat a *terminus post quem* as appears at first, since this type of lion's head originated in Assyrian art in the ninth century and became regular in the eighth: see W. L. Brown, *The Etruscan Lion* (1960), 13, who would date the deposition to the eighth century, while M. Pallottino prefers the seventh (*Antiquity* 1962, 205)

76 For the families see M. Pallottino, *Mon. Ant.* 1937, 543ff

77 For the elogia see P. Romanelli, *Not. Scav.* 1948, 260ff; J. Heurgon, *Mél. Écol. Fr. Rome* 1951, 119ff; M. Pallottino, *St. Etr.* xxi (1950–1), 147ff; U. Kahrstedt, *Symbolae Osloenses* 1953, 68ff. The two inscriptions mentioned above are:

> .... VS . S .... VR ...
> ... . ORGOL(ani)ENSIS
> ..... CAERITVM REGEM VI(cit
> ..... ARRETIVM BELLO ......
> De La)TINIS NOVEM O(PPIDA CEPIT.

The second runs:

> PR(aetor) IN EO MAGISTRATV A(d Caere
> EXERCITVM HABVIT ALTE (rum in
> SICILIAM DVXIT PRIMVS (ducum
> ETRVSCORVM MARE C(um milite
> TRAIECIT AQV(ila cum corona
> AVREA OB V(ictoriam donatus.

78 See R. Bloch, *Mél. Écol. Fr. Rome* 1958, 7ff and *The Origins of Rome* (1960), 139. Cemetery, *Boll. d'Arte* 1965, 106

79 For the rock-tombs see G. Rossi, *JRS* 1925, p. 1ff and 1927, 59ff. For San Giuliano, A. Gargana, *Mon. Ant.* 1929

80 For San Giovenale see the sumptuous volume entitled *Etruscan Culture* (1962), written with the collaboration of King Gustav Adolf of Sweden by A. Boëthius and others. For this preliminary description of the excavations, to which the account in the text above is much indebted, see especially pp. 277ff by K. Hanell, E. Welin and C. E. Östenberg. Also E. Berggren and M. Moreti, *Not. Scav.* 1960, 1ff

81 For Luni, see *Not. Scav.* 1961, 103ff, *AJA* 1964, 373ff

82 On Caere see M. Pallottino, *La Necropoli di Cerveteri* (Itinerari dei Musei e Monumenti d'Italia) 5th ed. 1960; R. Vighi, etc., *Mont. Ant.* 1955 (for some of the tombs); L. Pareti, *La Tomba Regolini-Galassi* (1947); Q. F. Maule and H. R. W. Smith, *Votive Religion at Caere* (1949); and for excavation reports, *St. Etr.* 1927, 1935–7

83 See J. Bradford, *Ancient Landscapes* (1957), 111ff

84 See J. Heurgon, *VQE*, 18off. Cf. *CIBA* 18off

85 See L. Banti, *ME*, 35ff

86 On La Tolfa see *St. Etr.* 1942, 229ff. On Monterano see L. Gasperini, *Études Etrusco-Italiques* (1963), 19ff. On Colle Pantano, J. Bradford, *Ancient Landscapes*, 139ff. On Etruscan tombs at Pian Sultano in the hinterland of Pyrgi, see G. Colonna, *St. Etr.* xxxi (1963), 149ff. There was an Etruscan sanctuary (from the end of the sixth century until the second) on the road from Caere to Pyrgi by Montetosto; see E. Colonna, *op. cit.* 135ff, *Boll. d'Arte* 1965, 107. For the discovery of an early Etruscan temple (from *c.* 550 BC), dedicated to Minerva, at Santa Marinella (Punicum), which continued in use until the third century, see *Boll. d'Arte* 1965, 125f. On Pyrgi, F. Castagnoli, *PSBR* 1957, 16ff; M. Pallottino, *Arch. Class.* 1957–9; *Not Scav.* 1959, 143ff

87 On the new finds at Pyrgi, see M. Pallottino, *Arch. Class.* 1964, 49ff, *Studi Romani* 1965, 1ff, *Illustr. Lond. News* Feb. 1965, 22ff; G. Colonna, *St. Etr.* 1965, 191ff; G. P. Carratelli, *id.* 221ff; G. L. della Vida, *Arch. Class.* 1964, 67ff, *Oriens Antiquus* 1965, 35ff. Colonna argues that temple B was built by Thefarie in honour of Astarte, that the 'sacred place' means the *cella* or *adyton*; the gold tablets will have been fixed on its doors which will also have been decorated with nails. He sees more Sicilian influence on temple B than on A, and suggests that the cult may have come from Eryx, with possibly its practice of sacred prostitution (*cf.* Lucilius' *scorta Pyrgensia*). On the other hand Vida believes that the Phoenician inscription points more to Phoenicia than to Carthage; he looks to Cyprus.

A fourth tablet has been discovered. It is in Etruscan, inscribed on bronze, and mentions Uni: J. Heurgon, *JRS* 1966, M. Pallottino, *St. Etr.* 1966, 175ff

It should be noted that Thefarie is the equivalent of the Latin Tiberius and that Velianas might mean a man from Velia: if so, this would give other possibilities of interpretation—a spectacular discovery is reported from Olivetta near Trevignano on the north of Lake Bracciano: several intact tombs were found, containing not only bodies but 'a rich equipment which started in the period and with the culture of the "princely" burials at Cerveteri, Palestrina and elsewhere' (see A. W. Van Buren, *AJA* 1966, 352)

88 We now have an excellent monograph, to which the account given here is much indebted, by one whose energy and wisdom have done so much to increase knowledge of the site and of southern Etruria in recent years,

the Director of the British School at Rome, Dr J. B. Ward-Perkins: *Veii. The Historical Topography of the Ancient City, PBSR* 1961. Cf. also *ibid.*, 1959 for the 1957–8 excavations. Unfortunately much of the older material has not yet been fully published; this applies both to the cemeteries and to the Portonaccio site. On the latter see *Not. Scav.* 1953, 29ff. Reference to Ward-Perkins' monograph makes fuller bibliography unnecessary here.

89 On Capena and the ager Capenas see the very detailed survey by G. D. B. Jones, *PBSR* 1962, 116–207

90 For Lucus Feroniae see Jones, *PBSR* 1962, 189ff and R. Bartocinni, *Atti del vii Congresso Internazionale Archaeol. Classica*, 1958

91 On Falerii see L. A. Holland, *The Faliscans in Prehistoric Times* (1925), M. W. Frederiksen and J. B. Ward-Perkins, *PBSR* 1957, 67ff and especially 128ff. Foundation legends: Cato apud *Plin. NH*, 3. 51; Dionysius, 1. 21. Greek potters, A. Blakeway, *JRS* 1935, 146. The temples and their remains, M. Moretti, *MVG*, especially 185ff

92 For the Ager Faliscus and its road systems see Frederiksen and Ward-Perkins, *op. cit.* note 91

93 For Nepet see *PBSR* 1957, 89ff. For Sutri, G. Duncan, *PBSR* 1958, 63ff. For the road-system of southern Etruria see J. B. Ward-Perkins *PBSR* 1955, 44ff, 1957, 67ff, *JRS* 1957, 139ff

94 See R. M. Cook, *Greek Painted Pottery* (1960), ch. xv

95 On Vulci see S. Gsell, *Fouilles de Vulci* (1891), *Fouilles dans le nécropole de Vulci* (1923); F. Messerschmidt, *Die Nekropolen von Vulci* (1930); *Jahrb. d. deutsch. Arch. Inst.* xii (1930): M. Moretti, *MVC*, 19ff; for recent excavations, Moretti, *op. cit.* and R. Bartoccini, *Atti del vii congr. internaz. d'arch.* II (1961), 257ff and as a pamphlet, and on the temple, *Études Etrusco-Italiques* (1963), 9ff. On the family inscriptions, see M. T. F. Amorelli and M. Pallottino, *St. Etr.* 1963, 183ff. On the date of the François paintings which have been assigned to various dates between the fourth and first centuries BC, see F. Messerschmidt, *op. cit.* 160ff and W. L. Brown, *The Etruscan Lion* (1960), 160 note 1 (against the late dating by von Gerkan and Pallottino)

96 For Cosa see F. E. Brown, etc., *Cosa*, I, II (1951 and 1960); for Orbetello, M. Santangelo, *L'Antiquarium di Orbetello* (1954); A. Mazzolai, *Mostra archaeologica del Museo Civico di Grosseto* (1958); for Sovana, R. Bianchi Bandinelli, *Sovana* (1929); for Poggio Buco, G. Matteucig, *Poggio Buco* (U.S.A. 1951); for Saturnia, A. Minto, *Mon. Ant.* xxx, 1925; for Marsiliana, A. Minto, *Marsiliana d'Albegna* (1921); D. Randall-MacIver, *VEE*, 181ff

97 J. A. Bundgard (*Analecta Romana Instituti Danici*, 1965, 11ff) in an interesting article, 'Why did the art of writing spread to the West? Reflexions on the alphabet of Marsiliana', has argued that writing was introduced into Etruria not for its possible literary merits, but 'because it was useful for

purely practical purposes: to facilitate the organization of that trade which was to lay the foundations of the country's prosperity in the following centuries' (p. 23). Indeed, it is argued, the Marsiliana tablet may have been sent to Etruria by a Syro-Phoenician merchant (of, *e.g.*, Tyre or Byblos) to teach an Etruscan a new technique for promoting trade.

98 For Heba, see A. Minto, *St. Etr.* 1935, 11ff

99 Procopius, *Bell. Goth.* 2, 20. He also implies that there were surrounding heights to which the city was connected by a narrow neck: this description would apply to many of the Etruscan promontory-fortresses, but certainly not to Orvieto. He must be referring to Orvieto and not to a long-deserted site at Bolsena because he distinguishes the two names: elsewhere he refers to Lake Bolsena (λίμνη Βουλσίνη καλουμένη, *Bell. Goth.*, 1, 4, 14). Thus presumably he is just mistaken on this point

100 On Volsinii see R. Bloch, *Mél. Écol. Fr. Rome* 1947, 98ff; 1950, 53ff; 1953, 39ff; *CIBA*, 50ff; *Arch. Jahrb.* 1957, 242; *St. Etr.* 1963, 399 (a general survey of his excavations); R. Enking, *PW*, s.v. Volsinii (1961), 828ff. For finds in Lake Bolsena see A. Fioravanti, *St. Etr.* 1963, 425ff. On Orvieto see P. Perali, *Orvieto etrusca* (1928); S. Puglisi, *Studi e ricerche su Orvieto etrusca* (1934); and for recent excavations in the cemetery of Crossifisso del Tufo, M. Bizzarri, *St. Etr.* 1962, 1ff, 1966, 3ff

101 See G. Dennis, *CCE*, ch. xiv; G. Foti, *Museo Civico di Viterbo* (1957)

CHAPTER V

102 On Rusellae see C. Laviosa, *St. Etr.* 1959, 33ff, 1960, 289ff, 1961, 31ff, 1963, 39ff, 453ff, 1965, 49ff; *Encyclopedia dell' Arte Antica* VI (1965), s.v. Roselle; R. Naumann and F. Hiller, *Mitteilungen des deutschen arch. Inst. Römische Abteilung*, 1959, 1ff, 1962, 59ff. 1965 campaign: *St. Etr.* 1966, 297
For the suggestion that the harbour used by Rusellae was at Telamon, 20 miles to the south, see R. Naumann, *Röm. Abt.* 1963, 39ff

103 On Vetulonia see I. Falci, *Vetulonia* (1891); D. Randall-MacIver, *VEE*, especially pp. 100ff; D. Levi *Mon. Ant.* xxxv (1933), 5ff (for necropolis dell' Acessa); *St. Etr.* 1931, 13ff (for plan of site), 41ff (ossuaries), 71ff (candelabra), 85ff (tripods); xxi (1950-1), 291 (plan). For a report of the excavations of 1959-62 see A. Talocchini, *St. Etr.* 1963, 437ff. These revealed walls of the late (Hellenistic) period in the north, a tomb of *c.* 600 on Colle Baroncio in the west, and the Circolo dei Leoncini in the Carrechio district. The last contained (see *St. Etr.* 1963, 67ff) two fine armlets of gold plate (of *c.* 650-25); the earliest burial within it belongs to the last quarter of the seventh century, and the rite appears to be cremation which thus continued through the orientalizing period to *c.* 600. Two tombs in the district of Diavolino have produced Attic vases of the second half of the fifth century and other objects which show the existence

of a necropolis during a period when life at Vetulonia was thought to have died out

104 On Populonia see A. Minto, *Populonia. La necropoli arcaica* (1922) and *Populonia* (1943); A. de Agostino, *St. Etr.* xxiv (1955–6), 255ff and (for cross-wall) 1962, 275ff; A. Minto, *St. Etr.* 1954, 291ff (iron-working). R. Cardarelli, *St. Etr.* 1963, 50ff, discusses the extent of Populonia's mainland territory (about 1,100 km²) and its harbour facilities. The Massoncello promontory, on which Populonia is situated, was originally an island; the process by which it was gradually linked to the mainland, by the formation of sand-bars and lagoons, is considered by Cardarelli in the context of harbourage. For the Tomba dei Colatoi, etc., see A. De Agostino, *Not. Scav.* 1961, 63ff, who confirms the survival of an Etrusco-Roman settlement in the first century BC

105 On Volaterrae see L. Consortini, *Volterra nell' antichità* (1940), which should be used with caution; Randall-MacIver *VEE*, 63ff; excavation reports in *Mon. Ant.* viii (1898), 101ff, *St. Etr.* 1930, 9ff, 1957, 367ff, 463ff; R. Enking, *PW*, s.v. Volaterrae (1961). On the *stelae*, see M. Pallottino, *Études Etrusco-Italiques* (1963), 145ff. Since another comes from Vetulonia, and another (unpublished) from Rusellae, their area of distribution appears to have been wide between the Arno and Ombrone. Pallottino emphasizes their resemblance to a fragment from Xanthus in Lycia. For Casale Marittimo, *St. Etr.* 1930, 54ff. For Casaglia, *St. Etr.* 1934, 59ff. For Val d'Elsa, see R. Bianchi Bandinelli, *La Balzana*, ii (1928). For Etruscans north of the Arno, see L. Banti, *St. Etr.* 1931, 163ff

106 On Clusium see R. Bianchi Bandinelli, *Mon. Ant.* xxx, 1925 (basic); D. Levi, *Il Museo civico di Chiusi* (1935); D. Randall-MacIver, *VEE*, 231ff; R. Bianchi Bandinelli, *Clusium: Le pitture delle tombe arcaiche* (1939). E. Paribeni, *St. Etr.* 1938, 57ff, 1939, 179ff, for archaic reliefs. D. Thimme, *St. Etr.* xxiii (1954–5), 25ff, 1957, 87ff, for late urns, sarcophagi and tombs. J. L. Myres, *Annals Brit. Sch. Athens*, 1951, 117ff, for 'Porsenna's Tomb'. G. Batignani, *St. Etr.* 1965, 295ff, for *bucchero pesante*. On the Val di Chiana see R. Bianchi Bandinelli and R. Biasutti, *La Val d'Amba e la Val di Chiana* (1927); M. Fazzi, *St. Etr.* 1933, 421ff

107 On Cortona see A. Neppi Modona, *Cortona* (1925). For the tombs, E. Franchini, *St. Etr.* xx (1948–9), 17ff (Camuscia); L. Pernier, *Mon. Ant.* xxx (1925), 89ff and A. Minto, *Not. Scav.* 1929, 158ff (tombs at Sodo)

108 On Perusia see C. Shaw, *Etruscan Perugia* (1939); L. Banti, *PW*, s.v. Perusia (1937), and *St. Etr.* 1936, 97ff (for its territory); A. M. Pierotti and M. Calzoni, *St. Etr.* xxi (1950–1), 275ff; A. von Gerkan and F. Messerschmidt, *Mitt d. deut. arch. Instit., Röm. Abt.* lvii (1942) for the Tomb of the Volumnii; U. Calzoni, *Il Museo preistorico dell' Italia Centrale in Perugia* (1956) for prehistory. On the bronzes, see L. Banti, *Tyrrhenica* (1957) 89ff (imports), and W. L. Brown, *The Etruscan Lion* (1960), 80ff (imported artists)

109 On Arretium see *St. Etr.* 1927, 99ff; 1932, 533ff. The brick wall is apparently accepted as Etruscan by M. E. Blake, *Ancient Roman Construction in
Italy* (1947), 277ff, but is regarded as Roman by L. Banti, *ME*, 115; the
references are to Vitruvius 2, 8, 9; Pliny, *N.H.* 35, 173. For the sculptured
heads see P. J. Riis, *Etruscan Art* (1953), 105ff. W. L. Brown, *The Etruscan
Lion* (1960), 155ff, would date the Chimera to the early fourth century.
For the episode in 302 BC see Livy 10, 3–5. For Maecenas: Hor. *Odes* 3,
29, 1; *cf. Sat.* 1, 6; Propertius 3, 9, 1

110 *Cf.* C. Hardie, *JRS* 1965, 122ff who dates the foundation of Florentia to
41 BC

111 On Quinto Fiorentino see *AJA* 1961, 385; G. Caputo, *Boll. d'Arte*, 1962,
109ff; *St. Etr.* 1959, 269ff. On the Fiesole stelae see *St. Etr.* 1932, 11ff,
1933 59ff; 1934, 401ff; *Arch. Class.* 1958, 201ff

112 On Faesulae see G. Caputo and G. Maetzke, *St. Etr.* 1959, 41ff; A. De
Agostino, *Fiesole* (1949). On the temple see *St. Etr.* xxiv (1955–6), 277ff;
the area north of the temple, *Not. Scav.* 1961, 52ff

CHAPTER VI

113 On Praeneste see *PW*, s.v. (1954) and Supplb. viii (1956), 1241ff. On the
contents of the tombs: Randall-MacIver, *VEE*, 209ff, M. Moretti *MVG*,
257ff. Fibula similar to the Manios fibula: Montelius, *Civilisation primitive
en Italie*, pl. 378 no. 2

114 On Tusculum see G. McCraken, *PW* (1948); M. Borda, *Tuscolo* (1958);
T. Ashby, *Bull. Com. Arch.* 1929, 161 (for cistern). Rutuli = Etruscans:
Appian, *Basil.* 1. *Cf.* Cato apud Macrob. *Sat.* 3, 5, 10; Varro apud Plin. *NH*
14, 88; Dionysius 1, 65

115 Treaty between Rome and Carthage: Polybius 3, 22. For discussion see
F. W. Walbank, *A Historical Commentary on Polybius* I (1957), 337ff

116 On Satricum see Moretti, *MVG*, 237ff, who comments that the material
in the museum 'provides a complete picture of all the manifestations of
the life of a Latin city'. On the inscription from Lavinium (*Castorei
Podloqveiqve Qvrois*) see S. Weinstock, *JRS* 1960, 112ff. Quotation from
Pallottino, *Etr.* 159

117 On Greek colonization in general see T. J. Dunbabin, *The Western Greeks*
(1948); J. Bérard, *La colonisation grecque de l'Italie méridionale et de la Sicile*[2]
(1957); G. Vallet, *Rhégion et Zancle* (1958), on which *cf.* M. Pallottino,
Arch. Class. 1960, 121ff; A. G. Woodhead, *The Greeks in the West* (1962);
J. Boardman, *The Greeks Overseas* (1964)

118 On Lipara and Pentathlus see Diodorus 5, 9; Pausanias 10, 11, 3 (based on
the historian, Antiochus of Syracuse); Thucydides 3, 88. See Dunbabin,
328ff, Vallet, *Rhégion* 161

119 On Greek pottery in southern Gaul see M. Pallottino, *Arch. Class.* 1949,

78; G. Vallet, *Rhégion*, 160; F. Villard, *La ceramique grecque de Marseille* (1960); H. Rolland, *Rev. des Études Anciennes* 1949, 90ff

120 On Alalia see Herodotus 1, 163ff; Diodorus 5, 13; Strabo 5, 2, 7 (slaves); and Diodorus 11, 88 (for 453 BC).

121 For possible later Phocaean trade see Vallet, *Rhégion*, 188; 191. Archaeological confirmation, *e.g.* for Elea, would be welcome

122 Etrusco-Carthaginian treaty: see Aristotle, *Politics* 3, 9; 1280a 35. Etruscan inscription at Carthage: E. Beneviste, *St. Etr.* 1933, 245. M. Pallottino, *Arch. Class.* 1964, 114, note 110, who has recognized a cippus of Caeretan type among the stelae of the *tophet* of Salammbo at Carthage

123 Strabo 6, 2, 2. The attempt of G. Vallet (*Rhégion*, 50; 104) to explain this reference to the Etruscans as a reflection of the activities of the people of the early 'Ausonian' culture of north-east Sicily, Rhegium and Lipari is not convincing. If these people were meant, they would be covered by Strabo's reference to the Sicilian 'barbarians' rather than to Etruscans. *Cf.* Pallottino, *Arch. Class.* 1960, 122

124 For Sardinia see A. Taramelli, *St. Etr.* 1929, 43ff; M. Pallottino, *La Sardegna nuragica* (1950), 37ff; M. Guido, *Sardinia* (1963)

125 Alleged Etruscan elements in place-names, see A. Schulten, *Ampurias* 1940, *Tartessos* (1945). Atlantic island: Diodorus, 5, 19ff. Imports in Carthage: E. Colozier, *Mél. Écol. Fr. Rome*, 1953, 77ff. Bucchero in Sicily, Vallet, *Rhégion*, 162. Etruscan exports to Greece, etc.: G. Karo, *Arch. Ephemeris*, 1937, 316ff. E. Kunze, *Studies to D. M. Robinson*, I, 736ff; E. Gjerstad, *The Swedish Cyprus Expedition* IV, 2, (1948), 404; P. Courbin, *Bull. Corr. Hellen.* 1953, 342ff

126 Etruscan occupation of Campania. In general: Polybius 2, 17, 1; Strabo 5, 4, 3; Pliny, *NH* 3, 60. Capua: Velleius 1, 7; Polybius 2, 17, 1; Livy 4, 37, 1; 10, 38, 6; Dionys. 15, 13; Serv. *ad Aen.* 10, 145. Nola: Cato apud Vell. 1, 7; Pol. 2, 17, 1. Nuceria: Philistus, apud Steph. Byz. (Meineke, p. 478). Herculaneum: Strabo 5, 4, 8; Theophr. *Hist. Plant.* 9, 16, 6. Pompeii: Strabo 5, 4, 8; Surrentum: Pliny *NH* 3, 70; Steph. Byz. S.V.; Statius, *Silv.* 2, 2, 2. Marcina: Pliny, *NH* 3, 70; Strabo 5, 14, 3. Salernum: Pliny, *NH* 3, 70. Ager Picentus: Steph. Byz. p. 523

127 For Pompeii see A. Maiuri, *Atti Ac. d'Italia*, Ser. vii, vol. iv, fasc. 5, 1943, 121ff; G. Patroni, *St. Etr.* 1941, 109ff. For Herculaneum, see G. P. Carratelli, *PP* 1955, 417ff, who suggests that the Greek element may have been Rhodian. For Pontefratte see A. Maiuri, *St. Etr.* 92, *Not. Scav.* 1952, 86ff. For Pontecagnano, see note 9 above

128 See M. Pallottino, *Etr.* 146f; *PP*, 1956, 81ff; *Arch. Class.* 1960, 120f

129 Foundation date of Capua. On Cato see Servius (*ad Aen.* 11, 567): 'Quod Cato plenissime exsecutus est'. According to Velleius (1, 7) Cato said that 'Capua had been in existence only about 260 years before it was captured by the Romans'; this capture was in 211, so the foundation date would be 471. Velleius could have misread Cato, who might have referred

either to Capua's capture by the Samnites in 423, and this would make the foundation 693 (*cf.* K. J. Beloch, *Griech. Gesch.* I, 245) or to the surrender of Capua to Rome in 343 or to its entering the Roman state in 338; this would make the foundation *c.* 600. J. Heurgon, *Capoue preromaine* (1942), 63, has rejected this as involving too violent a handling of the text. His own solution is to link the foundation with the Etruscan attack on Cumae which Dionysius dates to 524; he ingeniously argues, on the basis of certain links between Capua and Vulci and Clusium, that the initiative in founding Capua came from these two cities; a basic motive will have been to protect their trade links with Sybaris. For a criticism of this view see Pallottino, *St. Etr.* xx (1948-9), 328f. For Pallottino's own arguments in favour of 471 see *PP*, 1956, 81ff

130 See A. Alföldi *Early Rome and the Latins* (1964), 184ff, 420ff, and D. Mustelli in *Greci et Italici in Magna Grecia* (*Atti d. pr. convengo d. studi sulla Magna Grecia*) (1962) 182ff, 248; W. Johannowski, *Klearchos* 1963, 62ff, *St. Etr.* 1965, 655ff

131 On Capua see the valuable monograph by J. Heurgon, *Recherches sur l'histoire, la religion et la civilisation de Capoue preromaine* (1942). For the name see Heurgon, p. 135ff (*cf.* some reservations by Pallottino, *St. Etr.* 1948, 330)

132 For the Oscan inscription see Heurgon, *op. cit.* 101ff. For the painting, P. J. Riis, *Etruscan Art*, pl. 18

133 On Aristodemus see M. Pallottino, 'Il filoetruschismo di Aristodemo e la data della fondazione di Capua', *PP* 1956, 81ff. On the sources of Dionysius' account, see G. De Sanctis, *Storia dei Romani*, I² 438, Jacoby, *FGrH,* no. 576, A. Alfoldi, *Early Rome and the Latins* (1964), 56ff. Whatever other ingredients have gone into the making of Dionysius' story, these include a local chronicle of Cumae which may be regarded as a basically reliable source; further, it is of great value since, independently of the Roman tradition, it bears testimony to the general background of Porsenna and the Latins before the end of the sixth century

134 See Strabo 6, 1, 5. *Cf.* G. Vallet, *Rhégion*, 368

135 M. N. Tod, *Greek Historical Inscriptions*, no. 22. In 1959 a second helmet (Corinthian in type, rather than Italic as the first) was found at Olympia: it bears a nearly identical inscription. See G. Daux, *Bull. Corr. Hell.* 1960, 721ff

136 The date of the Samnite conquest of Campania is uncertain: Diodorus assigns the fall of Capua to 438, Livy to 423. See Heurgon, *Capoue*, 85ff

CHAPTER VII

137 On the Etruscans in the Po valley in general see G. A. Mansuelli and R. Scarani, *L'Emilia prima dei Romani* (1961) especially Ch. vi; *Mostra*

dell' Etruria Padana 2 vols. (2nd ed. 1961; full bibliographies in vol. II); R. Chevallier, *Latomus* 1962, 99ff; Mansuelli, *St. Etr.* 1965, 3ff

138 On Felsina (Bologna) see A. Grenier, *Bologne, villanovienne et étrusque* (1912); P. Ducati, *Storia di Bologna* (1928) and *Guida del Museo civico di Bologna* (1923); G. A. Mansuelli, *St. Etr.* 1957, 31ff. For the *stele* found in 1960 in Via Tofane see the catalogue of the *Mostra* (cited in note 137) p. 142 and pl. xix. *Cf.* also J. Kastelic, *Situla Art* (1966)

139 On Marzabotto see G. A. Mansuelli, *Comptes Rendus de l'Acad. des Inscr.* 1960, 65ff; *Illustr. London News*, 13th Oct. 1962, 556ff; *Mostra* 214ff. G. A. Mansuelli, *Röm. Mitt.* 1963, 44ff (for the houses); P. Saronio, *St. Etr.* 1965, 385ff (for potters' quarter). For Casalecchio, R. Bloch, *Comptes Rendues* 1963, 61ff. For finds in the Reno valley, *Mostra* 217

140 On Spina see S. Aurigemma and N. Alfieri, *Il Museo nazionale archeologico di Spina in Ferrara* (1957); P. E. Arias and N. Alfieri, *Spina* (Florence, 1958); *Spina e l'Etruria Padana*, supplement to *Studi Etruschi*, Atti del I convengo di St. Etr. 1959; *Mostra* 263ff. On Greek influence in the Adriatic see R. L. Beaumont, *JHS* 1936, 159ff. On the foundation see Hellanicus apud Dion. Halicarn. 1, 28 (*cf.* 1, 18); Strabo 5, 1, 7 (214); Pliny, *NH* 3, 120; Ps.-Scylax, 17

141 On Etruria Padana in general see note 137 above. On Adria see *Mostra*, 373ff; foundation, Justin 20, 1; Strabo 5, 1, 8 (214); Livy 5, 33. On Mantua see Pliny, *NH* 3, 130; Virgil, *Aen.* 10, 200; on Virgil and Mantua see M. L. Gordon, *JRS* 1934, 1ff; G. E. F. Chilver, *Cisalpine Gaul* (1941), 215ff. For the tomb at Castiglione delle Stiviere, *Not. Scav.* 1915, 302

142 On the Celts in general see T. G. E. Powell, *The Celts* (1958). On the date of their invasion of Italy see G. A. Mansuelli and R. Scarani, *L'Emilia prima dei Romani* (1961), ch. vii. Livy's source for his account of the Celtic migrations was almost certainly Greek, either Poseidonius or Timogenes: *cf.* R. M. Ogilvie, *Commentary on Livy I–V* (1965) 906ff. On the Etruscan material in Celtic tombs at Bologna see *Mostra*, 207f

CHAPTER VIII

143 'lucumones reges sunt lingua Tuscorum'. So Servius (*ad Aen.* 2, 278); he need not be doubted, either because elsewhere (*ad Aen.* 10, 202) he calls the magistrates in charge of the *curiae* at Mantua *lucumones* or because the Romans sometimes took *lucumo* to be an individual personal name as when Livy (1, 34) used it of Tarquinius Priscus before he went to Rome. For the two inscriptions see *TLE*, nos. 1, §9, and 131

144 For the *trabea* see A. Alföldi, *Der frührömische Reiteradel* (1952), 36ff

145 The traditional view that the early Roman nobility formed an aristocracy of knights and that they exercised their predominance through their

power as cavalry (as in early Greece), has now been challenged by A. Momigliano, to whom I am most grateful for letting me read his forthcoming article (*JRS*, 1966). He argues that the 'equites' were the bodyguard of the king and that the land-owning aristocracy through 'gentes' and 'clientelae' manned the infantry. If this view is right, it solves many problems such as the superior importance of the *magister populi* compared with the *magister equitum*, and the voting rights of the *sex suffragia*

146 See Festus s.v. rituales, p. 358L: 'Rituales nominantur Etruscorum libri, in quibus perscriptum est, quo ritu condantur urbes . . . quo modo tribus, curiae, centuriae, distribuantur'. *Cf.* A. Momigliano, *JRS* 1963, 109

147 Diodorus 23, 2; *Ineditum Vaticanum*, 3. See also above, pp. 237f. *Cf.* A. Momigliano, *JRS* 1963, 109

148 The *ordo* is mentioned in a passage of the translation of an *Ostentarium Tuscum* by a haruspex Tarquitius Priscus, which is preserved by Macrobius (*Sat.* 3, 7, 2). See J. Heurgon, *Latomus* 1953, 402ff

149 The Etruscan name for the Senate is not known. M. Hammarstrom-Justinen conjectured (*St. Etr.* 1937, 248ff) that *rathiu cleusinsl* in an inscription from Clusium (*TLE*, 488) means *ordinis Clusini*, *i.e.* the ordo was called *rath*

150 See the thorough work of R. Lambrechts, *Essai sur les magistratures des républiques Étrusques* (1959) for discussion of the inscriptions and monuments

151 See J. Heurgon, *Historia* 1957, 71ff. This view of Rome's good treatment of Tarquinii, however, is strongly rejected by L. Banti, *ME* 138ff

152 See A. Rosenberg, *Der Staat der alten Italiker* (1913)

153 The *marones* appear to have been civil magistrates who formed a college, and to have been inferior to the *uhtur* (who was the chief autonomous magistrate); they are attested in late inscriptions from Fossato, Foligno and Assisi (but, unlike the *uhtur*, not in the Iguvine Tables). See G. Camporeale, 'La Terminologia magistratuale nelle lingue Osco-Umbre', *Atti dell' Accademia Toscana* 1956, 104ff

154 See *TLE*, 91, which comes from the Tomba degli Scudi (third to second century). An earlier inscription (*TLE*, 84) from the Tombe dell' Orco (fourth to third century) seems to date the death of a man by the names of two magistrates. This need not cause difficulty, since at Tusculum eponymous dates are given by the names of either two or one aedile

155 So J. Heurgon (*Historia* 1957, 83ff) and Lambrechts (*op. cit.* 114ff). The title *purth* appears in nine inscriptions. The phrase *purth ziiace* from Tarquinii (Tomba dell' Orco: *TLE*, 87) appears to mean 'he exercised in the college of zilath the function of president'. Pallottino, however, regards *purth* as separate from zilath, though a very important magistracy (*Etr.* 226). Though the tombs of the *purth* are generally rich, those at Clusium are surprisingly modest. This may be due to the severity that Rome displayed towards the city (*cf.* Heurgon, *op. cit.* 73)

156 *Op. cit.* note 150
157 See S. Mazzarino, *Dalla Monarchia allo Stato Repubblicano* (1946), 58ff. This bold attempt has been criticized by A. Momigliano (*JRS* 1946, 197ff), Heurgon (*op. cit.* 66ff), Lambrechts (*op. cit.* 188ff) and L. Banti (*op. cit.* 140ff).
158 For the Musarna inscriptions see *TLE* 169–76. For their significance see Heurgon, *op. cit.* 96ff
159 See E. A. Freeman, *History of Federal Government*² (1893), 562ff, and for recent discussion Heurgon, *Historia*, 1957, 86ff. For the view of the political unimportance of the League see L. Pareti, *Rend. Pontif. Accad. di Archeologia*, 7, 1929–31, 89ff and G. Camporeale, *PP*, 1958, 4ff
160 See *CIL*, xi, 5265. G. Camporeale (*op. cit.*) argues that the Fanum Voltumnae was of limited importance: it lay in southern Etruria, near Veii. This can hardly be right, since (as pointed out by W. Eisenhut, *PW*, s.v. Voltumna, col. 851) Livy describes the council as meeting there in 389 BC, after Veii had been conquered by Rome
161 See Livy 1, 8, 3 (duodecim populis communiter creato rege) and Servius, *ad Aen.* 8, 475 (nam Tuscia duodecim lucumones habuit *i.e.* reges, quibus unus praeerat)
162 Excavations appear to have revealed the site of Panionion, near Mycale: 'the 60 foot long altar on top of Otamatik Tepe is now recognized as archaic and the meeting place of the Ionic probouloi in the historic councils of the sixth century' (*Archaeological Reports for 1964–65*, p. 49)
163 C. Roebuck, *Ionian Trade and Colonisation* (1959), 31; *cf.* 24ff. The evidence adduced for the leadership taken by Miletus may not convince all. Wilamowitz-Moellendorf (*Kl. Schr.* V, 1, 128ff) had argued that the league came into existence *c.* 700, but see Roebuck, *CP* 1955, 26ff
164 For the analogy with the Ionian League see Müller-Deecke, *Die Etrusker* (1877), 1, 329. The idea has been developed more recently by F. Altheim, *Der Ursprung der Etrusker* (1950). This view is accepted in principle, if not in detail, by J. Heurgon, *Historia* 1957, 87
165 See the important article by A. M. Snodgrass, 'The Hoplite Reform and History', *JHS* 1965, 110ff, and *Arms and Armour of the Greeks* (1967), ch. iii
166 See *CIE*, 1, 4143 and 4144, and E. Vetter, 'Die etruskischen Personnenamen lethe, lethi, lethia und die Namen unfreier oder halbfreier Personen bei den Etruskern' in *Jahreshefte des Oesterr. Arch. Inst.*, xxvii (1948), 57ff. This article amplifies the collection of inscriptions containing the words *etera, lautni* and *lautneteri*, by S. P. Cortsen in *Die Etruskischen Standesbund Beamtentitel* in *Kgl. Danske Videnskarbernes Selskab.* XI, i, 1925. See also Th. Frankfort *Latomus*, 1959, 3ff and J. Heurgon, *VQE*, 74ff
167 In describing how leading men from all Etruria gathered together against Rome in 480, Dionysius (9, 5, 4) adds that they brought 'their own Penestae'. By deliberately choosing this unusual word, which denoted the

serf population of Thessaly subdued by Dorian invaders, he was doubtless trying to find an equivalent for the term he found in his Latin source. It is tempting to think of a conquered Villanovan population and their Etruscan masters, but this would not fit into Dionysius' picture of Etruscan origins. For the view that he may have been thinking less of serfs than clients (etera? *Cf.* the *agrestes* whom the Etruscan *principes* hastily summoned from their fields to meet the Romans in 310: Livy 9, 36, 12), see Th. Frankfort, *Latomus* 1959, 3ff, and J. Heurgon, *ibid.* 1959, 713ff

168 For the inscriptions see, seriatim, *CIE*, 3705; 3001; 3692; 1288; 3088. H. Rix, *Das etruskische cognomen* (1963) 372ff, has argued for two grades of *lautini*; those with *praenomina* and *nomina* (gentile), and those with only an individual name—at least for northern Etruria in the late period

169 See M. Pallottino, *St. Etr.* xx (1948–9) 259ff, xxi (1950–1), 232ff

CHAPTER IX

170 A. Momigliano, *JRS* 1963, 95ff, with full bibliographical references to recent work. The proceedings of a conference on early Rome will be published in *Entretiens Foundation Hardt 1966*. For the article by Momigliano and others by him cited below, see now also his collected papers, *Terzo contributo alla storia degli studi classici* (1966)

171 Chalcolithic evidence: E. Gjerstad, *Acta Archaeologica*, 1961, 215ff and *Legends and Facts of Early Roman History* (Lund, 1962), 7ff. Bronze Age: Gjerstad, *op. cit.* and *Early Rome*, III, 378ff, 462ff. R. Peroni, *Bull. Com. Arch.* lxxvii (1959–60, published 1962), however, argues for a lower dating and believes that continuity of life can be traced from the late Bronze Age through a sub-Apennine phase to a proto-Villanovan (*cf.* also M. Pallottino, *St. Etr.* 1963, 10ff). But *cf.* Gjerstad, *Bull. Com. Arch.* lxxvii, 103

172 The archaeological evidence is published in the monumental work of E. Gjerstad, *Early Rome* I–III, (1953–60). It should be noted that what are here called Periods I, IIA, IIB and III are in all his later works (post 1960) renumbered I–IV: see *Opuscula Romana* 1962, 1ff

173 H. Müller-Karpe, *Von Anfang Roms* (1959), *Zur Stadtwerdung Roms* (1963). For criticism see M. Pallottino, *St. Etr.* 1960, 11ff, 1963, 3ff, *Arch. Class.* 1960, 1ff

174 In general see Gjerstad, *op. cit.* note 172. For the Esquiline burial, *Early Rome*, II, 232ff. For very recent attempts to discern Phoenician influences or even Phoenician traders in early Rome, and more precisely in the Forum Boarium, see J. Heurgon, *JRS* 1966, 2f and the articles cited there

175 G. Colonna, *Arch. Class.* 1965, 1ff

176 See E. Gjerstad, *Early Rome*, III, 357ff, for all this early material

176a The results of recent excavation at the Regia by F. E. Brown will, when published, throw further light on the chronology and development of the building

177 S. Omobono excavations: E. Gjerstad, *Early Rome* III, 378ff, *Bull. Com. Arch.* lxxvii (1959–60, published 1962), 33ff; R. Peroni, id 7ff. The early tracks leading to the site of Rome will have converged on the site of the Forum Boarium; when the Roman Forum became the centre of the community, adjustments will have been made so that from it all the roads radiated like the spokes of a wheel: see G. Lugli, *Études Étrusco-Italiques* (1963), 111ff

178 M. Pallottino, however, does not accept this argument from silence, and believes that some of the S. Omobono material may have come down from the Capitol: see *St. Etr.* 1963, 16ff

179 See M. Pallottino, *Bull. Com. Arch.* 1941, 101ff. For the second inscription, from the Palatine, see *St. Etr.* xxii (1952–3), 309ff. A third was found in 1963 in a pre-temple stratum of S. Omobono, and reads *UQNUS*: see G. Colonna, *Arch. Class.* 1965, 9. If a complete word, this might be a proper name, and conceivably a form of Ocnus, the legendary Etruscan founder of cities in Cisalpine Gaul: *cf.* M. Pallottino, *St. Etr.* 1965, 506ff. The earliest inscriptional evidence that Latin was spoken in early Rome seems to be the Duenos Vase of the second half of the sixth century: see E. Gjerstad, *Early Rome* III, 163ff. The *lapis niger* inscription in the Forum is probably slightly later

180 On the temple see E. Gjerstad, *Early Rome* III, 168ff, whose reconstruction is followed: in its details there is some controlled guess-work, but the total picture is probably not far from the truth. He has replied (Institutum Romanum Norvegiae, *Acta* 1, 1962, 35ff) to Boëthius' criticism (*op. cit.* 27ff) of his restoration of the elevation

181 The tradition is criticized by A. Alföldi, *Studi e Materiali* 1961, 21ff, *Early Rome and the Latins* (1964), 85ff. His views have been refuted by A. Momigliano, *Rendiconti dei Lincei* 1962, fasc. 7–12 and more briefly in *JRS* 1963, 106f; *cf.* also the criticism by R. M. Ogilvie, *Commentary on Livy, books I–V* (1965), 182f

182 See G. Säflund, *La mura di Roma Repubblicana* (1932); E. Gjerstad, *Opusc. Rom.* 1954, 50ff, 1960, 69ff, *Early Rome* III, 26ff

183 For the tradition about the kings of Rome see the standard works, *e.g.*, *CAH*, vii and R. M. Ogilvie, *A Commentary on Livy, books 1–5* (1965)

184 Ogilvie, *op. cit.* p. 142

185 *Cf.* A. Momigliano, *Claudius*[2] (1961), 11ff

186 *Cf* Ogilvie, *op. cit.* p. 181ff

187 *Cf.* A. Momigliano, *JRS* 1963, 119ff

188 A. Alföldi, *Early Rome and the Latins* (1965). Early criticism comes from A. Momigliano, *New York Review*, September 16th, 1965, and R. M. Ogilvie, *Cl. Rev.* 1966, 94ff. On the importation of Greek vases to Rome in the sixth century (with direct trade with Athens in the last third of the century?) see now E. Gjerstad, *Mélanges . . . A. Piganiol* (1966), 791ff

189 Porsenna's capture of Rome: Tac. *Hist.* 3, 72, 1, and Pliny, *NH* 34, 139.

According to Pliny, *NH* 2, 140, Porsenna came from Volsinii, while E. Pais has argued (*Storia Critica* II, 97ff) for a connection with Veii. De Sanctis (*Stor. d. Rom.* I, 375 and 446ff) identifies Porsenna with Mastarna, while L. Pareti (*St. Etr.* V, 155ff) equates them both with Servius Tullius. For bibliography *cf.* Momigliano, *Claudius*, 85ff

190 For recent discussion of various theories about the origin of the consulship and other constitutional matters, *cf.* E. S. Staveley, *Historia* 1956, 72ff and especially 90ff, and, very briefly, H. H. Scullard, *A History of the Roman World, 753–146 B.C.*[3] (1961), 428ff

191 *Cf.* A. Momigliano, *Rivista Storica Italiana* 1963, 882ff. Jacoby, *Fr. Gr. H.* no. 576, does not believe in a local chronicle of Cumae, but A. Alföldi (*Early Rome and the Latins*, 56ff) argues for it. The important aspect is the partial independence of Dionysius from the Roman annalistic tradition, whatever his precise source

192 See K. Hanell, *Das altrömishe eponyme Amt* (1946) and E. Gjerstad, *Legends*, etc., and his other works. For criticism see E. Meyer, *Mus. Helveticum* 1952, 176ff; M. Pallottino, *St. Etr.* 1963, 19ff.; A. Momigliano, *Riv. Stor. Ital.* 1961, 802ff, 1963, 882ff, *JRS* 1963, 95ff (*cf.* works cited on p. 103 note 42). R. Werner, *Der Beginn der römischen Republik* (1963) is a long, scholarly, but unconvincing work, in which the beginning of the Republic is placed in 472 BC. He argues that Pliny (*NH* 33, 18) fixes the dedication of the Capitoline temple in 507 BC, that in the fifth century time was still reckoned by the annual driving of a nail in the temple (Livy 7, 3 : Festus 49L) and not by eponymous annual magistrates; this latter system was adopted only in the third century by the *pontifices* who found a starting point for this list by equating the beginning of the Republic with the dedication of the temple. Hence they had, on Werner's theory, to invent a list of eponymous magistrates to fill up a gap between 507 and 472/70, at which date he believes the Etruscans to have been expelled and the consulate established. This new attack on the early consular Fasti, though pursued from a new angle and with ingenuity, has met with damaging criticism: see A. Momigliano, *Rivista Storica Italiana* 1964, 803ff, R. M. Ogilvie, *Class. Rev.* 1965, 84ff

193 Gjerstad's arguments are set out seriatim and discussed by M. Pallottino, *St. Etr.* 1963, 19ff

194 *Cf.* R. Bloch, *Revue des études anciennes* 1959, 118ff; *The Origins of Rome* (1960), 96ff; Appendix to *Tite-Live, Histoire Romaine, Livre II (1962), 101ff*, re-issued separately as *Tite-Live et les premiers siècles de Rome* (1965). For a discussion of these views, see M. Pallottino, *St. Etr.* 1963, 31ff

CHAPTER X

195 See R. A. L. Fell, *Etruria and Rome* (1924), 87ff; *Cambridge Ancient History* VII, 504ff, etc.; H. H. Scullard, *A History of the Roman World, 753–146*

B.C.[3] (1961), 70ff, etc.; R. M. Ogilvie, *A Commentary on Livy, Books 1–5* (1965), passim

196 See J. B. Ward-Perkins, *PBSR*, 1959, 43ff; R. M. Ogilvie, *op. cit.* 672f. M. Sordi, *I Rapporti Romano-Ceriti* (1960) argues that the basic source for the war with Veii was a lost Etruscan historian. Historical events at Veii will have lain behind the legendary war between Aeneas and the Etruscan Mezentius, which is told by Virgil; and since this story was known to Lycophron, it was known in the fourth century and will therefore derive from a pre-Roman, *i.e.* Etruscan, source. The analogy, however, between the Mezentius story and the events at Veii is far from complete

197 See M. Sordi, *op. cit.* For discussion *cf.* A. N. Sherwin White, *JRS* 1961, 240ff, A. H. McDonald, *CR* 1961, 268ff

198 See W. V. Harris, 'Roman *foedera* in Etruria', *Historia* 1965, 282ff

199 On these colonies, see E. T. Salmon, *Athenaeum* 1963, 16ff

199a E. S. G. Robinson (*Numismatic Chronicle* 1964, 47ff) has argued that the bronze coins with the negro's head and elephant, which are usually attributed to Hannibal *c.* 217 BC, may have been issued by Arretium some time in 207–8 as a pro-Hannibalic and anti-Roman gesture

200 On the Sullan colonies, see E. Gabba, *Athenaeum* 1951, 232ff, 271f

201 Cicero, *Pro Milone* 87; *ad Att.* 8, 12c

202 On Lucus Feroniae, etc., see G. D. B. Jones, *PBSR* 1962, 124ff, 194ff. He also argues (*Latomus* 1963, 773ff) that Octavian's forces may have attacked Veii in 41/40 before he closed in on Perusia. On the walls of the colony at Rusellae, see F. Hiller, *Röm. Mitt.* 1962, 59ff

203 On Etruscan literature, see J. Heurgon, *VQE*, ch. viii and for Tarquitius see Heurgon, *Latomus* 1953, 402ff

204 See Cicero, *de divinatione* I, 92; *CIL*, vi, 32439

205 On Claudius' Etruscan interests, see A. Momigliano, *Claudius*[2] (1961), 8ff, and on his Etruscan connections through his wife Urgulanilla, see J. Heurgon, *Comptes Rendues* 1953, 92ff

206 For Claudius' speech, see Tacitus, *Ann.* 11, 15. On the Ordo, see L. R. Taylor, *Local Cults in Etruria* (1923), 235 ff

207 Zosimus 5, 41

SOURCES OF ILLUSTRATIONS

The author and publishers are grateful to the many official bodies and individuals who have supplied illustrations. Pictures not otherwise credited are from Thames and Hudson's archives.

INDEX

(*n.* = a reference to Notes where some bibliographical information will be found; in a work covering so wide a field, no general bibliography has been attempted)